Charles Merivale

The Conversion of the Roman Empire

Boyle lectures for the year 1864 delivered at the Chapel Royal, Whitehall

Charles Merivale

The Conversion of the Roman Empire
Boyle lectures for the year 1864 delivered at the Chapel Royal, Whitehall

ISBN/EAN: 9783337302702

Printed in Europe, USA, Canada, Australia, Japan

Cover: Foto ©Andreas Hilbeck / pixelio.de

More available books at **www.hansebooks.com**

THE CONVERSION OF THE ROMAN EMPIRE.

THE BOYLE LECTURES

FOR THE YEAR 1864

DELIVERED AT THE CHAPEL ROYAL, WHITEHALL.

BY

CHARLES MERIVALE, B.D.

RECTOR OF LAWFORD;
CHAPLAIN TO THE SPEAKER OF THE HOUSE OF COMMONS.

LONDON:
LONGMAN, GREEN, LONGMAN, ROBERTS, & GREEN.
1864.

CONTENTS.

LECTURE I. (Page 1.)

CHRISTIAN BELIEF CONTRASTED WITH HEATHEN UNBELIEF.

ACTS XVII. 32.

And when they heard of the resurrection of the dead, some mocked: and others said, We will hear thee again of this matter.

LECTURE II. (Page 21.)

HEATHEN BELIEF DIRECTED TOWARDS A TEMPORAL PROVIDENCE.

ACTS XVII. 22.

Then Paul stood in the midst of Mars' hill, and said, Ye men of Athens, I perceive that in all things ye are too superstitious.

LECTURE III. (Page 40.)

EXPANSION OF HEATHEN BELIEF BY THE TEACHING OF THE PHILOSOPHERS.

ACTS XVII. 26.

God hath made of one blood all nations of men, for to dwell on all the face of the earth.

LECTURE IV. (Page 64.)

EXPANSION OF HEATHEN BELIEF BY THE IDEAS OF ROMAN JURISPRUDENCE.

GALATIANS III. 24.

The law was our schoolmaster to bring us unto Christ.

LECTURE V. (Page 85.)

THE HEATHEN AWAKENED TO A SENSE OF HIS SPIRITUAL DANGER.

1 JOHN IV. 21.

And this commandment have we from Him, That he who loveth God love his brother also.

LECTURE VI. (Page 106.)

EFFORTS OF THE HEATHEN TO AVERT SPIRITUAL RUIN.

ST. MARK IX. 24.

And straightway the father of the child cried out, and said with tears, Lord, I believe; help Thou mine unbelief.

LECTURE VII. (Page 129.)

THE DOCTRINES OF CHRISTIANITY RESPOND TO THE QUESTIONS OF THE HEATHENS.

ST. MATTHEW XXVIII. 19.

The name of the Father, and of the Son, and of the Holy Ghost.

LECTURE VIII. (Page 150.)

THE GODLY EXAMPLE OF THE CHRISTIANS COMPLETES THE CONVERSION OF THE EMPIRE.

ACTS XVII. 6.

These that have turned the world upside down are come hither also.

PREFACE.

THE CONVERSION of the Roman Empire to Christianity is a very comprehensive subject of inquiry. It is a subject not for a dissertation but for a history, for it involves a progressive change extending over three or more centuries, and is marked by a series not only of moral and intellectual, but of political revolutions. It embraces a multitude of events, and presents to us a long gallery of individual characters. It points backward to the origin and progress of thought and feeling on religious questions; and forward almost to the farthest expansion that they have hitherto attained. It is in itself the history of religion brought into one focus, for there is little probably in the later course of human speculation on the most interesting of all questions, of which the germ and often the full development may not be traced in the controversies of primitive Christianity with Paganism. In undertaking to give a sketch of this subject within the limits of eight lectures delivered from a pulpit to a mixed and fluctuating congregation, I have not supposed that I could do more than indicate a few of its most salient points, and suggest topics of reflection and possibly of inquiry that might lead some of my hearers or readers to a further and more fruitful consideration of it. With this view, in printing these Lectures according to the terms of the foundation on which they were delivered, I have appended to them some explanatory and illustrative notes which seemed to be required for the better understanding of my remarks; but still the volume which I lay before the reader does not pretend to be a formal disquisition on the subject—still less, I need hardly say, to be a history of the great transformation of opinion of which it treats.

It may be well to observe, however, that the conversion of the Empire seems, under God's providence, to have been affected principally in four ways:—

1. By the force of the external evidence to the truth of Christianity, that is, by the apparent fulfilment of recorded prophecy, and by the historical testimony to the miracles by which it claims on its first promulgation to have been accompanied.

The age indeed was uncritical, and little competent to weigh such external testimony with the accuracy which is now demanded. There was great proneness to accept the claim of miracles; but at the same time, and in consequence of this very proneness, very little weight was attached to it as an argument of Divine power. Greater stress was laid on the fulfilment of prophecy, but in this respect also the age was liable to be grossly imposed upon; and it must be allowed that the preaching of Christianity owes some portion, however trifling, of its success to the false pretensions of the so-called Sibylline Oracles, which form no part of its genuine credentials.

On these accounts, and because a discussion on this branch of the subject would have been ill suited to discourses from the pulpit, I have refrained from dwelling upon the effect of the external evidence of Christianity in the conversion of the Empire.

2. By internal evidence, from the sense of spiritual destitution, the consciousness of sin, the acknowledged need of a Sanctifier and a Redeemer.

This in the primitive, as in later ages, was undoubtedly the most effectual testimony to the Truth in Christ Jesus. It appeals to all men without distinction of class and nation. But it addresses itself more especially to men of intelligence and moral sensibility. It is the highest and the worthiest testimony, the most distinctive of the true religion, the most foreign to the character of the false religions of the heathen, yet bearing a mysterious affinity to some of the highest and worthiest aspirations of the heathen philosophy. It addresses itself with equal power to mankind in all ages, and establishes most vividly, by its applicability to ourselves, the moral connection which subsists between the men of the first century and the men of the nineteenth.

This is the branch of Christian evidences on which I have most emphatically insisted; for by this, I believe, the most refined and intelligent of the heathen were actually converted, and there is none to the action of which we can point so reasonably and justly as this.

And with this may be combined the results which flowed from the recognised want of a system of positive belief. The Greeks and Romans had generally discarded the dogmas of their old mythology. They had rejected tradition, and pretended to shake off authority in matters of faith. Swayed for a time each by his own conscience or sensibility only, they had yielded eventually, more or less implicitly, to the guidance of the Sophists, the perplexed and dubious inheritors of the science of the great masters of antiquity; and by a slow but inevitable decline, they had fallen once more under the dominion of newer and stranger formulas. The traditions of the East, of Syria, Persia, and Egypt, the worship of Belus and Mithras, of Isis and Serapis, had popularly replaced the traditions and the worship of Jupiter and Juno, of Hercules and Quirinus. Christianity, it should be clearly understood, did not succeed at once to the vacant inheritance of Olympus. Another religion had interposed: an exotic family of superstitions had demanded and received, for at least two centuries, the devotion of the pious, and been in its turn rejected as a mockery and a delusion. Christianity, in fact, was not simply the resource of a dissatisfied philosophy; it was not accepted as the only refuge from the blank negation of a creed. It was the tried and approved of several claimants to the sovereignty of the religious instinct among men — tried by reason and argument, and approved from its own manifest adaptation to human requirements. The world, I conceive, had long resolved, in spite of the philosophers, that a positive creed was necessary to its moral being; it had endeavoured in vain to satisfy itself with systems of its own invention; it yielded at last, under a divine impulse, to that which God Himself had revealed and recommended to it.

3. There is, however, a third kind of testimony, the character of which I would not be supposed to dis-

parage; a testimony which worked powerfully upon large numbers among the heathen, among persons perhaps of less critical acumen, but eminently susceptible of impressions from the contemplation of goodness and holiness—the testimony to the truth of Christianity from the lives and deaths of the primitive believers, from the practical effect of Christian teaching upon those who embraced it in faith. The godly examples of the Christians throughout the trials of life, and especially in the crowning trial of martyrdom, were, as we may be assured from history, productive of thousands, nay of millions, of conversions. On this subject I have been naturally led to touch, and would willingly have expatiated, but my limits and the scope of my Lectures did not allow of my dwelling upon it.

4. But further, among the multitude there was probably, after all, no argument so effectual, no testimony to the divine authority of the Gospel so convincing, as that from the temporal success with which Christianity was eventually crowned. The decline of the Empire, the discredit and overthrow of Paganism, the fall of Rome itself, did actually turn the mass of mankind, as with a sweeping revolution, to the rising sun of revealed Truth in Christ Jesus. Men of earnest thought and men of ardent feeling had already been converted by the evidence before adduced; but the great inert mass

of the thoughtless, the gross-minded, and the carnal, upon whom no legitimate arguments could make any impression, were startled, arrested, and convinced by the last overruling argument of success.

This success, however, was not assured till the time of Constantine, and up to the fourth century, at least, the multitude still continued to cling to the false gods whose overthrow was not yet manifestly apparent. The conversion of the more intelligent among the heathen, which encouraged the *coup d'état* of the first Christian Emperor, had been, I conceive, actually effected before the proved inefficacy of the heathen religions had caused them to be abandoned by the herd of timeservers. The Empire, as a political machine, was now transferred to the rule of Christ: its laws and institutions were placed upon a Christian foundation: the conversion of the Empire was substantially completed, whatever doubt or repugnance might long linger among some classes of its subjects. Accordingly, while I have pointed out the effect of the growing distrust of their own systems among the heathens, I have not thought it necessary to dwell upon a cause of conversion which, however ultimately effectual, had not yet begun to operate very powerfully within the limits of time to which these sketches are confined. Had my treatment of my thesis extended far into the fourth century, it would have been important to estimate the effect of the Imperial example, which in the Roman Empire, no doubt, as elsewhere, must have determined in innumerable instances the conversion or conformity of the people. To the Romans, as long as they retained a spark of ancient sentiment, the Emperor, in his capacity of Chief Pontiff—a title with which Constantine and Valentinian dared not dispense—seemed still the appointed minister of the national religion, still the intercessor for divine favour, the channel of covenanted mercies to the State, whatever form of ministration he might employ, to whatever Name he might address himself in behalf of the Empire. He was still on a large scale, and in the public behoof, what the Romans had been wont to consider the head of each private family to be in his domestic sphere. Cato the Censor directed the paterfamilias to offer prayers and sacrifices to Jupiter, Mars, and Janus, that they might be propitious to 'himself, to his house, to his whole family;' and throughout the bounds of the Roman's farm, there was no bailiff, hind, or bondman who would have ventured probably to offer a prayer or a sacrifice on his own account, still less to question the authority of his master to offer for himself and for them all whatever prayers, and whatever sacrifices, and address himself to whatever deity he might choose.[1] Nevertheless, the struggle of the Pagan conscience against the authority of the Emperor in religious matters is a marked feature in the history of the fourth century; and the effect of the Imperial example in the final conversion of the Empire was subject undoubtedly to important modifications. M. Beugnot's 'History of the Destruction of Paganism in the West,' published about thirty years ago, is still, I believe, the best and completest work we possess upon the later phases of the great transformation of religion; but the subject admits of profounder examination and a more extended survey.

[1] Cato's injunction to the Villicus, *De Re rust.* c. 143, may be taken as an epitome of the ecclesiastical theory of the Romans: Scito dominum pro tota familia rem divinam facere.

LECTURE I.

CHRISTIAN BELIEF CONTRASTED WITH HEATHEN UNBELIEF.

Acts xvii. 32.

And when they heard of the resurrection of the dead, some mocked: and others said, We will hear thee again of this matter.

To men of education, to men of academic training and accomplishments, to all who pretend to ground their religious faith on reasoning and argument, no study can be more interesting than that of the process by which Christianity has actually won its way in the minds of the intelligent and accomplished, the reasoners and philosophers, of ancient and modern times. The records of Scripture disclose to us a glimpse, and no more than a glimpse, of the form which the discussion assumed between the preachers of the gospel and the possessors of human wisdom, in the centre and reputed stronghold of ancient science. The account of St. Paul's address to the philosophers of Athens, which occupies but a portion of a single chapter of the sacred history, suggests, as it seems to me, more directly the fundamental question between God's revelation and human speculation than any of the ample apologies, or explanatory defences of Christianity, set forth by the fathers of our faith in the centuries next ensuing. The apologists, no doubt, knew what they were aiming at; they had their own special object, which they placed clearly before them; they met the objections or refuted the fallacies which they knew by their own experience to be the most critical and the most harassing of their own times. But neither their arguments in defence of Christ's revelation, nor their arguments against the pretensions of heathen superstition, are generally such as to engage the interest of our day; their value is historical rather than critical; we neither go to them to confirm our own faith, nor of course do we require their help to perceive what is false, absurd, impossible in the creeds of heathen antiquity. Tertullian and Justin, who lived in the ages of persecution, dwell with most force and fervour on the sanctity of the Christians' lives in attestation of the truth of the gospel message. Augustine and Lactantius, witnesses of the triumph of the new religion, expose to scorn the vain pretences of the priests of Jupiter and Apollo: but the preaching of St. Paul, in the short fragment before us, goes in one word to the root of the matter, and sets before us the question of questions, which all generations must ask and do ask of themselves—in private, in their own hearts, if not in public debate and controversy—namely, whether God has given us the assurance of His Being, of His Providence, and of His Righteousness, by the sure and certain promise of a Future Existence? For such is the way in which the apostle states the question of the resurrection.

'Forasmuch then as we are the offspring of God, we ought not to think that the Godhead is like unto gold, or silver, or stone, graven by art and man's device.

'And the times of this ignorance God winked at; but now commandeth all men every where to repent:

'Because He hath appointed a day, in the which He will judge the world in righteousness by that man whom He hath ordained; whereof He hath given assurance unto all men, in that He hath raised Him from the dead.'[1]

The moral government of God, the judgment of God, and the need of repentance to meet that judgment, are all assured to us by the fact of Christ's Resurrection, which is the type and pledge of our resurrection also.

How, then, did the philosophers of Athens meet the arguments of St. Paul, of which no doubt a mere outline has been preserved to us, but which were evidently based upon the fact, affirmed and demonstrated, of our Lord's own resurrection? 'When they heard of the resurrection of the dead,' says the same brief record, 'some mocked, and others said, We will hear thee again of this matter.'

I need not say how truly this concise statement represents the way in which the truths of religion are

[1] Acts xvii. 29-31.

very commonly received by the adepts in human wisdom in all ages: some who are possessed by a prejudice, whose minds are made up, who have been long persuaded that there is no new truth to be discovered, make a mock, courteously perhaps and blandly, of the doctrine propounded to them; others, touched at heart, distrusting themselves, perplexed and dubious, put off the day of conviction, and silence their uneasy doubts by promising to enquire further at some future time. But the words of the narrative are more remarkable, as foreshadowing the way in which the revelation of Christianity, the keystone of which is the doctrine of a future state, would be received generally in the heathen world, and more particularly by the philosophers and thinkers among the heathen; how many, to the last, would make a mock of it; how, in the midst of their own spiritual struggles and distresses, in all the agony of their search for spiritual consolation, they would still make pretence of derision or defiance at the preaching of the Christian Resurrection. Nevertheless others there were, many there were, at last a majority there was, who would *hear again* of the matter. The preachers of the gospel and of immortality, of God's justice and the final retribution, would never fail of listeners till the day should come when this great doctrine should attain its triumph, when upon this stone, upon the confession of this fundamental truth, the Church of Christ would be established in the Roman Empire, and the Truth as it is in Christ Jesus become the moral law of civilized men throughout the 'inhabited world' of the Greek or Roman.

We may take the statement of the text, then, as a type of the struggle between Paganism and Christianity, and of that transformation of religious opinion, by which the hopes and fears and spiritual aspirations of the Roman world, at the time of our Lord's appearance in the flesh, became absorbed in the faith of Christ—modified, purified, exalted, expanded. In the Lectures which are to follow I propose to sketch, as far as opportunity allows, the progress of this transformation, the most signal of all religious revolutions. The object of the foundation of the Boyle Lecture is to assert the truth of Christianity against unbelievers, and it may have been usual to give these discourses a controversial turn, to answer special objections against the facts of our religion, or urge direct arguments in its defence. If I take a somewhat different course in setting forth a historical survey of the change of religious opinion among the ancients, I believe I shall act not less in the spirit of my instructions. At the present day, at least, if I judge rightly the temper of my contemporaries, I am more likely to recommend the truth of Christianity by tracing the progress of conviction in the minds of men, than by combating again the old objections, or seeking weapons with which to encounter the most recent, the offspring generally of the old, and bearing a strong resemblance to their parents.

Many, I think, are agreed that, after all, the most striking evidence for the Divine origin of our faith lies in the patent fact of its existence, of its growth and diffusion, its proved superiority to all other forms of spiritual thought, its proved adaptation to all the spiritual wants of man. Nothing can be more interesting, nothing can more conduce to a just notion of its claims on our belief, than a critical examination of the state of thought and opinion with which it had to deal at the outset, and the nature of the intellectual struggle which it carried on. It is with this conviction that I propose to devote these Lectures to the consideration of that spiritual resurrection, that resurrection of faith and genuine piety, which marks the intellectual history of the early centuries of our era; to dash at least a few rapid sketches of the most salient features of the controversy between the wisdom of this world and the Truth as it is in Christ Jesus.

One indulgence your lecturer must crave. The line of enquiry thus marked out cannot be profitably followed in these discourses without the free use of the materials of secular history, without repeated reference to the names of men and of places of antiquity, without occasional allusions to worldly customs and modes of thought, without citation sometimes of secular books—in short, not except under the usual conditions of a critical investigation. I must be allowed to make these addresses, what they are in fact properly termed, *Lectures*, rather than *Sermons*. I must be pardoned if the exposition of the sacred text, or the topics of religious exhortation or instruction which form the usual staple of our discourses from the pulpit, give place for the most part, in my hands, to an examination of human opinions on matters of religious interest. For these subjects, too, I believe, 'are good and profitable unto men.'[1]

The transition from ancient to modern ideas of religion to which I call your attention extends over a period of three or four centuries: a long period, no doubt, in the history of civilized man; a long period, marked with many changes of progress or decline in arts and inventions, in intellectual interests, in literature and science. In many respects the fourth century of Christianity was a different world from the first century before it, though the long interval, the wide chasm, was spanned by the vast structure of the Roman Empire, the bridge of ages, one pier of which rested on the consulship of Cæsar, the other on the despotism of Constantine. But how wide was the moral space which divided the worshippers of Jupiter on the Capitol from the worshippers of Jesus Christ at the new Rome on the Bosphorus may be appreciated from the contrast of two historical scenes which I will now place before you.

The Roman senators were assembled on the fifth of December, in the year 63 before Christ, in the Temple of Concord, the pavement of which, at the foot of the Capitoline hill, uncovered in modern times, serves us even now to realize vividly the scene and the circumstances presented. The divinity to whom the temple was dedicated marked in itself a peculiar phase of the course

---

[1] Titus iii. 8.

of religious feeling among the Romans; for Concord—a mere moral abstraction, a mere symbol of a compact effected at an earlier period between the political orders of the State—was not an old popular creation of Italian sentiment, but eminently the invention of the magistrate, introduced by law into the national ritual. The Senate was itself the minister of the civil government, and on this occasion it met on the spot which thus eminently symbolized the civil religion of the Roman State. Nor less was the Senate the minister of the State-religion. It comprehended in its ranks the pontiffs, the augurs, and most of the great ecclesiastical officers of Rome. The place in which it held its meetings—wherever the consul might appoint, whether a temple or a hall for civil affairs—must be consecrated by the observation of the auspices. Never, then, were the civil and the religious character of the Senate more conspicuously represented than when it met in the Temple of Concord to deliberate on the punishment due to the greatest of crimes political and religious, the sacrilegious treason of Catiline and his followers.

Among the senators convened on that memorable day were men of the highest political renown,—men who had maintained or men who had daringly assailed the traditions of government on which the fortunes and the fame of the commonwealth had for centuries rested;—warriors and legislators, patriots and demagogues, leaders and partisans, orators and mere dumb but faithful voters; all influenced by the strongest political feelings, most of them absorbed in the great struggles of the day,—enthusiasts, fanatics,—ready to stake their fortunes and their lives in assertion of their respective watchwords ;—all full of reminiscences of the great men and the great deeds of old ;—not a few among them emulous of ancient fame, many setting glory and honour and duty high above every sordid or selfish consideration. Moreover, there were few or none of them who had not been trained in the philosophies of the day, and accustomed to look with intelligent interest upon the problems of human nature, and consider the claims of the higher spiritual life, and recognise the workings of man's soul within him.

It was on such an occasion, then, on such a spot, in such an assembly, that Cæsar pronounced the words which have been doubtless faithfully reported to us by no mean contemporary authority—the words which have ever since been marked and held in remembrance as the manifesto of Roman unbelief on the subject of future existence.

'In pain and misery,' he said, 'death is the release from all suffering, not suffering itself; death dissolves all the ills of mortality ; beyond it is no place either for pain or pleasure. Wherefore,' such was his argument, 'keep these criminals alive, to suffer a fitting penalty ; after death there is no more punishment for sin, neither is there any reward for virtue.' Cæsar himself, the chief pontiff, the highest functionary of the State-religion, the chosen interpreter of Divine things to the national conscience, declared peremptorily that there is no such thing as retribution beyond the grave, no future state of consciousness, no immortality of the soul. To him replied the grave and virtuous Cato, the devoted servant of his country, her laws and institutions; the most regular observer of the traditions of his class and order; the most *religious* man, I may say, at Rome, inasmuch as, of all the Romans of his day, there was none who set before himself so high a rule of life or so strictly kept it; a man whose aim it was to 'fulfil all righteousness' in the sense in which righteousness would present itself to him—a man, I will add, with a nearer sense of a personal inspiration, of the indwelling of a divine spirit, than any heathen, except perhaps one or two only, with whom we are acquainted:—to him Cato replied, following and refuting, closely and gravely, all his political arguments, but passing by this remarkable expression with just one sentence of what looks like polished banter, just enough to indicate a humourist's sense (for Cato too was a humourist) of the curious incongruity of such a sentiment in such a mouth;—but so lightly, so perfunctorily, as plainly to show how little there was in it to alarm the religious feeling of the audience, or to disgust the religious convictions of the speaker himself. But another great man took part also in the debate; another orator remarked on the daring assertion of Cæsar—daring, as with our habits of thought we can hardly refrain from calling it, though in the minds of the Roman senators there was clearly no daring in it at all. Cicero, the most consummate adept in the doctrines of the philosophical schools, the man who of all his order could most exactly weigh the amount of approbation which the denial of immortality would then and there carry with it—Cicero also, I say, refers to Cæsar's assertion, not as caring to give his own assent or dissent upon the question, but leaving it perfectly open to the learned or the pious, to the statesman and legislator, the pontiff and augur, to embrace or repudiate it as he pleases. We read of no further discussion upon the point, upon this blank negation of all spiritual faith and hope; the historian takes no personal notice of it; no writer of antiquity alludes again to it; it passes as a matter of general indifference. Such, in short, is the tone of sentiment among the highest intelligences of the day at Rome, in the century next before the coming of Christ, that the belief in a future state of retribution—the very foundation, as we regard it, of all true and rational religion—is allowed to be made an open question, to be treated as hardly worth question at all, in the gravest of assemblies, on the gravest of all public occasions.[1] Such was their proud devotion to the false show of this world, to the glories of a world-wide dominion, the enjoyments of a voluptuous luxury, the flatteries of a complacent literature; such their judicial blindness to the future, with all its aspirations and its terrors, its rewards and its punishments.

But 'blessed be the God and Father of our Lord Jesus Christ, which according to His abundant mercy hath begotten us again unto a lively hope by the resurrection of Jesus Christ from the dead.'[2]

[1] See Note A.   [2] 1 Peter i. 3.

For let the clouds of time settle upon the scene before us, and when the mist clears up let us find ourselves transported in imagination four centuries onwards, from Italy to Asia Minor, from Rome to the provincial city of Nicæa, from the Temple of Concord beneath the Capitol to a public hall of state over against the destined site of a second Rome on the Bosphorus. How changed is the scene which now meets our eyes; how changed—yet in some marked circumstances how like to the old scene renewed? The place of meeting is no longer a temple, but a town-hall or a palace; the government there enthroned is no longer a commonwealth, but an imperial autocracy; the men assembled before us in their robes of dignity and their ensigns of office,—the pallium for the toga, the crooked staff for the ivory sceptre,—are no longer senators but bishops; not fathers of patrician households, and rulers of provinces and legions, but fathers of the Church, elders of a spiritual congregation, abounding in exhortation and teaching, interpreting a rule of faith and practice, holding fast an already ancient ecclesiastical tradition. The ideas of the time, indeed, are changed : the faith and usages of the people have undergone a marvellous transformation. The matter in debate in the assembly to which the gravest affair of state is now committed is not a question of political emergency, of foreign levy or domestic treason, but of the deepest spiritual significance; the Council of Nice is met together to fix the creed of Christendom on a point of religious dogma, to close up an intellectual schism, and settle the faith of men on an everlasting foundation.

The chief who summons this council of Christian bishops is still the highest guardian of the national ritual, the head of the Church upon earth, but he comes not to prescribe his own views on points of religious faith, but to collect the suffrages of its recognised expounders, the depositaries of three centuries of interpretation and tradition, the chief pastors of the Christian congregations scattered over the face of the empire and even beyond it.

For there too were assembled, not the denizens of one imperial city, descending from their mansions on the seven hills into the Roman forum, but, in the words of the great historian of the crisis, 'the most eminent among God's ministers of all those Churches which filled all Europe, Libya, and Asia. And one sacred oratory,' he continues, 'enlarged as it were by God Himself, enclosed within its walls both Syrians and Cilicians, Phœnicians and Arabians, Palestinians and Egyptians also, Thebæans and Libyans, and those that come forth of Mesopotamia. There was present also at this synod a Persian bishop, neither was the Scythian absent from the quire. Moreover, there appeared here Thracians and Macedonians, Achaians and Epirotes, and such as dwelt far beyond these met nevertheless together.'[1]

And he goes on, as you might anticipate, to compare this varied assemblage to the multitude of many

---

[1] Eusebius Pamphilus, *Life of Constantine*, iii. 7.

nations that were gathered together on the day of Pentecost; a meeting inferior indeed, as he hints, to this in interest, for that was composed for the most part of laymen and neophytes, but this of ministers and teachers only.

The interest and importance, indeed, of this famous synod, it requires no theologian's rhetoric to magnify. Viewed as an event of human history only, dull indeed must be the imagination which does not see in the Council of Nicæa an incident of the deepest significance, the first launching of a vast spiritual engine on its career of conquest and dominion. However variously we may estimate the morals and intellect of the age, we cannot doubt that it was represented at this council by its best, its ablest, and its most intelligent. Whatever judgment polemics may hold of the soundness of the ecclesiastical traditions then current, there can be no question but that at that council they were faithfully expounded and fully developed. Whatever value some modern thinkers may set upon the abtruse dogmas which came under discussion in it, it is allowed that in these dogmas lay the breath of all spiritual life at the period; and especially the question of the Divine Son's relation to the Father, then elaborately defined, was a question of life and death for the scheme of theology then established, and ever since maintained in preeminence in the Church of Christ. Nor can we dispute that, if such transcendent mysteries can ever be profitably subjected to the test of critical discussion, there were men there met together of every temper, of manifold habits of thought, of various mental associations, of various intellectual powers; some trustworthy as witnesses to traditional usage, some respectable for their personal experiences, some to be admired for their keenness and subtilty, some to be revered for their illustrious piety; and that in such hands the subject in debate received as full and as worthy treatment as it has ever been capable of among men.[1]

The bishops, 318 in number, who met on this solemn occasion had all been swept over by the last storm of imperial persecution, the agitation of which had hardly yet subsided. Known to each other hitherto by the record of their trials and endurance only, they now met for a moment upon earth, trusting to be united finally in heaven—the witnesses to the faith in Rome and Antioch, at Trèves and at Carthage; witnesses to the same faith, the same law, the same sacraments, the same Lord and Master of them all. The most illustrious were soon distinguished: some were betokened by their strange dress and habits, some by their well-known reputation for zeal or for learning, some by the wounds and scars of their noble confession. Paphnutius, a confessor from the Thebaid, who asserted the right of the clergy to the society of their wives, had been blinded and maimed in the leg; Paul of Neocæsarea was crippled by torture in the hand. Ascetics from the Upper Egypt were clothed in the wild raiment of the Baptist; they had wandered forth in sheepskins and

---

[1] Socrates, *History of the Church*, i. 6.

goatskins, they had dwelt in deserts and on mountains, in dens and caves of the earth. The childlike simplicity of the primitive ages was instanced in Spiridion, the village bishop of Cyprus—the prototype, it would seem, of the model prelate of a recent fiction,—who, when brigands robbed him of his sheep, rebuked them meekly for not having rather asked him for them. The learning of the clerical order, which could compare with that of the Pagan orators and sophists, was represented among others by Eustathius and the two Eusebiuses; while for age and venerable bearing none were more remarkable than the Spanish prelate Hosius, and Alexander the patriarch of Alexandria. While again the neology of the period, and the leanings of secular learning towards notions which sprang from the lurking heathenism of the heart, found their artful expounder in the arch-heretic Arius, the real doctrine of the Church, such as it claimed to have been from the beginning, and such as it has been maintained for fifteen centuries onwards, was defended, above all others, with the keenest logic, with the most ardent rhetoric, and with indomitable energy, by the mighty Athanasius, —he who not long after stood alone, as it was said, against the world, and triumphed. The intellectual excitement of the day was not unfelt even by the heathens themselves; and many distinguished adherents of the old religion came,—some scoffing, some trembling, all wondering,—to hear how the Church of Christ, that strange confederation which had vanquished them at last after three centuries of conflict, would solve the most awful questions, which the human mind can encounter. These strangers to the faith were not indeed admitted to the scene of the sacred conference, but they hovered anxiously around it, and conversed from time to time with the members as they passed in or out, and were admonished sometimes with compassion, sometimes with yearning love, sometimes with grave and authoritative rebuke; and if some still mocked, and some hesitated and said, 'We will hear thee again on this matter,' others there were who were conscience-stricken and converted on the spot, and the Holy Spirit added unto the Church daily such as should be saved.

The Synod was assembled, every man in his place, when the Emperor Constantine entered, arrayed in gold and purple, and strode with his guards around him to the top of the Hall, where, standing for a moment before a golden throne, he looked hesitatingly around, as if to ask permission to be seated. When he took his seat all the ecclesiastics sat down likewise, according to the tradition of the Roman Senate, all the members of which were virtually equal. Then the Emperor rose and addressed the assembly in a set harangue, explaining the main object of their summons, using 'for the majesty of the empire,' as his predecessors would have phrased it, the sonorous tongue of Latium. 'When by the assent,' he said, 'and the aid of the Almighty, I had triumphed over my enemies, I hoped that I had nothing more to do than to give thanks to God, and to rejoice with those whom He had delivered by my hand. But as soon as I heard of the division existing among you, I judged it to be a pressing matter, which I must not neglect; and desiring also to apply some remedy to this new evil, I have called you together without delay, and great is my satisfaction in being present at your meeting.' With these, and such words as these, full of goodwill to the Church, its chiefs, and its concerns, but without venturing even to propound the subjects to which he invited discussion, did Constantine open that memorable council; giving the sanction of the highest civil authority to debates which ranged over topics of the deepest spiritual significance; setting the first precedent in recorded history, however moderate and reserved, of the action of a regal supremacy in matters ecclesiastical; giving the first fulfilment to the prophecy, that kings should be the fathers of the Church, and queens her nursing mothers. Deep indeed must have been the interest of the civilized world, Christian and Pagan, lay and clerical, learned and unlearned, noble and plebeian, in the questions which then agitated the Christian Church, when the deliberations of this new senate, of this novel confederation of the civil and ecclesiastical powers, of the emperor and the bishops, of the State and the Church, issued in the promulgation of a solemn rule of faith, of that form of sound words which has been recited daily in the Church for fifteen centuries, and still is recited with awe and veneration among us—the illustrious creed of Nicæa. A few years, as we have seen, before the incarnation of Jesus Christ, the Roman senators listened without shame or shuddering to the utter denial of man's spiritual being from the mouth of their sovereign Pontiff. Three hundred years after His resurrection, an assembly of priests, the august successor of that incredulous Synod, deliberately affirmed the most mysterious dogmas of revealed religion. 'We believe,' it said, ' in one God, the Father Almighty, Maker of all things visible and invisible ; And in one Lord Jesus Christ, the Son of God, of the same substance with the Father, by whom all things were made : Who for us men, and for our salvation came down from Heaven, and was incarnate and was made man, suffered and rose again the third day, He ascended into Heaven, He shall come again to judge both the quick and the dead :'— And further, 'We believe in the Holy Ghost, the Lord and Giver of Life : and in the Remission of Sins, the Resurrection of the Body, and the Life everlasting.'[1]

Here there are two great facts set before you : an immense revolution in human thought has been effected, a vast transformation of human feeling. Such change was not wrought upon the spot, not by a single miraculous stroke of Providence, not by a momentary decree of the Almighty, as when He said to chaos, ' Let there be light, and there was light ;' as when He said to Saul of Tarsus, 'I am Jesus whom thou persecutest.' If the conversion of the individual soul is rarely sudden and immediate, still more rare—still less,

[1] See Note B.

I may say, possible—is the immediate conversion of a people. No; there was an interval of four centuries, crowded with movements of changes outward and inward; all slow and gradual, and following justly one from another:—the falling away of many prejudices; the scaling off of many folds of inveterate error; the raising up of many footholds of truth and faith. There was life in death, energy in decay, rejuvenescence in decrepitude. The human mind continued to work by its old accustomed methods, but those methods of thought were themselves of God's original appointment; the Holy Spirit had brooded over their creation, and guided them gently to the end which to Him was present from the beginning. Let us seek, with His blessed aid and enlightenment, to trace in these Lectures the mode of this spiritual revolution, this conversion of the Roman Empire, of the civilized world of antiquity, of the natural human intellect in the pride of its highest acquirements, from a denial of the first principle of positive belief to the assertion of an entire system of revealed religion.

LECTURE II.

HEATHEN BELIEF DIRECTED TOWARDS A TEMPORAL PROVIDENCE.

ACTS XVII. 22.

Then Paul stood in the midst of Mars' hill, and said, Ye men of Athens, I perceive that in all things ye are too superstitious.

THERE is no need on the present occasion to discuss critically the meaning of the word here rendered 'superstitious,' nor of the fact from which the apostle particularly infers it of the Athenians, when he adds, 'For as I passed by, and beheld your devotions, I found an altar with this inscription, To the unknown God.' We will take the phrase 'too superstitious,' or literally 'god or spirit fearing,' to mean, excessively addicted to the worship of supernatural powers, over-prone to believe in and tremble before the influence of invisible existences, capricious or perverse in the apprehension of God's nature, and of the nature of His divine rule and providence. Superstition, as here spoken of, seems to be an excess or extravagant conception of religion: it is the fanatic issue of human thoughts on subjects too pure, too sublime, and too holy for human nature, unenlightened from above, to think of duly or worthily. Nevertheless, even such superstition does bear in a certain measure the character of religious belief; it is grounded upon the same fundamental principle—the apprehension of a spiritual world.

Now I would have you observe the juxtaposition of the religious feeling here ascribed to the Athenians with the mocking denial, or at best, the timid and doubtful anticipation of a future state which is imputed to them in what presently follows : 'And when they heard of the resurrection of the dead, some mocked : and others said, We will hear thee again of this matter' —a text on which I enlarged in my last Lecture, to show the imperfect apprehension or popular denial of a future retribution in the heathen world. Compare these two passages, and it will plainly appear, that in St. Paul's view the same people might have, and indeed actually had, a keen and conscious apprehension of a Divine government, together with a direct renunciation of the doctrine of a future retribution. I need not say how utterly this is inconsistent with the idea we as Christians entertain of religion. We Christians, trained from father to son in the teaching of Scripture, cannot, I imagine, divorce the two ideas. We cannot contemplate for ourselves, hardly can we conceive in others, the idea of religious belief,—of belief in God as a moral ruler, and in His providential government of the world,—apart from the conviction of judgment hereafter. The famous paradox of Warburton is founded upon this conviction, upon this instinctive assurance, as he maintained it to be, that belief in Providence cannot ordinarily subsist, that it cannot certainly be maintained among men in society, without a belief in a future state of rewards and punishments. The omission of this cardinal doctrine, as he argued, in the Mosaic economy, formed a conclusive demonstration that the law of Moses was no invention of the mere human mind; so manifestly, in his view, does such omission contravene the first principles of human reasoning on the subject of religion.

I perceive well enough the apparent presumption in favour of such a theory. I felt myself authorized to declare in my last Lecture that the open denial of immortality in the Roman Senate implied a general repudiation of a fundamental principle of religion. I contrasted this repudiation with the assertion of Christian dogma at the first of the great Christian councils, to mark, at one glance, the entire space of the chasm which separated the one age from the other, the heathen from the Christian, the Roman Empire from the City of God. Here we see, indeed, two great forces arrayed against each other—Belief and Unbelief.

Such, at least, is the broad and general view of the case presented to us. But let us look a little closer, and see whether the condition of the heathen mind was altogether negative in religious matters. Did the heathen deny all obligations, all objects of religious faith, in repudiating the cardinal principle of a future retribution? Can a man have no apprehension of a God because he has no apprehension of immortality? Our text points to a different conclusion. The Athenians, little as they certainly regarded a future life, were even too superstitious; full of a strong apprehension of unknown superior powers, they were blind and mean and gross in their conception of them. And the same might be shown equally of the Romans.

The heathen, as St. Paul says, were to be left without excuse, and therefore the eternal power and Godhead, at least, of the Deity were made manifest to their hearts by the inner witness of the conscience. Though they glorified not God in their acts, nor even in the justness and purity of their notions, yet they knew God so far as to apprehend the fact of His Being, His Power, and His Providence.

I repeat that, speaking broadly, the heathen of Greece and Rome, at least the intelligent classes among them—all above the common herd, the women and children—had no real belief in a future state. I speak not of the teaching or the private aspirations of a few philosophers, of which more may be said hereafter. Nor need I spend words in showing that the vulgar mythology, with its Hades and Olympus, its Tartarean blackness and Elysian sunshine, was an exploded and despised tradition. Whatever hankering after a positive belief on matters of such awful interest might linger in men's hopes and fears, and find utterance here and there in their popular literature, there was no real and living faith in such things; no intelligent man would have publicly acknowledged any such anticipations, no priest or preacher was appointed to teach them dogmatically; the rewards and punishments of a future state, as far as such a state pretended to be revealed, had become no more than mere poetic machinery.[1]

The heathens, then, had no popular belief in a future retribution. Nevertheless, they had their temples, and their altars; their gods were represented by images, and service was done to them by priests and ministers. A comprehensive and intricate ritual prescribed the names and characters of hundreds of divinities, specified their various attributes and functions, interpreted their will, interceded for their favour. 'He that cometh to God,' says the Christian Scripture, speaking of mankind generally, 'must believe that He *is*, and that He is a rewarder of them that diligently seek Him.'[2] This is the universal and fundamental condition of religious belief. If the heathens of Rome did thus come to God, even to a God of their own imaginations, with religious service, however blind and carnal, they did then assuredly believe in the Being of God, a God of power and intelligence; and did apprehend in some way, however faintly and imperfectly, the fact of His providential oversight of man. And accordingly the Gospel had to combat not a mere blank negation of all belief, but a living and substantive principle of religion.

[1] See Note C. [2] Heb. xi. 6.

Let me then first place clearly before you the fact that this religious service was really made a matter of conscience, enjoined and enforced by ecclesiastical authorities, accepted and acknowledged by the heart and understanding of the worshippers.

We read how, not many years after the above-mentioned debate in the Roman Senate, the factions of the Republic culminated in a great political apostasy. An impious son raised his hand against his parent's bosom. The crossing of the Rubicon, the march of Cæsar upon Rome, was denounced as an act, not of rebellion only, but of impiety and schism. It must be met with human arms indeed, but before human arms were tried, or while human arms were being tried, it might be met also with a solemn religious ceremony— by an act of lustration, of expiation, of national humiliation before the insulted powers of the other world. Policy and religion joined hand in hand. The Consul takes counsel with the Pontiff; the Philosopher enquires of the Augur; they revolve the ancient books, and resort to the prescribed usages, and marshal with one accord a long procession of priests and statesmen, of magistrates and citizens, of Vestals, Salians, and Flamens, to stalk around the sacred inclosure of the city, and purge its dwellings with a holy lustration. The whole population, in an access of superstitious fervour, is moved to appease the national divinities by an act of national devotion. Men and women, young and old, the learned and the vulgar, unite in this solemn function with a common will and conscience.

How far they believed in the idols to which they bowed themselves; how far they duped one another; how far they were duped themselves, who shall say? The scene itself stands before us, a great and impressive fact, a fact surely not without a meaning. The mighty multitude of the greatest of cities, in an age when none believed in a resurrection, none regarded a future retribution, was moved by a common impulse to make this striking demonstration of its religious instincts and spiritual convictions. We cannot shut our eyes to the fact. Whatever abatement we may make from the entire genuineness of the sentiment by which this multitude was animated, we must allow that there did exist, even at this time, among the heathen at Rome a principle of religious belief. Christianity, I say, had a real living enemy to encounter.[1]

But this, it may be urged, was a sudden outburst of feeling, a paroxysm of alarm, a transient panic of unreflecting superstition. Not so: we may judge of its depth and reality from the marked revival of religious usage, and apparently of actual persuasion, which ensued in the next generation. The conviction of the existence of Powers unseen, on whose due propitiation the safety of the State (in which was enwrapped the safety of every citizen) depended, was still deeply rooted in the heart of the Roman even of this latter age. Choked it might be, and stifled amid the cares of government; forgotten it might be in the turmoil of war; it might be thrust contemptuously aside in the

[1] See Note D.

flush of victory and triumph, in the selfish enjoyment of success, amid the orgies of sensual luxury; nevertheless, the stress of circumstances might at any time revive it, the call of an astute or ardent ruler might evoke it. When the religious principle among the Jews of the olden time had been perverted by evil influences, they had fallen away to the snares most tempting to their peculiar weakness, to the idolatries and harlotries of Edom and of Moab. The Romans, when the same principle was corrupted among them, surrendered themselves to the charm of their most seductive neighbours, the Greeks, and the love of the gods of the Capitol waxed cold under the spell of sceptics, rationalists, and philosophers. But among both Jews and Romans the religious sentiment was again and again revived. The process was alike in both cases; the history seems to repeat itself. The example or command of pious kings effected more than once a religious revival in Israel and Judah. Asa and Hezekiah removed the high places and brake down the images, and restored the worship of the God of their fathers. The people followed in their steps and turned again to the service of Jehovah. 'And Josiah,' we read, 'stood by a pillar, and made a covenant before the Lord, to walk after the Lord, and to keep His commandments. . . . . And all the people stood to the covenant.'[1] Such were the acts of the good kings, influenced by pure religious feeling, prompting them

---

[1] 2 Kings xxiii. 3.

to please God by their own conversion, urging them to lead their people to propitiate Him by a willing service. But Jehu, again, is an instance of a wicked king, a politic and selfish man, impelled by mixed and impure motives of gain, or fear, or statecraft, to put on a show of godliness, to effect an imperfect and one-sided reformation. 'Thus Jehu destroyed Baal out of Israel, while at the same time he did not himself depart from the sin of Jeroboam, who made Israel to sin.'[1]

Now the obligation and responsibility thus felt by the chiefs of Israel and Judah, was confessed not less openly by some of the Roman Emperors. When Rome became a monarchy, the spiritual headship of the people was assumed by the Cæsar as definitely as if he were the anointed of Jehovah. It might be mere craft and policy that induced Augustus to call for a restoration of national religion; he knew well that religion is the safeguard of thrones, and sought doubtless to clench thereby the obedience of his subjects. It might be superstition, for Augustus was the victim of many an abject superstition. Great conquerors, the realizers of great projects—great favourites, as we call them, of fortune, and we almost sanction the sentiment ourselves in calling them so—generally are superstitious. And again, there might be some real belief, some genuine religion in it; for Augustus was too great a man not to be strongly and devoutly impressed with the depth and breadth and height of the mission to

[1] 2 Kings x. 28, 29.

which he was appointed. At the same time, from the innovating spirit of the theorists and philosophers Augustus was singularly free, if not absolutely hostile to it. While the educated men of Rome were banded, as it were, in the contending camps of the Stoics and Epicureans and Platonists; while almost every eminent statesman among them announced himself the disciple of some dogmatic teacher, as publicly as he declared himself the follower of a party-leader, it was remarked that this man, the most eminent of all, stood scornfully aloof from all the schools of thought and moral doctrine. The religion of the genuine Roman had no sympathy with them; the personal aspirations they might engender, the yearning after the invisible, the ardent gaze upon an ideal of virtue and holiness; these sentiments in which, imperfect and partial as in the mere natural heart they must be, we as Christians still place the first seeds and germs of religious principle, had no connection with the train of thought and basis of feeling on which the system of the Priests and Pontiffs, the Augurs and the Flamens, was established. Such were not the pillars on which the conqueror could build his Empire. He must revert to the old foundations: he must stand upon the ancient ways.

Hence, then, his propping of the falling temples, his repair of decayed and smoke-soiled images; hence his erection of thrice a hundred shrines in the city, his revival of old religious usages, his enforcement of the sanctions of property and marriage, his correction of social irregularities, his Pantheon, his Secular Games, his incessant sacrifices and lustrations. Such were the elements of a religious revival, which Augustus deemed requisite for the gaining of Divine favour, for the safety of the State, for the perpetuation, it may be, of his own government and power. The man who in his youth, when himself an aspirant and an adventurer, had mocked the gods of his country with indecent ribaldry —a Jehu in ambition, in bloodshed, in every personal impurity—in mature age, when accepted, as it seemed, for the favourite of heaven, the first child of Olympus, acknowledged that his own rule, like the sovereignty of Rome herself, depended on the Powers above, and was founded on the confession of their mighty name. Nor was this a mere personal feeling. The general consent of the writers of the time, admitting this principle of a providential government, accords fully with it, and reflects the temper of the age as faithfully as of the sovereign.

There was then a deep religious feeling among the Romans, however blind and narrow we must esteem it, in which their chief himself partook, even while he profited by it. This feeling is attested, among many other tokens, by the outburst at the time of pretended prophecy, by the general augury of a spiritual manifestation; showing that it was no mere outward pretence, no mere ceremonial reformation, not a revival only of masonry and upholstery. Paganism had indeed no tap-root of moral renovation. A religious revival in the age of Augustus may have been but the maudlin remorse which follows on a surfeit of sin and selfish indulgence. Yet for a moment at least the nation's heart was stricken, its conscience agitated; and the chief who rejected the exotic doctrines of the ideologists; who restored the cult of the national divinities; who sate once a year at the gate of his palace, and propitiated Nemesis by the begging of alms; who appealed to the bystanders at his death-bed with a smile, 'Have I played well my part in the show and drama of life?' was, I conceive, a signal example of the native power of the religious sentiment of the Roman people.

It was necessary to examine this example closely if we would estimate the work which it was appointed for the Gospel to effect on the heart of the heathen. I will not detain you with a survey of a similar revival, impelled a hundred years later by another Cæsar, another profligate, another tyrant, yet another anxious votary of the gods of Rome. It was the boast of Domitian that in his youth he had waged the wars of Jove, in defence of the Capitol; that in a later age he had scaled the heavens for himself and his family, by piously restoring it. He too enforced the religious code of antiquity with the ruthless barbarity of a Jehu; he too rejected every spiritual innovation, persecuted the Christians and expelled the philosophers. The heart and conscience of his countrymen, alarmed by many signs and sufferings, responded to the impulse he gave it; and the student of history cannot fail to appreciate the sense of religious responsibility evinced by the Roman people under the rule of the Flavian dynasty.

What then, we may ask, was this religious idea which was before Christianity; which was so widely spread, so deeply rooted, so keenly felt, so importunate in its assaults on the conscience even of worldlings and sensualists; which all the vice, and sin, and carnal abominations of the natural heart could not extinguish or allay; which Christianity was sent into the world to combat, to try as with fire, to purge its dross and draw forth its residue of gold; which was so hostile in its outward form to Christianity that the two could not endure together, but its rites must be abolished, its mysteries suppressed, its vanity demonstrated; while it still held fast the true foundation of the fear of God, and confession of His providence?

Look back for a moment at the early world, in the aspect of nature and the works of man; at the woods in which men planted their first stockades, the rocks on which they founded their primeval fortifications, the lakes in which they raised their first amphibious dwelling-places. Look at the masses of Cyclopean masonry, piled upon rugged cliffs; the solid bulk of earthworks, stretching from hill to hill, and from sea to sea. Do not these glimpses of society in infancy point, and nowhere more plainly than in Italy itself, to a state of existence in which men lived together in constant apprehension of other men, in which combination for mutual protection was the first and paramount object of all; in which mutual fear was the common bond of union, and every nation, tribe, and clan was banded together against all its neighbours?

This is not a description, perhaps, of the patriarchal and pastoral communities of the plain of Shinar and the banks of the Euphrates; but looking westward to Greece and Italy, we observe how the necessary conditions of civil society issued in the most jealous of all national institutions, the most exclusive of all national beliefs. The idea of Greek and Roman religion was to secure by a national worship the enjoyment of national advantages, protection, favour and reward, escape from national disasters and national punishments. This was the political religion of states and peoples. Their priests were the mediators between God and the Nation, between Heaven and the City. The Citizen was merged in the State; for the State he was born, he lived, he married, he tilled his land, he bequeathed his goods, he perpetuated his family. The Roman worshipped for his country rather than for himself. To the gods of the enemy he opposed the gods of Rome; and if he conquered the enemy he was anxious to propitiate his gods though baffled, and draw them by craft, by flattery, even by force, to his own side. His idea of religion was of a national, not a personal covenant with God. His rule of right was framed on views of public expediency. If his principles were narrow or corrupt, his strictness in maintaining them was often worthy of a better code and a higher sanction. But whatever his idea of duty, whatever his law, he recognised no future retribution for his deeds. Like the Athenian, he was even too superstitious in his apprehension of a Divine Power; believing in God, he believed in Him as a Rewarder indeed of them that diligently seek Him; but the care of the gods, he imagined, was for the nation rather than the individual worshipper, their favour temporal, their rewards and punishments of the earth earthy. Starting, I say, from the notion of the gods as national patrons, he could scarce conceive in his mind—surely he could not logically conceive of them—as ushering the man, the citizen, into a personal immortality.

The tendency of such a fixed idea of religion was to resolve the essence of piety into the fulfilment of ceremonial observances. Its main object was to preserve the traditions of immemorial antiquity, to hand down intact from generation to generation the forms and usages of the past. The popular belief of Rome pointed to a period long since past, when the people was exemplarily religious, when the Divine services were punctually performed, when the gods were always propitious, when the State was always prosperous, when her men were brave, her women chaste, her legions triumphant. In every crisis of terror or disaster the heart of the multitude turned with unutterable yearnings to the tradition of that happy age; and sought to recover, were it but possible, by fond recurrence to the ancient practice, the favour and happiness they seemed to have foregone. The piety of the Romans looked ever backward: its ideal lay behind it, not before it. It aspired to present safety or enjoyment by a faithful imitation of an imaginary Past; but it had no standard of future excellence or future blessedness to attain unto, no rising star to follow, no expansion, no development to anticipate. With no yearnings for consummation and perfection hereafter, it took no heed of advance or improvement here. Of whatever greatness or goodness man was by nature capable, he was supposed to have already attained to it; enough, and more than enough, if he had not fallen from the height of his early attainments, and forfeited his privileges for ever. How obscure the Past! how comfortless the Present! how blank the Future! A Divine power with no adequate subject for its exercise! A Divine Providence with no consistent scheme of creation and government! And yet, so strong, so lively was this corrupt conception, this narrow view of God and Providence, this nervous apprehension of temporal rewards and punishments, fostered by long ages of political success—that not only was it made the subject of a national revival under an Augustus and a Domitian, but it continued to struggle on under many a mortal discouragement—retaining its hold of the throbbing heart—animating the body of expiring Paganism, for many a century after them. The last phase of the worship of Olympus was the personification of Rome herself as the patron deity of the Romans, and of Victory the embodied symbol of their national power and success. To the last moment the simple theory of the Gospel—which the Apostle required a vision to conceive and realize—that God is no respecter of persons, but that in every nation he that feareth Him and worketh righteousness is accepted of Him, was strange and abhorrent from the prejudices of the heathen. The City of God, in the Christian dispensation, is neither Rome nor Athens, nor even Jerusalem, but the society of believers on earth in spiritual communion with the saints in heaven. It has no promise of temporal favour, no assurance of defence against the world or the flesh; its promises point to a future reward, its terrors respect an impending retribution. It was to this belief, simple to us, but strange to him, that the heathen was to be brought—slowly, painfully, under stress of manifold influences, which I hope on future occasions to unfold. But he had still, at the time of our Lord's coming, a substantive belief of his own; a belief most alien from the Gospel, most visionary to the enlightened reason; a religion of temporal views and sanctions, a religion of national not individual import. To this he had been led by the first necessities of his social condition; in this he had been confirmed by the success which had long seemed to attend upon it; to this, if ever forgetful of it in his prosperity, if ever disgusted with it in his adversity, still from time to time he passionately recurred, full of horror at his own backsliding, full of hope for his tardy resipiscence. Three hundred years after the first preaching of the Gospel the chastened eloquence of the Christian Lactantius was still employed in exposing this spiritual perversion, this sacrifice of the soul to the lust of the eye, and the pride of life.

'And now,' he says, 'to sum up the Christian theory briefly. The world was made that man might be born into it. Man was made that he might recognise God the Maker of the world, and of himself. We recognise Him that we may worship Him; we worship Him that we may earn immortality through the works which are His peculiar service; we receive the reward of immortality that, being made like unto the angels, we may serve our Lord and Father for ever, and be His everlasting kingdom. This is the sum of all things; this the secret of God, the mystery of creation, to which they are strangers who, following present lusts, have abandoned themselves to things frail and earthly, and have plunged in deadly pleasures, as in the mire, souls born for heavenly occupation.

'But what sense can there be in the worship of the gods of the heathen? If they are many in number, if they are worshipped by men for the sake of wealth, honour, victory, which profit for this life only; if we are created for no purpose; if we are born by chance for our own selves and for pleasure only; if after death we are nothing, what so vain, so foolish, so frivolous as man's life and being, and the whole world itself, which, infinite as it is in magnitude, and wonderful in structure, is thus abandoned to vanity? For why do the winds blow and collect the clouds? why gleam the lightnings? why roar the thunders, and descend the rains for the increase of earth's manifold offspring? why, in short, doth all nature labour, that nothing may be wanting of the things by which man's being is sustained, if life be empty, if we wither to nothing, if nought be in us of greater interest to God? But if it be sin to say, nor possible to believe, that that which we see to consist with the highest plan and purpose, was not itself for some great purpose constituted, what sense can there be in these errors of the false religions, and in this persuasion of the philosophers that the souls of men do perish? Surely none whatever.'[1]

[1] See Note E.

LECTURE III.

EXPANSION OF HEATHEN BELIEF BY THE TEACHING OF THE PHILOSOPHERS.

ACTS XVII. 26.

God hath made of one blood all nations of men, for to dwell on all the face of the earth.

FEW declarations of Holy Writ have sunk more deeply into the heart and conscience of Christendom than this, by which we confess the unity of the human race in its claims on man and God, on the sympathy of our fellow-beings, and on the justice and mercy of our Creator. This is the point to which all Scripture seems to lead up. The doctrine which is plainly set forth in the first chapter of Genesis, which is affirmed repeatedly in the record of God's dealings with the Jewish people, when He chose them out from among other and mightier nations, for no merit or superior character of their own, but for the special purposes of His providence, to be merged again once more in the general mass of mankind, Jew and Gentile, among whom the Church and spiritual people of Christ should be established—this doctrine, I say, of the essential unity of our race is again dogmatically asserted in the text of St. Paul, and asserted or implied elsewhere throughout the volume of the New Testament—made in fact the very foundation of the promised preaching of salvation to the Gentiles. Such is the thorough consistency of the Word of God from one end to the other; such the Divine inspiration of truth breathed into it from the beginning, and continued to it even unto the end. And this doctrine, I repeat, is one which all Christendom has uniformly accepted as certain and divine. There has been, I suppose, no doubt of it at any time in the Church; so entirely does it seem to harmonize with our own moral convictions, as well as with the express declaration of Scripture. Nevertheless, this doctrine is far from being one of which men can be said to have a natural and instinctive apprehension. It is a truth engrafted upon the human stock. Let us see how the matter stood at the time when the apostle thus definitely announced it.

I explained in my last lecture the principle on which the religion of Rome was founded, and on which it still continued to rest, fixed by its weight, if not grappled by the roots, at the period of our Lord's actual teaching. This principle was the belief in national divinities, the patrons of the State, in the protection of one favoured race against all others, the maintenance of a federal compact between Heaven and the City, in which the individual worshipper had but a relative and proportionate interest. This was the hostile principle with which the Gospel was to make no terms, to hold no peace; to combat it, first where it lingered in the bosom of the descendant of Abraham, but more especially, more permanently, to combat it where it was enthroned in the prejudices, enwoven in the selfishness of the Roman and the Greek. Till this principle was overthrown, Christianity could not triumph; as long as it held sway over the human heart to which it was naturally congenial, Christianity could make no sound or palpable progress in the world. At this moment it was a formidable foe to the Gospel. It not only dwelt in the hearts and persuasions of the people, but was supported by all the powers of political interest; it glowed with the pomp of ceremonial observances; it was hallowed by the charm of long possession, by its pretended appeal to actual experience, and the demonstration it affected to derive from the worldly success of the Roman Empire. It was still a living and active principle, for it was capable of a marked revival, a new growth and development, as proved more than once in the course of the Roman history. But God's word had gone forth that His Church was founded upon a rock, and the gates of hell should not prevail against it. He had launched His Gospel into the world; the apostles were bearing the good tidings from land to land, and the motto they inscribed on their banner when they offered to do battle with all the powers of the false religions was such words as those of the text, 'God hath made of one blood all nations of men for to dwell on all the face of the earth;'[1] 'By one Spirit are we all baptized into one body, whether we be Jews or Gentiles, whether we be bond or free;'[2] and, 'God is no respecter

---

[1] Acts xvii. 26.   [2] 1 Cor. xii. 13.

of persons; but in every nation he that feareth Him, and worketh righteousness, is accepted with Him;'[1] and again, 'There is neither Greek nor Jew, circumcision nor uncircumcision, barbarian, Scythian, bond nor free: but Christ is all, and in all.'[2]

In fact, however formidable was the front which the power of the false religions advanced against the first preaching of the Truth, the principle on which it stood was already sapped from within by the circumstances of society around it, and the slow and gradual influence of social opinion. Four centuries before Christ a doctrine had been promulgated in which the Fathers of the Christian Church recognised a faint adumbration of some lineaments of Christian Truth, in which the spiritual character of God as the common source of all human spirituality, the reality and nearness of His providential government, the possibility at least of a future state of retribution, and the duties of repentance and devotion towards God, of love and general charity towards men, had been set forth in pleasing though uncertain colours.[3] Lofty indeed, and spiritual as the teaching of Plato was, it was baffled in its operation, and degraded by the inveterate prejudice of the Grecian and the Pagan—their prejudice against the natural equality and unity of man, his equal claim on God, his common right to social and political freedom, his right to live in personal relation to his Maker through his own conscience, and not merely in a political relation to him through the state of which he was socially a

---

[1] Acts x. 34, 35.   [2] Col. iii. 11.   [3] See Note F.

citizen. The actual division, it would seem, of Greece into rival communities operated so forcibly on Plato's imagination, that he could not conceive of mankind as living in a single or a widely diffused community; and his ideal of a political Utopia was not a broad cosmopolite association of men of various races, creeds, and colours, and climates, but the narrowest and closest combination of a few select thousands — even the number he expressly limited — to keep themselves apart in all their public relations from all the rest of mankind. So only could he imagine that the practical end of true philosophy and religion could be attained. So only could mankind, in his partial view, acquire or retain a just conception of their relation to the Divine, and fulfil the spiritual object of their being. His theory fell short of his principles, and whatever in his religious creed was truly expansive and liberal, stood in glaring contradiction to his political doctrines. The combination of the two in one system could result only in a strange and disappointing inconsistency.[1]

It would seem that this inconsistency did not escape the penetrating vision of the next great master of heathen philosophy, Aristotle. Warned by it, this teacher took a step backward. Instead of carrying on the great spiritual theory of Plato, and making it logical by widening the basis of humanity on which it rested, he yielded still more to the prejudices of his countrymen, and was content to regard man and his spiritual claims still more exclusively from the narrow

[1] See Note G.

Grecian stand-point. He avowed without remorse the preeminence of one race over every other; he declared the distinction to be natural and necessary between man and man, Greek and barbarian; as far as in him lay he would have fixed once and for ever the limits beyond which truth and knowledge, political rights, spiritual privileges, should not pass. He would have confined the work of God in the soul of man to one petty province, and thereby have practically abolished the work of God in the soul of man altogether. This single step backwards, so rashly, so inopportunely taken, would have destroyed the first germ of true religion in the world of Pagan antiquity.[1]

Rashly indeed, and inopportunely; for while the philosopher was baffling himself by the acuteness of his own logic, God was doing a work in the world which from the mere force of circumstances would utterly refute and discredit it. While the philosopher in his closet was mapping out the nations of the earth, by their political divisions, and civil constitutions, the conqueror in the field was bringing them, far and near, under one sceptre, one law, and one name. Aristotle was dividing and discriminating the hundred and fifty polities of the civilized world; Alexander was laying broad and deep the foundations of the Macedonian Empire. It was the work of God: not merely in the ordinary sense in which we reverently and justly ascribe to Providence every movement among men on the face of His earth, and the more confidently so, the wider

[1] See Note H.

and more permanent it is; but God Himself has claimed this work as His own by the indication He gave of it in the records of His Word, by the mouth of His prophet Daniel.

God, who hath made of one blood all nations of men for to dwell on the face of the earth, and hath determined the time before appointed, and the bounds of their habitation; God, who by a vision revealed to His Apostle Peter that He is no respecter of persons, was pleased by a dream, and the interpretation of a dream, to foreshadow the establishment of the third great Empire, which, after the Assyrian and the Persian, ruling much more widely, founded far more deeply, operating more gravely and permanently than they, should combine the nations of the world together, and force upon the understanding and conscience of men the truth of this great spiritual doctrine, the essential unity of the human race; the doctrine which, true long before Christianity, has been accepted, diffused, and perpetuated by Christianity itself.

It was vain to teach this doctrine by the lips of a heathen master, however wise and gifted. The pure and spiritual Plato had tried and failed. Aristotle had shrunk from the attempt. But what Plato could not do, and his successor abandoned as an illusion, was effected by a political revolution, long prepared but suddenly executed, by the establishment of the world-wide empire of Alexander, foretold by God's prophet, and recognised on its occurrence as the work of His far-designing Providence.

The prophecy of Daniel, accepted by the Jews as the inspired word of God, points clearly to this event as a great epoch in the history of God's spiritual dealings with mankind. Its full import and significance appear when we regard it in its direct consequences, not as the triumph of one set of heathens over another, not as the exultation of the West over the East, of Europe over Asia, of one type of civilization over another, of one form of political society over another, of one family of languages over another, great as the effect of each and all of these revolutions has been on the progress of human thought—but as the authoritative promulgation of the doctrine of the natural equality of men before God, and the fusion of many peoples, many laws, many ideas in one universal mould.

Nebuchadnezzar dreamed, as we read in Daniel, of a third kingdom of brass, which should rule over all the earth;[1] and this was interpreted in the time of Josephus, and by the Jews themselves, of a people coming from the West, clad in brazen armour—not in the gilded silk or cotton vestments of the East—which should destroy the empire of the Medes and Persians. The conqueror claimed for himself the title of king of all the world, and appeared in his own conceit, and to the imagination of the millions around him, as he stood on the confines of the habitable globe or plunged his courser's hoofs in the waves of the Indian Ocean, the master of all the land and sea.

Of the action of this conquest no description is given

[1] Daniel ii. 39.

in the bare outline of the Scripture record; but we may add that the influence of Grecian conquest was eminently soothing and civilizing; it diffused ideas of humanity and moral culture, while the conquerors themselves imbibed, on their side, the highest of moral lessons, lessons of liberality, of toleration, of sympathy with all God's human creation. 'Alexander,' says Plutarch, 'did not hearken to his preceptor Aristotle, who advised him to bear himself as a prince among the Greeks, his own people, but as a master among the barbarians; to treat the one as friends and kinsmen, the others as animals or chattels. . . . But, conceiving that he was sent by God to be an umpire between all, and to unite all together, he reduced by arms those whom he could not conquer by persuasion, and formed of a hundred diverse nations one single universal body, mingling as it were in one cup of friendship the customs, the marriages, and the laws of all. He desired that all should regard the whole world as their common country, the good as fellow-citizens and brethren, the bad as aliens and enemies; that the Greek should no longer be distinguished from the foreigner by arms or costume, but that every good man should be esteemed an Hellene, every evil man a barbarian.'[1]

Here, in a few rapid touches, enforced by a vivid illustration which we may pass over, is the picture of the new humane polity, the new idea of human society flashed upon the imagination of mankind by the establishment of the Macedonian Empire. Such at

---

[1] Plut. de fort. Alex. See Note I.

least it appeared to the mind of a writer five centuries later; but there are traces preserved, even in the wrecks of ancient civilization, of the moral effect which it actually produced on the feelings of society much more nearly contemporaneous. The conqueror indeed perished early, but not prematurely. He had done his work as the instrument of Providence; and Providence broke at once and threw away the instrument which, selfish in its aims and arbitrary in its actions, had perhaps, humanly speaking, no claim on its forbearance. But the providential work survived. The great empire was split into many fragments, but each long preserved a sense of the unity from which it was broken off. All were leavened more or less with a common idea of civilization, and recognised man as one being in various stages of development, to be trained under one guidance and elevated to one spiritual level. In the two great kingdoms of Egypt and Syria, which sprang out of the Macedonian—in the two great cities of Alexandria and Antioch, to which the true religion owes so deep a debt—the unity of the human race was practically asserted and maintained. Alexandria invited all nations to meet together and exchange in her common mart the products of every land, and enjoy the material fruits of God's creation. Antioch was for ages the chosen home of science and philosophy, and fused the religious ideas of many peoples, which she discriminated and harmonized with a zest peculiar to herself. In Alexandria the Jews were welcomed and domiciled, and encouraged to diffuse the knowledge of the law of Israel by the translation of the older Scriptures: in Antioch the fact was first recognised that a new religion had appeared in the world, that a new revelation had been made to men; the difference between the Jews and the followers of Jesus, Jews themselves by birth and by religion, was perceived and appreciated: at Antioch the believers in our holy faith were first called by the name of Christians.

But intellectual ideas which were received and cultivated at Antioch and Alexandria could not fail to receive admittance at the home of all intellect, Athens. The doctrine of human unity became a cherished doctrine in the schools which had resounded not long before with the utterance of the exclusive and selfish Hellenic sentiment, that the Greek is not as the barbarian, the bondmen not as the free. Three centuries of preparation passed away, and St. Paul, the first preacher of the gospel to the Greeks, could declare without a murmur of disapprobation, without a whisper of disgust, the fundamental doctrine of the true and universal faith, that 'God hath made of one blood all nations of men for to dwell on the face of the earth.' But was this the Athens of Solon and Pericles, and Plato and Aristotle? By no means: such a declaration could have had no place in an address to the Athenians of those earlier ages. To them it would have sounded strange and barbarous; it would have been received with mockery or clamour; it would have been repudiated with amazement and indignation; it would have made no spiritual impression at all. Such an idea was then unknown and unimagined. Conceptions of religion were then strictly local and national; conceptions of philosophy, though they might ostensibly reject the restrictions of positive faith, were not the less confined, by early mental training and still imperious prejudices, to a circle in this respect little, if at all, wider. The bond of positive belief was indeed broken; but the philosopher dragged after him, at each remove, no light portion of his chain. But, after three centuries of national amalgamation, the result of a wide-spread political revolution, after the diffusion of Grecian ideas among every people from the Ionian to the Caspian or the Red Sea, and the reception in return of manifold ideas, and in religious matters of much higher ideas, from the Persian, the Indian, the Egyptian, and the Jew, the people even of Athens, the very centre and eye of Greece, were prepared to admit the cardinal doctrine of Paul's preaching—to take at least some common ground with him on the very foundation of true religion—to look, perhaps, with the more favour upon him, that he, a Jew, one of a tribe notorious for their exclusiveness and national prejudices, came before them bowing, as they might suppose, to the majesty of their own Catholic creed, with what was now in its turn exalted into a philosophical doctrine— with what was serenely contemplated as a great and fruitful truth, revealed to the wise and prudent, if even yet regarded askance by the vulgar and illiberal among men.[1]

[1] See Note J.

A great and a fruitful truth! fruitful in spiritual conceptions of the Godhead, fruitful in lofty views of human duty and obligation, in glorious aspirations regarding the nature and destiny of man—a great and fruitful truth, the sole hope and stay of man in the contest of the heart and conscience against the narrow and debasing influence of superstitious dogmas, until the coming of Christ and the preaching of the gospel, and the shining of the day-spring from on high upon the soul!

I can give but a few words to a sketch of the principles derived from Plato, and developed by the later philosophy of the Stoics, which placed the higher minds among the heathen in antagonism with the popular and political religion, and might bring them, both at Athens and at Rome, into sympathetic relation with the preaching of the Apostle.

The ethical speculations of Plato and his followers led them to conceptions, hitherto unimagined, of man's position here below, of duty and responsibility, of sin and virtue, of penitence and assurance, before God, of the obligation to suffer—nay, even to seek and court the chastisement of sins for the sake of a spiritual blessing. The Christian mystic is not more entranced in the contemplation of the Supreme Holiness—the Christian ascetic does not more fervently denounce the sinfulness of the flesh, and the need of subjecting the body to the spirit—than Plato and the Stoics who derived from him. Sins and Virtues, in the view of the higher Greek philosophy, are to be measured by their agreement or contrast with an ideal of Justice, Wisdom, Temperance, or Fortitude—an ideal placed as high as mere human reason could exalt it. From these lofty abstractions they seemed to realize a Supreme Existence, one and universal, eternal and immutable—the image of every virtue, the source of all good, the sole unerring judge of every approximation of human actions to the normal standard of goodness and holiness. Sin they punished by the stings of conscience, and thus gave a spiritual colour to the gross traditions of the vulgar; while the expiations, the fasts, the lustrations of ritual religion expressed to their minds the necessity of reparation for crime, and the terrors which naturally haunt the souls of the guilty. It is the offence, and not the punishment, they said, that men ought to dread; the corruption of the moral sense by sin, not the loss of favours and blessings, that men ought to abhor and flee from. Like John the Apostle, they would have men do well for love, for love of goodness and justice, not from fear. And virtue, in their view, has its reward in a good conscience, which suffices in every extremity; virtue is the fulfilment of a rule, the realization of a harmony, the accomplishment of a divine purpose. Virtue is divine, and witnesses to the divine nature within us.

Now, such ideas as these, refined and exalted as they were under the system of the Stoics, may transport us beyond the sphere of Greece and pure Grecian speculation. They breathe the spirit of Ebionites in the wilderness, of Persian Magi in the plains of Media, of Brahmins by the banks of the Indus and the Ganges;

and it was, no doubt, by all these and kindred elements that they were modified or coloured. The fusion of nations under one political yoke tended, I say, to the fusion of ideas, and resulted in a marked elevation of heathen sentiment. Compare for a moment this teaching with that of a Socrates and a Xenophon, the most direct representatives of pure Grecian thought. How profound the difference! That which makes the value of temperance, for instance, in the eyes of these earlier masters, is that it assists men to act with manliness and energy; while to the Stoics its merit consists in its detaching us from the flesh, the body, and the earth. Courage again, in the one view, has for its end the attainment of empire or of liberty; in the other, it is the complement of temperance, and fortifies us in the struggle against the world and the senses. Love, in the one doctrine, is the expansion and purification of mere human sensibility; in the other, it raises man to aspire after the superhuman, to yearn for communion with an ideal, to seek absorption in God. It is the passion for the Eternal and the Infinite; it is the presentiment of Immortality.[1]

This presentiment, this aspiration, this hope, and almost faith in immortality, is the point at which the highest Grecian philosophy culminates. Belief in a future state is the touchstone of all spiritual conceptions of human nature. Towards this they climb step by step, even if they cannot fully attain to it, or keep it when attained for a moment; from this, as they fall

---

[1] See Note K.

away, they faint and fade into the earthly and the sensual. This is the great point of distinction between moral and ceremonial religions, between a rule of action and a cult, between personal and political conceptions of our relation to God and to Providence.

This aspiration, this belief, reveals to us our personal relation to a Higher Being. It equalizes men in their nature and condition; it discovers to them an essential unity in the whole race of mankind. It impugns and overthrows the natural and vulgar demand for an exclusive patron Deity, and a national compact with him. In the more spiritual doctrine of Plato and the Platonizers lay undoubtedly the germ of that transformation of heathen opinion which resulted, under the teaching of St. Paul and the Christian Church, with the effectual working of the Holy Spirit, in the conversion of the Roman Empire.[1]

Yet how faint, how feeble, how imperfect was this doctrine! how surrounded by prejudices, how enfeebled and confined by the counteracting influence of opposing ideas! Let us examine a little more closely the idea of immortality as taught by Plato, and accepted rather than firmly held by the more spiritual of the Stoics.

First, the soul, they said, was immortal, because it is one and simple, without parts or material elements, and therefore indivisible and indissoluble. It is not a mere harmony, resulting from the contexture of the body, with which it is here found in connection; for it

[1] See Note L.

commands and dominates over the body as an independent substance. It has nothing to fear, then, from the dissolution of the body, which is not itself essential to its existence. Nor has it any principle of decay or corruption of its own; for sin is its only infirmity, and sin, as an abstract principle, has no tendency to destroy it.

Again, the eternal truths or the ideas which are simple, immutable and divine, are the natural objects of the soul of man. The soul is therefore analogous and conformable to things that do not change, and accordingly has itself, like them, a principle of immortality.

Such are, the one the physical, the other what I may call perhaps the sentimental argument, on which Plato strongly insists, and to which we may continue to attach such weight as is really due to them, without depending wholly or even principally upon them. For there is a third demonstration from the moral nature of man, and this the strongest of all unrevealed arguments for the permanent existence of the soul, which rests on the need of a future state of retribution to equalize human conditions, to recompense virtue and punish sin, to relieve man from the intolerable anguish of beholding the sufferings of the good, and the prosperity here on earth of the wicked. This is the common argument of Christianity, which declares the vindication of God's justice and moral government as a main object of revelation. But turn to Plato and the Stoics, and but little reference will you find to any argument of this kind. They may, indeed, set forth the fact of a future retribution as the explanation of certain ancient traditions; they employ the machinery of the old mythology in this particular, however little regard they pay to it in others, to recommend what they believe to be a real moral truth, under the veil of a poetical illustration. But this is merely playing with the subject. It is dallying with the truth, not embracing and earnestly maintaining it. And whence does it appear that the philosophers had no earnest faith in a future retribution? From the pertinacity with which they still cling, even Plato and the most spiritual among them, to the low and popular notion that virtue must certainly be adequately rewarded, vice adequately punished, under God's providence, even in this life. They insist on the paradox, common, I say, to the sages and to the vulgar of old, to the paradox necessary to all moral systems which deny a future retribution, but required least of all by that of a Plato, which in terms at least admits it, that the virtuous man is necessarily happy, and the vicious necessarily wretched; that virtue is its own reward, and sin its own punishment; that the tyrant on the throne is always, by the law and nature of things, miserable—miserable, at least, in comparison with the triumphant happiness of the good man, even in the dungeon and on the scaffold. So far were the heathen teachers of immortality from the feeling of St. Paul, that the Christian saint, the man who has attained the highest pitch of grace and godliness, would be, in times at least of worldly trial and persecution, were his hope bounded by this life and its recompenses, of all men most miserable.

But the fact is, that it is with faint surmises and stammering lips only that even Plato and the most spiritual of his followers could enunciate the dogma of Immortality. Even under the humanizing sway of the Third Empire, amid the development of cosmopolitan sentiments which that sway, as we have seen, engendered, the philosophers could with difficulty keep hold of the sense of Human Equality—of the common claims of all men on a common God and Father of all—which is essential to a stedfast and consistent view of so spiritual a belief. It is upon the doctrine of human equality in the forum of conscience, in the view of a retributive justice, that the conception of a real immortality must actually rest. The philosophers, aristocrats as they generally were (from Plato downwards), could not shake off the notion of an aristocracy among souls. They might see, indeed, in the noblest specimens of humanity, some beings, outwardly not unlike to the rest of their kind, yet inwardly, as they imagined, different and superior, bearing a nearer kinship to Divinity itself, of whom they could imagine that after death they might be received into the bliss of the Divine Being, absorbed in His nature; of whom they could not, perhaps, conceive it possible that, so noble, so generous, so godlike, they should utterly perish along with the baser clay around them. But such instances, in their view, were rare; the mass of men could not hope to attain to such distinction : the difference between man and man seemed to them coeval with their birth, or anterior to it, to lie in the very essence of their natures, as much as if they descended originally from various stocks. And when they looked around them, and observed the social institution of slavery always like a ghost or shadow at their side,—the skeleton in their house, the death's head on their table,—ever crying out for an explanation and a justification, and of which no explanation, no justification could be given, but the presumed superiority of race to race, a higher calling and an ampler destiny ;—when they saw this fact, and were driven to this apology for its existence, no wonder if their ideas of immortality were vague, imperfect, and precarious.[1]

At the best, then, the Stoic conception of a future state was of reward and glory due to *some* men—to a select class of men—to a few men perhaps in each generation, leaders in thought or action, heroes, demigods ; but it left the case of the multitude wholly out of consideration. It maimed the whole doctrine of future compensation. It threw the philosopher back, against his will—against the tenor of his general reasoning— in spite of the plain inconsistency in which it involved him, upon the rash and crude paradox of a recompense here below—upon the fallacious assertion that the good man is necessarily happy in this life, the bad man necessarily miserable. It drove him to forced and extravagant definitions of the highest good, and the

[1] See Note M.

genuine character of virtue, and set his hand at last against every sensible man, and every sensible man's hand against him.

To resume, then: the philosophy of the Stoics, the highest and holiest moral theory at the time of our Lord's coming—the theory which most worthily contended against the merely political religion of the day, the theory which opposed the purest ideas and the loftiest aims to the grovelling principles of a narrow and selfish expediency on which the frame of the heathen ritual rested—was the direct creation of the sense of unity and equality disseminated among the choicer spirits of heathen society by the results of the Macedonian conquest. But for that conquest it could hardly have existed at all. It was the philosophy of Plato, sublimed and harmonized by the political circumstances of the times. It was what Plato would have imagined, had he been a subject of Alexander.

It taught nominally, at least, the equality of all God's children—of Greek and barbarian, of bond and free. It renounced the exclusive ideas of the commonwealth on which Plato had made shipwreck of his consistency. It declared that to the wise man all the world is his country. It was thoroughly comprehensive and cosmopolitan. Instead of a political union, it preached the moral union of all good men—a city of true philosophers, a community of religious sentiment, a communion of saints, to be developed partly here below, but more consummately in the future state of a glorified hereafter.[1] It aspired, at least, to the doctrine of an immortal city

[1] See Note N.

of the soul, a providence under which that immortality was to be gained, a reward for the good—possibly, but even more dubiously, a punishment for the wicked. So, in theory at least, it seemed to rise to the ideas of Christianity; it might seem a precursor of the Gospel, it might be hailed as an ally in the wars of the Holy Spirit. But the weakness of its support, the barrenness of its alliance, became manifest on a nearer inspection. For the immortality it augured was limited in time to a certain cosmical revolution, which should close in a general conflagration, in which gods and men, bodies and souls, earth and heaven, should perish. It was limited in subject; for it was after all limited, according to the concurrent voice of all Grecian theory, to a select class—an aristocracy, as I have called it, of souls: those who could scale the heights of excellence here might alone expect a higher exaltation hereafter; those who stumbled and fell at their base, would lie there forgotten or perish altogether. It was limited, further, in the nature of its promised retribution; for generally, though with much fluctuation and variety of opinion, it was held that the only punishment of the wicked was the common fate of the less worthy—annihilation. Once more it was limited in its conception of God; for its aspirations after Providence alternated with an apprehension of Fate, which it sometimes confounded with the Deity, sometimes set over Him and against Him.

Nevertheless, when St. Paul, standing on Mars's Hill at Athens, proclaimed that ' God hath made of one blood all nations of men,'—when, addressing the Romans, he declared that 'we, being many, are one body in Christ, and every one members one of another,'[1]—he knew that in the loftiest school of Gentile philosophy he should strike a chord of sympathy. He recognised the Spirit of God brooding over the face of heathenism, and fructifying the spiritual element in the heart even of the natural man. He felt that in these human principles there was some faint adumbration of the divine, and he looked for their firmer delineation to the figure of that gracious Master, higher and holier than man, whom he contemplated in his own imagination, and whom he was about to present to them. And such is the vision, such the augury, to which the great Augustine appeals, when in words of rude impassioned energy, with which, as a vessel ploughs the deep with unequal plunges, he seems to fall or rise, to shoot forward or stagger in his career, he exclaims:[2] 'Now, had one of his disciples asked of Plato, when he was teaching that Truth cannot be witnessed by the bodily eyes, but by the pure intellect only—that every soul which thereto attaches itself becomes happy and perfect—that there is no hindrance so great to beholding Truth as a life abandoned to sensual passions—that therefore we should heal and purge the soul, to contemplate the immutable forms of things, and this beauty ever the same, without bounds in space, without change in time, in the existence of which men believe not, though alone it exists and reigns;—that all things are born and perish, flow away and are lost, while as far

---

[1] Romans xii. 6.   [2] See Note O.

as they do possess reality, and thereby only, they belong to God eternal, who creates and sustains them; that, among these, it is given to the soul and pure intelligence only to enjoy and apprehend the contemplation of eternity, and hereby to merit eternal life;— but that when the soul is corrupted by the love for things created and perishable, it fades away in its vain imaginations, mocking forsooth at those who speak of a Being who is not beheld by the eye or conceived under sensible images, but is seen by the mind only:— had, I say, at the moment when Plato was preaching ideas so lofty, one of his disciples asked of him, saying, Master, if one so great and godlike should ever appear, who should persuade men to *believe* in these things at least, even though they could not *understand* them, would you deem him worthy of divine honours?— Plato, I believe, would have replied, that such things could not be effected by man, unless the very Virtue and Wisdom of God should withdraw him from the common nature of things, and, not by human teaching, but by its own divine illumination, so adorn him with grace, so establish him in power, so exalt him in majesty, as that, despising all that men desire, enduring all they shrink from, effecting all they admire, he should convert mankind to this most wholesome faith, by the highest love and authority.'

And there, *Ecce homo!*—Behold the man!—Jesus Christ, the Son of God, conceived by the Holy Ghost; to whom, three Persons and one God, be ascribed, &c.

LECTURE IV.

EXPANSION OF HEATHEN BELIEF BY THE IDEAS OF ROMAN JURISPRUDENCE.

GALATIANS III. 24.

The law was our schoolmaster to bring us unto Christ.

OUR version of this text may suggest to the English reader a notion not quite consistent with the sense which the Apostle's language seems really meant to convey. The law is here represented, not as the master, the teacher, the men in office and authority, the διδάσκαλος of the school, but as the παιδαγωγὸς, the faithful attendant, who brought the scholar to the master, guiding and urging his steps, bearing his satchel for him, by the direction of the parent whose servant he was. St. Paul, speaking here directly and primarily to the Jewish residents in Galatia, compares the province of the Jewish law, the law of Moses, in relation to Christ, to that of the pedagogue. For its proper office was thus to direct and control, under a special appointment, the wandering steps of God's own children, and see that they came without fail to the presence of the master, who was to take the place of their heavenly Father as the teacher and educator of their souls. St. Paul does not pretend that the old law taught the children of Israel any spiritual lessons itself, but merely that it brought them to the point at which their spiritual teaching was to begin. And that teaching was the discipline of Christ's holy faith.

Such, it seems, in the Apostle's view, was the ministry of the law of Moses. But does he here or elsewhere confine his view of the law, of which he speaks so much in relation to its contrast or subserviency to the gospel, to the law of Moses? When he speaks of the law, there is generally an ulterior object in view, just as, when he addresses himself directly to the Jews, he has generally other classes of hearers in his mind also.

Let us regard, then, more particularly the composition of the congregations to which he was wont to address himself. We must bear in mind how closely the Jews of the dispersion, the men of Hebrew birth and lineage who were settled in every land and city throughout the East, and far into the West also, were connected with native proselytes—men of Greek, or Syrian, or Italian, or other parentage, who had been received as converts into the Jewish synagogues—made in many cases Jews themselves by baptism, by circumcision, by abstinence, by fulfilling all the requirements of the law—admitted not less seldom, perhaps more commonly, to a status of partial communion with it, without being subjected to its most onerous obligations. Even among the 'Galatians' to whom the Apostle writes—though these are evidently for the most part genuine children of Israel, we cannot completely separate the Jews by birth and breeding from the proselytes of the gate or the proselytes of righteousness. The Apostle is anxious to impress upon them that the Jew and the Gentile among them are both one in his sight—that the rite of circumcision is not required to effect complete equality in their spiritual privileges in Christ—that there is henceforth no distinction between Jew and Greek, but all who are baptized into Christ have put on Christ. 'And if,' he says, 'ye be the seed of Christ, then are ye Abraham's seed,' whatever your actual parentage has been, 'and heirs according to the promise,'—that is, to the promise made to Abraham that in his seed all the families of the earth should be blessed. Even the 'Galatians,' then, were a mixed congregation of Jewish and Gentile believers.

The Epistles of St. Paul are all, I think, directed more or less to such mixed congregations (the pastoral Epistles, of course, excepted), and all, as coming from him who declared himself to be especially the Apostle to the Gentiles, breathe more or less the same Catholic spirit. But the character of this preaching most clearly appears from a reference to the Epistle to the Romans. We may picture to ourselves the Jewish synagogue at Rome as crowded with devotees of Jewish, of Greek, and of Roman extraction; of Jews who had migrated from the land of their origin, perhaps of their birth, to carry on their business of various kinds in the capital of the empire; of Greeks, who, like them, flocked in vast numbers to the same great centre of all employments, of all opinions and teaching, to hear and speak of every new thing; of Romans, who, after conquering and making tributary both Jews and Greeks, began to open their eyes to the wondrous gifts, intellectual and spiritual, of their Hebrew and Hellenic subjects,— to acknowledge that, with all their own power and greatness, they had much—yea, everything to learn, and that it was from Greece and from Palestine that their destined teachers had come.

Of the sympathy, indeed, of both the Greeks and Romans with the Jews at this period, history affords abundant evidence. The influence exercised by the children of Israel, in the court and in the market-place, over the minds and the manners of the Gentiles around them, was singularly strong at this period—a period of great intellectual and spiritual excitement; but, strongly as these Jewish habits of thought now affected the seekers after spiritual and moral truth among the Gentiles, stronger still was the impulse they received from the first breathing of the accents of a new revelation in Christ—a revelation within a revelation, a spiritual empire within a spiritual empire. The proselytes of the Jewish law, Greek and Roman, scarcely yet recovered from the excitement, the intoxication, of finding themselves admitted to communion with a religion of real signs and wonders, of genuine inspiration and enlightenment from above, were suddenly invited to take a step further, to penetrate beyond the veil, to receive a higher initiation, to share in a holier covenant, and enjoy a nearer and an ampler manifestation of God. They were called to Christ, and they came to Christ. The synagogues of the Law, so lately thronged with admiring converts from Greece and Rome, were again abandoned for the more private and retired churches, the little spiritual reunions, of the converts to the Gospel. The Synagogue itself was carried over to the Church. Even from the names of these earliest disciples whom the Apostle specially greeted, we may fairly infer, though the argument, I am aware, is not conclusive, that the Church of Rome, the Church of St. Paul's Epistle, the Church of the first imperial persecution, embraced communicants from each of the three rival nationalities.

In all ages of the separation the Jews have kept up close and active correspondence with their brethren, and the settler or exile on the Tiber or the Euphrates was made familiar with every movement, political or spiritual, in the city of David. And hence we may divine, though we cannot trace, how these people derived their knowledge of the ferment of religious convictions which was now taking place in Palestine. It was communicated, no doubt, through various channels, coloured by the prejudices of various narrators, received in various tempers. The truth was at first but imperfectly understood, but partially accepted. The Apostle addresses converts and believers in the revelation of Christ,—but as men infirm in their faith, imperfect in their lesson, ignorant of much saving knowledge, as yet hardly prepared to embrace without reserve the tidings which they deemed too surely to announce the overthrow of an ancient and august religion. What a further pang would they feel in the abruptness of the announcement! Jews who had so lately received into their fold not a few of the choicest spirits among the Greeks and Romans around them— men, I doubt not, of learning, women of fervour and godly zeal; Jews who, expatriated from their own conquered country, could retaliate upon their conquerors with the keen gratification of a spiritual triumph; Greeks and Romans, who had swallowed the bitter pill of a religious abjuration—who had nerved themselves to renounce their national faith, national usages, national ideas, by which the spiritual pride of both Greek and Roman was equally fostered: Jews, I say, Greeks and Romans, in this hour of high-wrought feeling, were required suddenly to abandon together the very creed which the one had imposed, the others had accepted, to bow their knees to the crucified Lord set up for their future Master, and acknowledge that all that appears to be wisdom and honour and majesty and power in the sight of Jew or Gentile is but foolishness with God! Such were the people—and such the feelings which animated them—to whom St. Paul addresses the Epistle to the Romans.

What, then, was it that he had to say unto them? What was the central idea, by explaining and enforcing which he might hope to reconcile them to the faith he preached? 'The law,' he says, ' of the spirit of life in Christ Jesus hath made me free from the law of sin and death.' . . . 'What the law could not do, in that it was weak through the flesh, God sending His own Son in the likeness of sinful flesh, . . . condemned sin in the flesh.' 'I delight in the law of God after the inward man.'[1] In these and other passages that might be cited, you find the same idea as that of our text, from Galatians—that the law is our pedagogue, leading us unto Christ the Master. 'The law' is the teaching of the human conscience, generally—whether enlightened by a revelation given unto men through Moses and the prophets, or by any other less special illumination from above—by the habits and ideas of human society in all its various phases: it is every moral principle of action whereby we feel ourselves allowed, forbidden, or excused, in our dealings with men and our behaviour towards God. If St. Paul in the Epistle to the Romans, and throughout his Epistles, points primarily to the contrast between the law of Moses and the law of Christ—making the one the preparation or pedagogue for the other—not less may we trace in them the bolder and broader idea of a distinction between the law of man in general and the law of God, and the way in which the first leads up to and introduces the second. He reveals the appointment of a new law to supplant and supersede the older—or, more properly, to explain, expand, and imbue it with a new spirit; to vivify the letter; to be a liberal gloss upon a rigid text, adapted at first under God's appointment to special ends and confined within narrow limits. Such

---

[1] Romans viii. 2, 3; vii. 22.

was the form under which the Holy Spirit directed the saving truths of the gospel to be promulgated, in the first instance, at Rome, to a mixed congregation of Greek and Roman proselytes, asking dubiously for the new light which had arisen in the eastern horizon, the dawn of which had as yet hardly streaked the clouds beyond the Ionian and the Egean.

Let us regard the text, then, in this wider sense; that the law of the Roman world, the law which ruled the hearts and hands of the subjects of Cæsar's empire, Greek and Roman, was in itself a schoolmaster, or rather a pedagogue, leading men to Christ, to the knowledge and acceptance of the gospel. I wish to show how the progress and development of the Roman civil law assisted in the transformation of religious ideas among the heathen, and in that conversion of the Roman empire which is the subject before us.

In my last address, I referred to Daniel's prophetic interpretation of the vision of the third or Macedonian empire. I showed the important part that empire had played in preparing mankind for the reception of the great gospel truth of the unity of man, and the equality of all classes and races in the sight of God their Creator; I remarked how worthy such a polity must appear to become the subject of an inspired communication from the Author of Divine Revelation.

Of the announcement, similarly conveyed, in the same place in Scripture, of the fourth kingdom, the Roman empire, a similar view may be taken—of the beast, dreadful and terrible, and strong exceedingly, with great iron teeth, which devoured and brake in pieces, and stamped the residue with the feet of it; which, according to the interpretation of the prophet, should be a fourth kingdom upon the earth, diverse from all kingdoms, and should devour the whole earth, and tread it down and break it in pieces.[1]

The part performed by the Roman empire in the course of religious history is great, and may be traced in many directions. I speak now of the preparation it made for the reception of Christian ideas in one particular only. The Macedonian empire tended to create, to foster, and fix in men's minds the conviction of spiritual unity, by the mild influence of the Grecian civilization, by softening and humanizing men's manners after a single type; by bidding them look to a common standard of art and science, of moral and social culture; by diffusing a social harmony throughout the various races of mankind, now first brought under a common political organization. The character of the Roman conquest was 'diverse' from this. It is well described in the sacred record as devouring, breaking in pieces, and treading under foot. The tribes of serfs and barbarians might hail the Greek as a deliverer and a civilizer; the same nations cowered before the Roman as a tyrant and a destroyer. The union with which the Roman legions threatened them was not the union of social quality and mutual improvement, but the bond of a slave to his master, of a captive to his enthraller. The world seemed for a moment to suc-

[1] Daniel vii. 7, 23.

cumb without hope for the future under the yoke of brute force and violence, tearing and destroying rather than consolidating. Nevertheless, Providence had its blessed work of union to carry to its accomplishment, and it could use even this cruel and destroying kingdom for that beneficent purpose, even against its own apparent nature. The conquering Roman long carried with him his peculiar law and usage, and imposed them upon the subject peoples; but his conquests rapidly outran his power to fuse and consolidate; and at last against his will, in contradiction to his political principles, in despite of his religious convictions, against every appearance and natural expectation both of the conqueror and the conquered, he found his own law and usage turned against himself, and that which was the narrowest and most selfish and most exclusive of all human codes of jurisprudence expanded by an unseen power and an irresistible tendency, till it became the most potent of all human instruments in establishing the conviction of unity and equality among men.

We have seen how strongly national and exclusive in its sanctions, its warnings, and its promises, was the character of the Roman religion; how the religious convictions of the great conquering race were founded upon the assurance of the special favour of their national divinities, confirmed to them by a long succession of national triumphs. We have seen how deeply this sentiment was seated, and how quickly it responded to the appeal of an astute or fanatical ruler.

Nowhere did this narrow creed and selfish sentiment find a plainer and more powerful expression than in the original constitution of the civil law. The civil law of the Romans, like the canon law of Christian communities, was the creation of the priesthood, and bore a deep impression of its sacerdotal origin. It was founded on a religious tradition. It treated all the great subjects of jurisprudence—the relations of family, property, marriage, testaments, and contracts—as matters of religious import. It placed men under the guardianship of the national divinities; it regarded them all as means to one chief, all-engrossing end—the conservation of the State, the advancement of the presumed designs of the special Providence which kept eternal watch and ward over Rome and the Roman people.

I cannot enter now into details, but you may remark how from this crude original germ, from this unpromising stock, this wildest of wild olive trees, the primitive law of the Roman commonwealth, of which even the Twelve Tables were a liberal expansion, has sprung by successive grafts, by additions and modifications, and glosses and commentaries—by the casting off of the old slough or rind in one place, by the assimilation of new ideas in another, by growth and obsolescence, by corruption and renovation—sometimes, possibly, through caprice—more commonly, more regularly, more systematically, from shrewd observation and philosophical reflection,—has sprung, I say, the world-wide elastic system of jurisprudence by which the great Roman empire, with all its boundless variety of races, creeds, and manners, was for ages harmoniously and equitably governed; which was accepted and ratified as an eternal possession by the same empire when it found itself Christian, and has been proved to satisfy the principles of law and justice announced by a religion which alone proclaimed and maintains as its foundation the unity and equality of men; the impartial providence of the Deity; the abolition of all national distinctions in the Divine economy; a city of God and a kingdom of heaven; finally, a jurisprudence which has been incorporated into the particular legal systems of, I suppose, every modern nation of Christendom.

How marvellous a development is here! We cannot now inquire into details; but it will be well, for the full understanding of our argument, to point out summarily one or two particulars in the general process. You must mark, then, in public law, the extension, step by step, through many a social disturbance, many a civil commotion, of the full rights of citizenship from the narrow circle of a few score of favoured families to the entire sphere of the free subjects of the empire—a secular revolution of eight hundred years;—in private law, the equal communication among various classes of the rights of property and dominion over the national soil; the abolition of territorial privileges; the readjustment, by gradual and peaceful manipulation, of the cadastral map of the empire; the relaxation, by slow and experimental process, of the patriarchal authority of the head of the family; of the father over the son, whom at first he might punish, sell, or slay;

of the husband over the wife, whom at first he received from her parents as the spoil of his own spear, and ruled as the chattel he had plundered; of the master over the slave, absolute at first, final and irresponsible to law, custom, or conscience; the gradual replacement of the strictly national or tribal ideas on these and kindred subjects by views of right, justice, and virtue, common to mankind in general; the slow but constant growth of principles of natural and universal law, and their application, searchingly and thoroughly, to every subject of jurisprudence, and to all the dealings of man with man.

Now for this gradual revolution and transformation of views and principles, and social institutions, various causes have been assigned.

First—an opinion has found favour in many quarters, and has been put forward with some notes of triumph by our Christian apologists, that the rude selfishness of the Roman law was humanized by the influence of Christianity only, at first unconsciously, when Christian sentiments were silently making an impression upon a world which refused to recognise them—afterwards openly and notoriously, when Christianity became enthroned on the seat of Cæsar in the person of Constantine, Theodosius, and Justinian. But while we allow its due effect both to the avowed and the tacit influence of the Gospel in this matter, while we trace with interest and delight the softening and refining pressure of God's law upon human and even heathen society, we must acknowledge that the first impression of His providential hand was given at a much earlier period; that the law of Rome was already a pedagogue, leading the nations unto Christ even before Christ Himself had appeared in the world, and held up to its admiration the principles of His catholic jurisprudence.

Some, again, ascribe this revolution to the influence of philosophy, to the teaching of the Platonists and Stoics, to the ideas of humanity and sympathy disseminated by the mild persuasion of the schools, when the rude Roman warrior sate meekly at the feet of the Grecian sages. We acknowledge the fact, and we admit its influence in its season: but the relaxation we speak of was anterior to this.

Once more, it has been attributed to the natural enlightenment of the conscience among the Romans themselves, to increased cultivation and the growth of moral sentiments, to the example of the wisest and most liberal-minded of their own chiefs, to the sense of security giving more room to the play of generous and humane feelings. But neither here do I find a full and satisfactory explanation of the phenomenon before us.

The account I would give of the matter connects it even more directly with what we may venture to regard as God's providential guidance of human affairs. It was the immediate and inevitable effect of the establishment of that kingdom of iron, of which God in His prophetic Scriptures spoke. It was the very condition of victory and conquest, which bore within themselves the germ of this moral transformation. The little fortress in the hills, in an obscure corner of Europe, was predestined to grow into the widest and mightiest of empires, and level by its force and pressure a clear and ample space for the edifice of the Christian Church. The Providence which directed the assimilation and fusion of conquered clans and tribes and nations successively with their conquerors, decreed the inevitable result—the combination and fusion in one general code of their several ideas of law and polity. Even from the first, as far as we can trace it, there existed this irrepressible conflict between the formal principles of municipal and national law—the civil law of the Romans,—and the principles of law, manifold and diverse, in force among their subjects and their clients. It was the same conflict which we have witnessed and moderated ourselves in the government of our own empire in India. Roman law was adapted only for the regulation of Romans dealing with Romans. It was often impossible to apply it to the dealings of the Roman with the stranger; it was never practicable to impose it as a rule for strangers dealing with strangers. Hence practically three laws in force at the same time on the same spot, —the pure Roman, the mixed, and the foreign: hence confusion, hence delay and misunderstanding: hence, in due course, the vague and desultory attempts of the strong man and the prudent man to select, to combine, to create a law common to all: hence the introduction of examples and precedents, the groping darkly for wide and general views; at last, the arrival of the reformer and codifier, the prætor, the proconsul, or the emperor. Hence, in short, the gradual conception of the idea of normal equity, of a natural and universal law, of a law of nations contrasted with a national law. Italian and Grecian, Jew and Syrian, Heathen and Christian, philosopher and preacher, all contribute to this ultimate conclusion, and help forward the establishment of the great religious principle of the moral equality of all men in the sight of a common God and Father, a common Ruler and Judge of all.[1]

You may imagine how fiercely the pride of the Roman would struggle against this conviction; how it would jar against his personal sense of preeminence, and the solitary grandeur in which he towered above his fellows,—against his religious sense of a Divine mission, which still abided in him, and constituted his last moral principle. For he, too, believed that his laws and usages were given him from above, that the favour of the heavenly powers was secured to him by their perpetual observance; and every blow directed against them, every slur cast upon them, startled and distressed him as an act of sacrilege. But practical necessity not to be put by, first reconciled him to the transformation of his law. Use and habit satisfied and convinced him. The daily progress of the new ideas, the gradual familiarization with new principles of thought and conduct, with other views of life, of duty, of the ends and objects of civil society, worked upon his awakened conscience with the charm of a new inspiration. They revealed to him the idea of new gods, or of a new dispensation from the gods;

[1] See Note P.

of a greater rule and order of affairs. They foreshadowed the announcement of a new and universal creed. At the time of St. Paul's arrival, men of earnest thought and wide reflection at Rome were already half prepared to accept the preaching of a new revelation, and lo! a new revelation was flashed upon them. Law had been as a pedagogue, bringing them to the Master, Christ. Philosophy had been such a pedagogue also. Standing sullenly on the old ways, they had felt the ground tremble under them—they saw the world drifting away from them. In spite of occasional reactions, of violent and forced revivals, of grim fanatic ecstasies, of many a grasping and clutching at the shadows of a waning theology, at the altars and the temples, the vows and the sacrifices of antiquity, they were getting day by day more inured to the conviction that old things were indeed passing away; behold! all things were becoming new.

That St. Paul was indeed well aware of this state of feeling at Rome, may easily be supposed. Although the words of the text were addressed to the Galatians, the thought which underlies them would naturally present itself to his mind when writing to the Romans. If at Ephesus or Ancyra, the Jew, the Greek, and the Roman dwelt and worshipped side by side, and apprehended in common the impending abrogation of the older law by the authority of the Gospel, still more did the Church at Rome collect men of all these nations together, and acknowledge, under the Apostle's teaching, that 'the law of the spirit of life in Christ Jesus had made them free from the law of sin and death.' But it would seem that the Apostle of the Gentiles, the Roman citizen, the man of heathen as well as of Jewish learning, had a special aptitude for thus shaping the argument of his Epistle to the Romans. He was, I am persuaded, personally well versed in the principles of the Roman law itself. In the first place, it was natural that he, a citizen of Rome, though of provincial extraction, by the admission of his forefathers to the franchise, should take care to inform himself of the laws which constituted the charter of the class he belonged to. Roman citizenship was a birthright of which he was proud, as he seems himself to acknowledge, and which he cherished as the safeguard of his person and his property. It gave him certain privileges; it assured him of protection and of freedom. He tells us as much himself. He appeals more than once to his rights as a citizen, and shows that he is well aware of the advantages they confer upon him. But more than this, there is in some parts of his teaching a direct application of Roman legal principles in illustration of his doctrine, which none but a Roman could be expected so to apply, none unless versed in Roman law would be able to employ.

Thus St. Paul dwells with emphasis on the position of the divine Son towards the Father, in terms which savour of a full appreciation of the power given to the parent over the child by the civil laws of Rome. His view of the subjection of the wife to the husband as her 'head,' which he uses as an apt illustration of the position of the Church to Christ her Lord, is conceived in the spirit of a Roman rather than of a Hebrew. Even in his account of the mutual duties of the married pair, compared with that furnished us by St. Peter, we may trace, I think, a shade of difference : the one breathes the austere reserve of a Scipio or a Cato ; the other the tenderer gravity of Abraham, of David, or of Boaz. The illustration, again, of a marked doctrine of our religion by the forms of Testation, is such as might actually suggest itself to a Roman jurist, but would not so readily occur to a mere Syrian or Jew ; for the notion of Testation, the technical and formal making of a will, with the covenant therein implied with the nation, and with all the rights and powers thereto annexed, was, in fact, almost a creation of Roman jurisprudence. And once more I would remark the interesting analogy St. Paul suggests in describing our relation as believers to our heavenly Father, as that of sons by adoption. The process of legal adoption, by which the chosen heir became entitled, through the performance of certain stated ceremonies, the execution of certain formalities, not only to the reversion of the property, but to the civil status, to the burdens as well as the rights of the adopter,—became, as it were, his other self, one with him, identified with him ;—this, too, is a Roman principle, peculiar at this time to the Romans, unknown, I believe, to the Greeks, unknown to all appearance to the Jews, as it certainly is not found in the legislation of Moses, nor mentioned anywhere as a usage among the children of the elder covenant. We have ourselves but a faint conception of the force with which such an illustration would speak to one familiar with the Roman practice; how it woud serve to impress upon him the assurance that the adopted son of God becomes in a peculiar and intimate sense one with the heavenly Father, one in essence and in spirit, though not in flesh and blood.[1]

This subject would bear some further amplification; but our limits to-day will not allow me to dwell longer upon it, and the next lecture must be devoted to another branch of the general argument. I will only ask you now to remark, in conclusion, how instruction conveyed thus in language suited to the comprehension of Roman citizens, of a class, at least, familiar with the privileges of citizenship,—whether Jews, Greeks, or Romans,—whether at Rome or in the provinces,—was plainly addressed to the cultivated and intelligent among men. St. Paul, a man himself of no mean social rank, and of high intellectual culture, spoke, I cannot doubt, directly to the intellect as well as to the heart of men of refinement like his own. His converts were among the wise and prudent, as well as among the impulsive and devout. I reject then the notion, too hastily assumed, too readily accepted, from a mistaken apprehension of the real dignity of the Gospel, that the first preaching of the faith was addressed to the lowest and meanest and least intelligent, the outcasts and proletaries of society. Many reasons, I am convinced,

[1] See Note Q.

might be alleged for concluding that it was much the reverse. As regards the Christian Church at Rome, at least—the direct statements of the Apostle himself—the evidence of existing monuments of antiquity—inferences of no little strength from the records of secular history—and inferences not lightly to be rejected from the language and sentiments of contemporary heathens—all tend to assure us that it embraced some devoted members, and attracted many anxious inquirers amidst the palaces of the nobles, and even in Cæsar's household. If such be the case—if high-born men and women—if well-trained reasoners and thinkers —if patricians, and patrons, and counsellors-in-law, with their freedmen, their pupils, and their clients, did read and appreciate the Apostle's letters—did visit him in his bonds, and listen to his teachings—did accept Gospel-truth from his lips, and ask for baptism at his hands; we may fairly assume, I say among other motive influences, that the law, the civil law of Rome, protesting as it did against the narrow jurisprudence of primitive antiquity, and the political religion on which that jurisprudence was founded—the civil law, refined and modified as it was into the expression of universal reason on the great principles of equity and legal use—the civil law, in short, the image in the Roman's view of the mind of God Himself—had been truly a pedagogue bringing men by gentle force and pressure to Christ the Master of Truth, and the Judge of Righteousness.[1]

[1] See Note R.

LECTURE V.

THE HEATHEN AWAKENED TO A SENSE OF HIS SPIRITUAL DANGER.

1 John iv. 21.

And this commandment have we from Him, That he who loveth God love his brother also.

WE are examining the process whereby the selfish national prejudices on which the heathen religions were founded, were gradually sapped, and the soil prepared for the seed of Christianity—the process whereby the engrossing idea of the city upon earth was exchanged for the anticipation of a city of God in heaven. We have observed how the progress of philosophy, of inquiry, that is, into the moral condition of man, led the Greeks and Romans, in the ripeness of their national life, to broader views of the unity of man, the natural equality of races, the common bonds of sympathy by which they are mutually connected. We have further traced the process by which, under the pressure of political necessities, the Romans were compelled to relax the exclusive spirit of their jurisprudence, and practically to make their city—what they learned at last with pride to denominate it—the common city and mother of nations.

Two great steps, then, have been taken towards the recognition of Christian principle: the one is the theoretical acknowledgment of human equality in the sight of God—the other is the practical admission of men to equal rights and common franchises in relation one to another.

So far have men been brought on their appointed march towards the stand-point of Christian revelation, which requires as the first condition of its acceptance—as the condition of all spiritual intuition, and of the knowledge and love of God—the fullest sympathy between man and man, perfect harmony and concord, or, in the language of the Apostle, 'Love.' 'Love thy neighbour as thyself,' was the golden precept of Jesus Christ. 'Bear ye one another's burdens, and so fulfil the law of Christ,'[1] was the commentary of St. Paul, of the practical teacher who contemplated religion in its actual exercise, and the works by which faith is known among men. 'Above all things have fervent charity among yourselves, for charity'—that is, love—'shall cover the multitude of sins,'[2] was the commentary of St. Peter, the brave and impetuous soldier of the Lord. 'In this the children of God are manifest, and the children of the devil: whosoever doeth not righteousness is not of God, neither he that loveth not his brother,'[3]—is the commentary of St. John, the self-

---

[1] Gal. vi. 2.   [2] 1 Peter iv. 8.   [3] 1 John iii. 10.

inquiring, self-devoting friend of Jesus, looking beyond the outward token of works to the inward feeling of the heart. And again and again, with redoubled fervour: 'Beloved, let us love one another: for love is of God; and every one that loveth is born of God, and knoweth God.' 'God is love; and he that dwelleth in love dwelleth in God, and God in him.'[1]

Now, bearing in mind these texts, and considering the principle of self-control and self-denial for God and conscience' sake which they involve—the principle of human sympathy springing from the love of the heavenly and divine,—we may see at once how far as yet the heathens were from the position of Christ's true disciples. Certain common rights of man as man have been hitherto acknowledged theoretically by the philosophers, and admitted as matter of political expediency by legislators and statesmen. Another and more important step remains to be taken. The heart must be awakened, the conscience roused to a sense of duty, and the feelings to a sense of thankfulness for mercies received. Love must be given for love, sympathy to man in return for the sympathy of God. Man must come to feel that he lives under a law of charity, under a commandment from above written on the fleshly tables of his heart—that he who loveth God must love his brother also.

But we can hardly feel the obligation to bear one another's burdens, which is the law of love, until we have acquired the sense of a personal burden of our

[1] 1 John iv. 7, 16.

own, of a personal debt and duty to One who alone is able to bear our burdens and share our infirmities. We cannot exercise fervent, hearty, and zealous charity towards others, till we have felt the reality of sin, and the need of Divine charity to excuse and to cover it in ourselves. Therefore it is that the sense of duty to God comes first, and brings after it a sense of duty to our neighbour. And such again is the declaration made to us throughout the epistle of St. John, who begins with the recognition of God the Father and the divine Son Jesus Christ the righteous, and the sense of sin, and of duty towards Him; and thence leads us on to recognise the duty of brotherly love: 'He that saith he is in the light, and hateth his brother, is in darkness even until now.' 'This commandment have we from Him, That he who loveth God love his brother also.'

The consciousness, then, of our own sin is the first step to the fulfilment of the law of love. This is the Christian's view. Let us now examine what progress the heathen had made in this direction, and how far it had led him to the fulfilment of this commandment.

The general impression we receive from the records of the New Testament is assuredly that they were written under a prevailing sense of human misery. The world seems to assume to the writers the aspect of a wreck and a baffled purpose. Deep shades flit over the face of human society, from the uneasy possessor of wealth and power to the humblest occupant of the cottage. Sickness and infirmity of every kind are brought painfully prominent; the brighter scenes of life—with one or two notable exceptions—are kept studiously in the background. Over bodily pain and mental suffering of all kinds broods a vague and terrible apprehension of the wrath of God, and the inheritance of an indefinable curse. The general impression, I say, of life there depicted is one of pain, sorrow, disappointment, defeat—of the vanity of human cares, the nothingness of human objects, the awfulness of the inexplicable Present, the fearfulness of the unimaginable Future. We are ever reminded of the yearnings of the Psalmist, and are compelled to feel with him that it were better, far better—even for the best and happiest among us—to flee away and be at rest. Smitten with the gloom of these mournful records of our existence, we throw ourselves fervently into the feeling which dictated the solemn language of our Burial Service, when we heartily thank our heavenly Father that He has delivered our departed brother from the miseries of this sinful world. Of this pain and sorrow the faithful disciples are represented as themselves experiencing the greatest share; as far as this world is concerned they are declared to be of all men the most miserable. There are, indeed, outward circumstances of alarm or privation, of mocking and persecution even unto death, which may seem at first sufficient to account for this; but this is not all; this is not the real foundation of the gloomy prospect of the world as depicted in the Gospel, but sin, and the knowledge and consciousness of sin. If sin has brought death into the world, and the curse of sin has made the world miserable, it is the consciousness of this sin that has made men sensible of their misery, and most anxious for the means of escape from it, and from its curse. No man is so sensible of this as the Christian; no man feels so much the horror and the misery; but to him this knowledge brings with it the hope and anticipation of escape. The pain more keenly felt by him—the pain which colours and darkens every page of his sacred records—which issues in sad cries of agony from his inspired preachers at every crisis of their sorrowing pilgrimage—that pain is first sanctified, then softened, at last transformed into joy and peace in believing, by the assurance of a Redeemer who has overcome sin and death, and taken away the punishment and the curse. For such a transformation, for such a recompense of suffering the heathen could not look. There was nothing in the face of things around him to indicate it; there was nothing in the records or legends of the past, nothing in the hopes and pretended prophecies of the future to lead him to such an aspiration. The fixed persuasion of the heathen was that the world was bad—that it had once been better, but could only become worse. Hints might be obscurely given, or fondly imagined, of a coming Ruler, a divine Conqueror, a mysterious Revealer of God's will and nature; but of a Sanctifier and Redeemer, of a Conqueror of sin, an Assuager of pain, of an Averter of the evil which is born within us or gathers round us, and clings to us always from the cradle to the grave, and poisons life, and blasts pleasure, and mortifies pride, and corrupts love, and makes everything desired and hoped for turn out other than what we had desired and hoped—of an Averter of this eternal immedicable evil the heathen had no conception, no anticipation at all.[1]

I have spoken of the sadness which pervades the atmosphere, so to say, of the New Testament; deeper sadness, deeper because unrelieved by the revelation of a greater gladness, pervades not less completely the atmosphere of secular history under the sway of declining heathenism; deeper because of the contrast of the inner spirit of heathen society, and the gaudy colours in which society invested itself, with the blaring noise of the trumpets and the cymbals with which it sought to drown its accusing conscience. St. Paul is sad; St. John is pensive;—but the Christian St. Paul is not so sad as the philosopher Seneca; the Christian St. John is not so pensive as the philosopher Aurelius. For this sadness there was no relief in the creed of the old mythology, there was no relief in the creed of the political religion. Nor was there any relief in the aspect of the times, notwithstanding the show of splendour which adorned it, and the grandeur of the position to which mankind might seem to have attained.

The popular voice, indeed, the voice of poets and orators and declaimers, the voice even of philosophers themselves, is one long and varied chant of triumph— of triumph over man's submission to a great conquering

[1] See Note S.

empire, of triumph over nature's subjection to a great civilizing society, of triumph over barbarism, over the elements, over mind, and over matter. Cæsar and Jove hold coequal and divided sovereignty. The world has become the Roman Empire, and the Roman Empire has become a palace of Art, a palace reared and decorated for the habitation of the human soul. Few and slender indeed were the conquests of the Roman over material things, compared with the conquests on which our later age now plumes itself, which swell it with pride, excessive perhaps and vainglorious. But his triumphs in the realm of Art may fairly be set against our victories in Science; he had quite as much reason to boast of his intellectual achievements as we of ours; and great indeed was the satisfaction with which he looked around on the creations of his power, his skill, and his imagination, and pronounced them very good. But in the midst of all this outward glory he was stricken at heart; alarmed and terrified at he knew not what; distressed and disconsolate, he knew not why; 'noises as of waters falling down sounded about him,'—'sad visions appeared unto him of heavy countenances.'[1] 'They that promised to drive away terrors and troubles from a sick soul, were sick themselves of fear, worthy to be laughed at.' 'For wickedness, condemned of her own witness, is very timorous, and being pressed with conscience always forecasteth grievous things.' 'And whosoever there fell down was straitly kept, shut up

[1] Wisdom xvii.

in a prison without iron bars.' And this because, according to the stern reproof of the Apostle, 'when they knew God, they glorified Him not as God, neither were thankful; but became vain in their imaginations, and their foolish heart was darkened. Professing themselves wise, they became fools . . . changing the truth of God into a lie, and worshipping the creature more than the Creator.'[1] For such is the reward and the end of Pantheism, whether in the first century or in the nineteenth.

In some of the most thoughtful spirits of those days, this gloomy sense of dissatisfaction vented itself in murmurs and rebellions against the public conduct of affairs, against the Government, against the Cæsars. The contrast, half stifled, half avowed, between the philosophers and the empire, is a marked feature in the history of the times. But this was but a symptom of the malady, not the malady itself. The malady lay deep in the spiritual nature of man, deep in the foundations of sentiment and conscience, in feelings which are opened and explained to us by religion, which are tended, comforted, and transmuted by faith in a revealed Saviour only.

It was from this sense, however, of depression and discontent with the frame of the outward world, that arose the remarkable change which now appears in the expression of heathen philosophy, that is, of all that could now be called in any spiritual sense, heathen religion.

[1] Rom. i. 21, 22.

We open now on an era of preaching instead of discussion, of moral discourses, of spiritual improvement drawn from events and circumstances, of the analysis of virtues and vices, of exhortations to the one, warnings against the other. The philosopher is no longer a logician with an essay, nor a sophist with a declamation; he is a master, a preacher, a confessor or director of souls: he is not a speculator, inquiring after truth, but a priest, a minister, a hierophant of the divine Source of truth, guiding and controlling, as with authority, the conscience of his disciples. He is a witness of God, bearing testimony to a divine law, and charged as it were with the cure of souls intrusted to his teaching. We meet no more among the masters of human wisdom with subtle enquiries into the operations of the intellect; but addresses straight to the heart and spirit; advice tender or severe, remonstrances indignant or affectionate; exhortations to fervent prayer and self-enquiry; enticements to love and charity; earnest declarations, as from a higher source of knowledge, of the unity of man with man, and the common ties of sympathy which bind all the families of the earth together. Such are the topics handled in the pulpits of Seneca and Epictetus, of Dion and Juvenal, of Plutarch and Aurelius.[1]

'My friend,' says Epictetus, 'you would become a philosopher: then train yourself first at home and in silence; examine long your temper and weigh your

---

[1] See Note T.

powers. Study long for yourself before you preach to others. Plants ripen only by degrees, and you too are a divine plant. If you blossom before the time, the winter will nip you; you will fancy yourself some fine one, but you are dead already, dead even to the roots. . . . . Suffer yourself to ripen slowly, as nature prompts. Give the root time to take the soil, and the buds time to blossom; then nature herself will bear her own fruits.'

And again :—' Strive to heal yourself, to change your nature; put not off the work till to-morrow. If you say, To-morrow I will take heed to myself, it is just as though you said, To-day I will be mean, shameless, cowardly, passionate, malicious. See what evil you allow yourself by this fatal indulgence. But if it be good for you to be converted, and to watch with heart and soul over every action and desire, how much more is it good to do so this very moment! If it is expedient to-morrow, how much rather is it to-day! For beginning to-day you will have more strength for it to-morrow, and you will not be tempted to leave the work to the day after.'

Or hearken to Seneca :—' To acquire wisdom do we not plainly want an advocate and adviser, who shall enjoin us contrary to the behests of common opinion? No voice reaches our ears without some evil effect. . . . . The good wishes of our friends, the curses of our enemies are equally harmful to us. . . We cannot go straight forward; our parents draw us aside; our servants draw us aside; no man errs to his own hurt only, but scatters his own folly round him, and imbibes of the folly of others. Making others worse, he becomes worse himself. He has learned worse things, and straightway he teaches worse things; and thus is created the vast mass of our wickedness, by the accumulation of all the little wickednesses of us all. Oh! may there be some guardian ever about us, to dispel false conceits, and recall our attention from popular delusions! For thou errest—thou errest,'—here mark the false wisdom of the heathen,—' thou that thinkest that our vices are born in us; no, they have come upon us, they have been thrust into us. We were born sound from sin, free to righteousness. Then let us restrain, by constant exhortations, the vain imaginations which ever surge around us.'

Or to the mild Aurelius, severe to himself as no other heathen, indulgent as no other heathen to others: ' Beware, O my soul, of imperial habits, nor contract the stain of the purple. Keep yourself simple, good, sincere, grave, a lover of justice, a worshipper of God, kind but resolute in all your duties. Strive always to maintain the temper which philosophy seeks to engender. Fear God—protect men: life is short, and of this mortal life the only fruit is sanctity of temper, sympathy in deed. Approve yourself in all things a disciple '—of whom? not, alas! of Christ,—not of a perfect and divine exemplar, but—' of the best of men you have known, of Antonine the Pious.'

Such is the general tone of moral teaching under the Empire, varying with each individual teacher. With

Epictetus it is familiar and subtle; more pompous, more vague, with Dion Chrysostom; more vehement and penetrating, more various in application, with Seneca; more elevated again, and more tender, with Aurelius. But in all there is the same general tone of pressing exhortation, or of lively remonstrance; very different assuredly from that of the old Grecian sages, of Plato and Aristotle; more practical, more moral, more spiritual: addressed to the heart rather than to the head—to the conscience, not to the intellect of the disciple. But of exhortation to virtue there was less, inasmuch as a true exemplar of virtue was wanting: there was more of remonstrance against vice, for of instances of vice there was no lack on any side. This was the great defect of the heathen teaching, a defect for which there was no remedy among them. They felt themselves how fruitless it was to set before their pupils a mere theory or abstraction of goodness, where there was no effectual standard of goodness to be shown. And so a man of great note in his day among them implicitly confessed, when he charged his disciples to treat themselves as confirmed invalids in godliness, nor so much as seek to attain the normal state of spiritual health and soundness.[1]

But what is it that has thus taught men to take this practical view of the scope and functions of philosophy? It is their growing sense of the miseries of the world; of the trials and perturbations to which men are

[1] See Note U.

subjected by the insufficiency of human aims, the weakness of human resolves; by the opposition of human nature to the eternal rules of right; by a sense, however faint and dubious, of sin inherent in our mortal being, a sense of sin and no augury of redemption. 'Great is the conflict,' cries Seneca, 'between the Flesh and the Spirit.' 'O this accursed Flesh!' is the exclamation of Persius.

Accordingly Seneca rejects with vivacity the dialectic subtleties of the schools. Life, he feels, is too grave a thing to be so trifled with. 'Would you know,' he says, 'what it is that philosophy promises? I answer, practical advice. One man is at the point of death, another is pinched with want; one cannot bear his adverse fortune, another is wearied of prosperity; one is afflicted by men, another by the gods. Why do you thus trifle with them? This is no time for jesting, no place for grimaces. You are adjured by the miserable! You promised that you would bring succour to the shipwrecked, to the captives, to the sick, to the starving, to the condemned and perishing! Whither away then? What are you doing? The man you thus sport with is in agony. Help him! The lost, the dying, stretch their hands towards you; they implore you, they cast upon you all their hopes and aspirations. They entreat you to draw them forth from such abject misery; to show them their errors, and enlighten their perplexities, by the bright effulgence of the Truth. Tell them then what nature declares to be necessary and what superfluous; how easy her laws; how pleasant life, and how free to those who accept them; how bitter and perplexed to those who follow their own fancies rather.'[1]

'O wretched man that I am, who shall deliver me from the body of this death?'[2] Such is the cry at this same moment of the Apostle, in his address to the Romans, to the believers or inquirers collected from among the devoutest spirits of Rome, Gentile no less than Jew; and doubtless he well knew what response this cry would awaken in their hearts. For to many a lord of a patrician palace this cry of agony would sound as the echo from his own walls, the echo to the sighs and adjurations he had himself uttered in solitude, or confided to the ears of his own private adviser, his domestic philosopher. For it was from no vain pride that the Roman magnate furnished himself with a friend and director at his table, or by his couch, with whom to converse in the intervals of business on the concerns of his soul, and from whose tuition to imbibe his soundest lessons on the conduct of life and preparation for death. The highway of history is thronged with a gorgeous procession of figures, military or royal, marching on with the solemn tread of destiny to the accomplishment of great secular revolutions; but her byways afford us many a glimpse of private life and personal character and domestic usage, and show us men like ourselves at every shifting of the scene, under various institutions, moving about on their affairs just as we do ourselves. And so, in the

---

[1] See Note V. [2] Romans vii. 24.

byways of Roman history at this period, we see how the men who had rejected as baseless and unsanctioned the law of Pagan morality, became a law to themselves in this crisis of spiritual need, and sought to work out that law, not without fear and trembling. We see the statesman who has been doomed to execution, and required to submit his neck to the swordsman, or plunge the poniard in his own bosom, summon his friends, arrange the benches, invoke the aid of his spiritual adviser, and invite the party to a final discussion on the aim and purpose of human life, the real nature of dissolution. We see him rise from the debate with an affecting farewell, as one who is about to find in person a reply to the unsolved riddle of existence. Or, again, we see the sick and weary veteran, who has been long the victim of bodily infirmity, and suffered many things of divers physicians, consult the director of his conscience; shall he end at once all his pains by the momentary pang of a voluntary death?—his friends interceding with the sage for a decision which shall deter the patient from the irrevocable stroke, and persuade him still to bear the ills he has rather than fly to others that he knows not of.

Such was the honour paid, such the authority ascribed to these physicians of souls; to the philosophers, who feeling keenly in themselves, and observing all around them the miseries of this showy but empty pageant, searching subtly into the cause from whence they sprang — apprehending, however faintly and vaguely, the nature and effects of sin—spent their lives in teaching men to sympathize with their fellows, as all lying under the same inscrutable defect and baffling of existence. The whole world they felt to be akin to them, and to the world they went forth, as upon a holy mission, to teach and preach a message self-imposed, a message of love and pity, of rebuke to the proud, of comfort to the suffering. In earlier times the sages of ancient Greece—a Pythagoras, a Plato—made the pilgrimage of science to Ionia, to Italy, to Egypt, to learn from the lips of priests and eremites the truth embalmed in a precious tradition, or ascertained by old experience. There was no such freshness of faith now, no such hope of moral discovery, no such confidence in the existence of positive truth at all. But the heart and conscience were awakened, and with narrower ends and fainter aspirations the disciple of the schools now glided forth, not as a searcher for transcendental verities, but as the preacher of practical philanthropy, to make men better and happier, not to make himself wiser. While the Apostles of the Saviour and the elders of the Church whom they had ordained to the same holy mission—they who could embrace Paul's holy aspiration, 'I thank God through Jesus Christ our Lord'—preached from land to land the commandment of the blessed Jesus that he who loveth God love his brother also—the same principle, the same instinct of love, the same sympathy in a common danger, sprang spontaneously, and without a sanction but that of nature, in the bosom of many a soul-stricken watcher of the wants and miseries of men. Christian preaching found its shadow in heathen preaching; the sermons of bishops and confessors had their faint accompaniment in the discourses of philosophers; an Apollonius and a Dion, and many others, expelled from city to city, exposed to persecution, threatened with death for their doctrine's sake, might exclaim with the Apostle, that they too had been in journeyings often, 'in perils of waters, in perils of robbers, in perils in the city, in perils in the wilderness . . . in weariness and painfulness . . . in cold and nakedness.' One of them could beard the tyrant on his throne, in bold reproof of cruelty and oppression; another could assuage the terrors of a sedition, and the fury of the legions, and plead the cause of the debased and trampled slave, and rebuke the vanity of the mob of Alexandria; a third would shame the Athenians, when they proposed to desecrate their city with a show of gladiators, exclaiming, 'You must first overthrow your venerated statue of Mercy.'[1]

How far was this preaching of love spontaneous? —how far was it caught from the tone of Christian preaching, which I cannot doubt was beginning in the second century to make impression upon the heart of stone of the heathen? Who shall say? Thus much at least we may accept as unquestionable, that wherever Christian preaching really penetrated, the greater ardour with which it was delivered, the stronger assur-

[1] See Note W.

ance by which it was accompanied—above all, the higher sanction to which it appealed—gave it a force, a life, a power far beyond anything that could fall from mere heathen lips. But this, I think, we must admit —and this in carrying on the argument of these lectures it is important to urge—that independent of Christian preaching and Christian revelation, and of all special working of God's Holy Spirit on men's minds, the heathen world was at this time gravitating, through natural causes such as we have already traced, towards the acknowledgment of the cardinal doctrines of humanity which the Son of God dwelt among us in the flesh to illustrate, to expand, and to ratify. For it is not among the philosophers only, among men bound by their profession, as truth-seekers, to know something of the teaching of the Christians, that this movement of philanthropy is found. The alleviation of slavery by law and custom; the recognition of the common rights of man by man; the softening of the brutal usages of the amphitheatre; the elevation of the social rank of women; the increase, not perhaps of restraints upon vice, but of horror open and avowed at its practice and permission; a greater show at least of respect for morality and virtue; a growing preparation for accepting the purer law and higher standard of God's holy ordinances; a preparation, in short, for receiving at the hands of God's ministers, not a system of theological doctrine—of that I am not now speaking, I shall have to speak of that in its place hereafter—but a republication of the law of nature, the law of love and mutual consolation; this movement, I say, in all its various phases, may be traced, not to the special intuition of the wise and prudent only, but to the sense and instinct of the multitude, gradually constrained, under God's providence, by disgust, by fear, by spiritual apprehension, by scorn for the world, by consciousness of sin, by the augury of a greater curse impending.[1]

The empire of the heathen, the empire over mind and matter, the highest culture of the natural man, had gone forth into God's world as a brave vessel upon the ocean, painted and bedecked and spangled at the prow and at the helm, and had accomplished half its voyage in pride and security. But the winds were now arising, the heavens were lowering; the muttering of thunders was heard above the hissing and seething of the waters; her masts were groaning, her planks were starting. Among the crew was fear and sorrow, and confusion of faces; they felt their common danger, and each gave a hand to the common work; each cheered his fellow with whisperings of comfort which he but faintly felt himself. The terror of the moment bound the crew, and the master, and the passengers all more closely together. There is still hope, brave crew, there is still comfort! In mutual help and sympathy your hope of safety lies. Then courage all!—to the oars, to the wheel, to the pumps! The vessel yet rides the storm; all may yet be well! Then love, and aid, and encourage one another.

[1] See Note X.

And here we must leave them for the present. Another and a wilder scene will shortly be presented to us—a scene of desolation and dismay and frenzy; of prayer hoarsening into imprecation; of the cutting away the boats, of breaking in twain the oars, of rushing madly to the spirit-room. They will lash themselves into fury; they will quarrel, fight, and threaten to slay; they will prepare to go together to the bottom, with fire in their brain and defiance on their lips. But when the Apostle was tost on the waves of Adria, and 'neither sun nor stars had for many days appeared, and no small tempest lay on them, and all hope that they should be saved was then taken from them,' the Angel of God stood by him in the night, saying, 'God hath given thee all them that sail with thee.'[1] And so, even now in that tormented bark of heathenism, the Spirit of the Almighty will be present. Lo! the crew is in His holy keeping! let them but turn to Him, and be converted, and abide in His faith; there shall be no loss of any man's life among them, 'but only of the ship.'

[1] Acts xxvii. 24.

LECTURE VI.

EFFORTS OF THE HEATHEN TO AVERT SPIRITUAL RUIN.

St. Mark ix. 24.

And straightway the father of the child cried out, and said with tears, Lord, I believe; help Thou mine unbelief.

CHRISTIANITY appeals to the heart as well as to the head, to the feelings no less than to the judgment. It teaches us that faith depends upon the will as much as upon the understanding, and therefore that it is to be attained by the exercise of the affections, by love and prayer, as well as by the exertion of thought and mind. This Christian paradox is illustrated by the familiar text above cited, 'Lord, I believe; help Thou mine unbelief;' a text familiar to all Christians at every step in their religious experience; for the feeling which it indicates of the insufficiency of the intellect to comprehend the mysteries of God, or to retain at all times and under all trials its hold of a constant and fervent faith in the Invisible, belongs not to the mere novice only, not to the recent convert, not to the first hearer of the Truth. It belongs to all who are really earnest in examining their own hearts, and jealous of a lapse, however transient, from the fulness of spiritual assurance. The text relates the occurrence of a particular incident, but is registered for all time; and the thoughts it suggests may be useful for all time, and for manifold situations.

The father of the afflicted child yearns for the promised relief. The condition is Belief. He will believe. He makes an effort of the will. His imagination, on the wings of love and prayer, transcends the limits of the visible and the possible. He flings himself into another world of higher existences, and powers, and possibilities. He sees the man Jesus before him dilated to Divine proportions, and shutting out from his field of view the gross realities of the world, with its material laws and its narrow limits. The spirit is willing, but the flesh is weak; the vision, the dream of faith, vibrates before his eyes; the realities of the world return again and again, they thrust themselves importunately upon him, and threaten to recover all their former vividness. He feels his faith yielding, his spirit fainting, his nerves relaxing; and he cries out for help, for strength to hold on yet a little longer, for light to see yet a little longer; he cries out with tremblings that shake his strength, with tears that blind his sight, 'Lord, I believe; help Thou mine unbelief.'

Such were the struggles of the human conscience when Jesus Christ appeared in the world, and held forth the hopes of His healing power to the afflicted and miserable both in soul and body. Such are the struggles, constantly repeated through all ages, when the knowledge of Him, and of His revelation of mercy, is set forth to the sinners and the spiritually-stricken among men; the same struggle of the will and the understanding, of faith and fear, is ever going on among us, and is the condition of our advance in spiritual light and experience.

But there was a time when the mercy of Jesus Christ was not yet made manifest to man; a time when, though he had actually come in the flesh and dwelt among men, the world was not yet prepared to acknowledge it; when his appearance had not yet been preached to all nations, and the offer of salvation through Him not yet generally published. Nevertheless, in the first ages of Christianity, in the decline of heathenism, there was among those who knew not Christ, nor perhaps had yet heard of him, the same struggle going on, the same opposition between the will and the power to believe. There was even then, at least among some meek and tender spirits, a will to believe in something, they knew not what; a cry for relief from some quarter, they knew not whence; a suspicion—a hope—an assurance that there was a revelation somehow to be made, a revelation of grace and mercy to the spiritually afflicted, and at the same time an earnest wish to be helped against their own unbelief; an effort, with groans and tears, against the deep despondency in which the absence of any visible object of faith had plunged them.

The father in the narrative deeply loved his son, but

his son was afflicted with a devil. The generation of declining heathenism deeply loved the world around them—the brilliant cities, the joyous country, the temples and the forum, the baths and the festivals, the objects of art and luxury with which their homes were stored to overflowing, the tranquil ease, the leisure for study or meditation, the security of their long-established civilization, the treasured results of philosophy and science; but the world they so loved was afflicted with a devil. All its pleasures appeared hollow and unsound; sweet to the taste, they left a sting of bitterness; its vices were flagrant, and seemed to call aloud for chastisement; pain and fear had taken possession of it. There was something radically amiss with it, some defect in its constitution, which plainly threatened it with dissolution. The physicians had been consulted, but without avail. The devil had torn them, and driven them away. The patient had himself struggled feverishly against it, but it had ofttimes cast him into the fire, and into the waters, to destroy him; he had fallen upon the ground, and wallowed foaming. Such is a picture of the misery of the heathen world at the moment of its highest outward culture; at the moment when it had lost its faith in the heathen religions, and not yet acquired faith in Christ; at the moment when its eyes were opened to its spiritual destitution, and the chastened feelings of humanity led it to recognise the corruption of the flesh, and the desperate condition of the soul that lives without God in the world. Anxious to find some one who could do anything to relieve this sickness of the world around them, the heathen knew not yet on whom they might call, and who would have compassion on them; who there was who could address them with those blessed words, 'If thou canst believe, all things are possible to him that believeth.'[1]

Yet, in this anxiety and despair, the heathen sought out a healer for themselves. The sentiment of mercy and pity, of mutual sympathy, of an ever-widening humanity, which, as we have before seen, was gradually prevailing among them, the sentiment of the equality of men in God's sight and of the equal claims of men on one another accordingly—this sentiment seemed to give them the first glimpse of an idea of divine grace and mercy, of a law of love, of some spiritual existence fulfilling that idea, and itself appointing that law and declaring it. They felt about, as men still dazzled or purblind, for the Being invisible and inaccessible to whom they might appeal, to whom they might exclaim— in their conscious weakness and uncertainty, and amidst the struggles which they felt within them of the flesh against the spirit, of the understanding against the reason, of the head against the heart, and through the tears which blinded them for the failures and vanities of the world, and its pomps around them—'Lord, I believe; help Thou mine unbelief.'

To whom should they apply? How should they image to themselves the Being whom they longed for, the realization of their spiritual consciousness? The

---

[1] St. Mark ix. 23.

Gods of the heathen had lost all significance, even with their accustomed votaries. Mars, and Quirinus, and last Rome, and Victory last of all—the many names of one idea, the idea of a local and temporal Providence—had all faded from the imagination, and remained only palpable to the senses in their images of wood and stone. There was no more use for them but to hurl them bodily from the walls of the city upon the heads of the assailing barbarians. The old mythology had long fallen to the ground, and the temporal religion, the fiction of the magistrate, which had more recently replaced it, while it still stood erect in apparent strength and majesty, had been tried by the earnest and spiritual-minded, and had been found wholly wanting; discredited by its results, disproved by the event, by its manifest defect of spiritual energy to chasten and control, by the apprehension of its temporal weakness to shield from disaster and discomfiture.

The civil religion of the Romans, then, has virtually come to nought, or survives only in vague unreal generalities, in poetry or in rhetoric. The personification of the genius of the empire, the deification of the emperor himself, is a mere make-believe of religion, a mere artifice or shift to save the appearance of a political continuity.

The place of this political religion has been occupied by the personal hopes and fears of the individual worshippers. Mankind—the spiritual portion of them—are too really anxious, for their own conscience' sake, to be swayed by such phantoms of expediency. There is spiritual peril around them. They feel that they have souls to be saved. The deepening earnestness, the anxious spiritual excitement of the heathen world, as it nears the period of its absorption in Christianity, is a fact of solemn import. It may teach us to apprehend how great was the impending revolution, how wide, how deep, the spiritual movement which transferred the faith of mankind from the old to the new foundations. But why all this earnestness?—why these spiritual apprehensions?—whence this ever deepening solemnity of feeling? The world gliding gently down the current of circumstance—rippling, running, rushing onward—yet knew not of the Niagara plunge it was about so suddenly to take. No! but the teaching of the philosophers had gradually permeated society, and sunk into the minds of thoughtful and earnest men; the events and facts of life around them had forced on them a nobler view of human nature, a sense of nearer connection with the divine, of the independence and immateriality of the soul, subject to higher laws, derived from deeper sources, directed to grander and more enduring purposes. The baffling of worldly pride, the dashing of worldly hopes, the gradual closing in of the political curtain, commotions within and the barbarians without, the ghastly blankness of the aspect of the future, all deter men from too much brooding on the world before them, and direct them with feverish haste to more spiritual aspirations. Amid the impending wreck of civil society creeps in a distrust of man and man's assistance; an instinctive cry of 'Save Thyself,' heard in the recesses of the conscience, drives men to look to their personal interests in regard to spiritual things. There springs up among them a feeling of mutual repulsion, in place of that mutual attraction which in ages of hope and faith brings them from all quarters together, builds their cities, founds their commonwealths, and establishes their national religions. Common creeds are disintegrated and split into a thousand fragments. And ever and anon, in every lull of the all-absorbing tempest, penetrates at hand or at a distance, the whisper of the Christian preaching—a still small voice, heard by many a heart-stricken heathen, above the song of the festival, and the blare of trumpets, exerting even over the worldly and the godless a silent, unacknowledged, disowned influence, and leading all men, more or less, some faster, some slower, some consciously, others against their will or without their knowledge, to a vague impression of a spiritual existence, inviting their faith and commanding their obedience. Viewed on every side there is no period of history, as it seems to me, when men were more in earnest about spiritual hopes and fears than in the third century of our era.

Baulked of his carnal hopes, distrustful of all human aid, the natural man now sought vehemently for a personal connection with God. Renouncing the idea of national communion with the Invisible, of personal protection or salvation, through the federal compact with his countrymen, he strove to unite his own soul to the spirit of the universe. He threw himself on the Infinite and Invisible in prayer. He cast from him the trammels of pride and prejudice, which in more cheerful and frivolous days had withheld his fathers from the self-humiliation of the prayer of faith and devotion. He tore asunder the cobwebs woven by the human understanding, which had been wont to intrude importunately between him and the mystery of Infinite Power, Mercy and Grace; and whisper that Infinite Power cannot undo what it once has done, Infinite Mercy may not save what has been once condemned, Infinite Grace will not condescend to the affections of poor human infirmity. True that Socrates and Plato had not refused to bend the knee and move the lips in prayer; that devout and spiritual men of old time had acknowledged a truth in reason beyond the conclusion of the purely logical understanding; but such masters as these had seemed to stand apart from the common nature of men; their speculations were deemed to transcend the practical wants of the human soul; their doctrines had been admired, and passed from mouth to mouth as men admire an ideal work of art, but were never taken to the bosom, and made the household possession of the multitude. Prayer had never been accepted as a great spiritual engine by the Western mind. This new and worthy conception of prayer, its nature, power and privileges, was Oriental, Syrian, and Jewish. It was through the synagogue, I doubt not, that this idea of prayer, of the prayer of the righteous man availing much, was propagated in the Roman world. The synagogue of the dispersion was the substitute for the Temple at Jerusalem; and the incense of prayer, the sacrifice of the lips, replaced among the Jewish worshippers abroad the incense of myrrh and spices, and the blood of bulls and rams, which could be offered only in the holy place at home. The influence of this Jewish practice, thus stimulated, upon the heathen mind, can hardly perhaps be overrated. The Jews penetrated every rank of Roman society. Their manners, their rites, their religious records and religious experiences, their moral and spiritual ideas; worked their way into the high places as well as the low places of Rome, and prepared a high road for Christianity by refining and spiritualizing the religious instincts of the heathen. We may not be able to trace a direct effect of Christian teaching upon the mind of a Seneca; but with the Jews and their religious notions there can be no doubt that he was well acquainted; and when he remarks with admiration, not unmingled with awe, that the Jews, subdued by the Romans, had in turn given laws to the conquerors, what laws could he mean, but the law of mind and conscience, the law of philosophy and religion, the law of worship and the law of prayer? And thus the teaching of this sage, and of the schools that symbolized with him, owed doubtless no small portion of their spiritual character to God's Revelation of His attributes to the Jews.[1]

In the Emperor Marcus Aurelius, in the slave Epictetus, placed at the opposite extremes of social rank, we observe almost at the same moment the

---

[1] See Note Y.

same devout attitude of thought. Both equally regard the received mythology as absurd and baseless, though they feel bound to abstain from direct attacks upon it; it suffices at least to represent to them as in a parable, the idea of a Divine superintendence—a moral Providence, to which their religious emotions may be safely directed. To this Being, this Essence, they address themselves, a being more obscure, more mysterious than the Invisible Jehovah of the Jews, but accessible enough to the conscience—palpable, as it were, to the touch of faith—when they throw themselves before Him in spirit, and seem to embrace His knees in the attitude of prayer. Their prayers are not the crude and fantastic effusions of the worshippers of a deity in the form and likeness of man, who regard their God as endued with parts and passions such as their own—the mere reflex of their own grovelling nature, and composed of selfish appetites and unholy imaginations, whose aid and favour they invoke in every enterprise of lust or malice. They do not exclaim, 'O God, avenge me of my enemy!' They do not whisper, 'O God, indulge my cupidity!' they do not say, 'Grant me health, wealth, or prosperity, or power;' but rather, 'Keep me from all evil desires, even towards those who have done me evil; guard me from too fond a wish for the benefits of fortune; make me resigned under calumny, content in poverty, cheerful in sickness.' They are well aware of all the subtleties by which doubt and perplexity are cast on our natural yearnings for prayer; but they rest secure in the conviction that there is One who hears the prayer of faith—who approves it—who takes it up into Himself, and through some inscrutable agency does truly reply to it. They are not cowed, like the hypercritical logician, by the great paradox of faith; but are ready to exclaim, with the simple eagerness of the Christian proselyte, 'Lord, I believe; help Thou mine unbelief.'[1]

I have cited the emperor and the slave as the two most conspicuous instances at this period of the incipient faith which seeks to exhale itself in prayer to a God unknown to it; the most conspicuous in our eyes, from their respective positions; the most conspicuous also from the frequency, the fervour, the force and freedom of their heavenward aspirations; the nearest in their day to Christianity among the heathen. But the heathen world, even in its scanty remains bequeathed to us, abounds at this time with indications of the same pious yearning. The spirit of prayer has gone abroad, and leavens the mass of the thoughtful and devout among the heathen. The effusions of the philosophers answer in this respect to the preaching of the Christian fathers; answer so far, that we see they belong to the same age: that the one in some degree reacts upon and tempers the other, and each is reflected by the other. The face is not the same, not one; but like, as that of brethren should be; as of brethren of one family, the family of God. The Father recognises His children on

[1] See Note Z.

the right hand and on the left; the child of the bond-woman and the child of the free woman: the minds of men, however separated by accidents and conventionalities, are evidently working under a common influence unto a common end. The goal, to the ken of angels, is already almost in sight, though men will still obstinately shut their eyes to it, and in their passion struggle to efface the lines of convergence and analogy, to deny the identity of origin and purpose, to foster repulsion and discord in the elements which should combine for the production of unity and love.

Much yet remains to be done and suffered before this unity can be effected, before the absorption of heathen devotion in the higher and holier devotion of the Christian. There are still more turns in the way, more fallings into error, more aversion from the light of God and prostration before phantoms of the human imagination. There is still a dark hour, the darkest of the night of heathenism, to be passed, before the dawn of the sun of the Gospel, and the rise of true religion in the soul. The spirit of prayer, the yearning for communion with God, have been awakened; but this spirit, this yearning, will surely generate error in the heart of the natural man, unenlightened, unconverted, unsanctified by the Holy Spirit, who is God Himself. A new sense of religious need has been awakened, and straightway it creates a new superstition, a development of the religious sense the more curious and instructive as it runs parallel with the historical career of Christianity, and seems to be consciously and even studiously opposed to it.

Of this new religion, the religion of the purest and most spiritual-minded of the later heathens, of this combination of a creed and a philosophy which is known by the name of the New Platonism, I have little room here to speak. I would only remark upon it as a special, and in the West an unique example of a dogmatic faith evolved from the pure reason. A religion professedly based on the historical records of a revelation we can fully understand; a religion resting upon mere unhistorical tradition is too common to excite our surprise; again, a philosophy which seeks for spiritual truths in the light of the natural reason may be a legitimate effort of the human mind; but such a philosophy makes no pretensions to be a religion. But the New Platonism was different from all these, for it combined with such a philosophy the gratuitous assertion of a dogmatic creed, the issue of mere caprice or guess-work. It was in fact the engrafting of the Oriental Mithraism upon the moral philosophy of the Platonists and Stoics. It asserted the existence of a divine hierarchy, culminating in a supreme essence, a triple godhead involving Unity, Soul and Intelligence, but descending again from development to development, from emanation to emanation, through a long series of divinities, of genii, good or evil, opposed or in alliance—still descending till they touched upon the confines of humanity, and reached even to man upon earth; thus not raising man to God, but bringing God down to man.

But with this Oriental divination of a personal godhead were combined the spiritual aspirations of the Grecian philosophy. The school of Alexandria accepted and sublimed the loftiest dogmas of the Stoics; they held that man might also be raised upwards to God, even to the eminence of the absolute Being, by study and virtue: what reason could not acquire in knowledge and spiritual power, might be revealed by enthusiasm or ecstasy: the individual man might lose himself in the contemplation of the infinite God, from whom he originally came, and to whom he might thus ultimately restore himself.

It is not the soul, they said, that comes to know God: God descends into the soul; a touch, a sympathy, a union; man for a moment becomes God. Thus ecstasy is the ultimate term of all knowledge, the crowning of perfect virtue. It is to be attained by patience in well-doing; by mortification of the senses; by extinction of the passions; by repudiating the flesh and the earth. Thus the sage or saint comes to be independent of the common laws of matter—he gets a foretaste of disembodied spirit—he can rise above the earth into mid-air—he can work miracles—he becomes a magician.[1]

This wild scheme of human religion, this last utterance of expiring heathenism points, it seems to me, to two things. First, it points to the need men evidently began now to feel of a personal relation to God. It was the completion, as far as human reason could go, of the efforts of the conscience to ally and unite itself with

[1] See Note A A.

God, upon whom it had thrown itself in all the energy of prayer. It had implored of God to reveal Himself to His believers. 'Lord,' it had said, 'we believe in Thee, but yet we do not know Thee: help Thou our unbelief: reveal Thyself—make Thyself known to us—let us not burst in ignorance.' And then it had gone on to imagine and invent a God for itself. It had guessed a God after its own conceit. It had framed a religion out of the depths of its own awakened conscience; a religion, not licentious, I admit, but rather painful and mortifying to the flesh at least, however it might pamper the pride of the heart; a religion requiring a long and searching initiation, demanding trials of fortitude and patience, giving glimpses of moral regeneration, promise of a remission of sins, hopes of a future life.

And this leads us to the second point we have to notice, the evident imitation of Christianity, the conscious plagiarism upon gospel truth, which marks the last development of religion among the heathen. It is sufficiently plain that the teaching of the Christians has been making way in the world. Even in the increasing sympathy of man with man, and in the development of the spirit of prayer, and in the demand for communion with God, we might fairly infer that such an influence had been operating obliquely; in the diffusion of the Mithraic and Gnostic superstitions, with the germs or shadows of Christian truth which they unquestionably embrace, we may recognise without hesitation its more direct and more powerful effect.

But if even the most spiritual among the heathen, permitted thus to enjoy a breath, however faint, from the sources of truth and knowledge, were given over to believe a lie, to grope in a world of darkness, to groan under the yoke of their own wild exaggerations, far grosser was the lie, far blacker the darkness, far wilder the extravagance under which the more vulgar and carnal of them laboured in their efforts to hold communion with God. The exercise of prayer has led men to a nearer conception of the Deity, to a closer sense of the reality of His being, His presence, His providence. It impels them to yearn for Him, to draw and drag Him down, as it were, to themselves. What then does the heathen do? He cannot wait for Him or feel for Him at a distance, he cannot address Him afar off, he will not brook delay or impediment, he must find a royal road to approach Him, he will make Him his own at once, and possess Him. He invents, or rather he revives, he multiplies, he exaggerates long familiar methods of divination and augury. He dreams dreams, he observes omens, he imagines sights and sounds of fateful import, he fancies that he works wonders, and requires wonders to be worked for him, he surrounds himself with all the artifices and instruments of magic, and exults or trembles—exults while he trembles, and trembles even while he exults—in the assurance that his faith has made all things possible, and brought God down to him, or raised him perchance up to God. The age of heathen prayer and devotion was the antecedent to the age of Thaumaturgy and Theurgy. The one followed, it would seem, as the immediate corollary from the other. The natural man had discovered the necessity of a god, of a providence, of a moral authority and sanction, of judgment and retribution; and he rushed precipitately forward to seize upon God, to bind Him, as it were, and secure the means of access to Him, and of compelling Him to appear at the summons of his votaries. As a ruder age had bound its idols to the city walls with chains of iron to prevent their deserting it, so the later heathens, more refined in their conceptions, but not more truly enlightened, sought to clasp the invisible and impalpable to their souls by the craft of magical incantation. The germ of a spiritual conception of God had been cast into the heathen world by the hands of Jews and Christians, but such was the strange and prodigious harvest it produced, when left to grow untended by the skill of the Divine husbandman.

The impulse thus given to the practice of divination was accompanied by a revival of the use of oracles. The impostures which had died to the roots under the neglect of genuine unbelief, sprang up again, renewed in life and vigour, amidst the cravings of superstition. The misery of the present time, the prospect still more gloomy beyond it, seemed to impel all men of devout sentiment to anxious enquiries into the future. To the happy and contented God is love; to the alarmed and miserable God is fear. To decrepit heathenism God was fear, dismay, and confusion of faces. The priests themselves, stricken with the universal panic, swept along in the common vortex of despair, amidst the fall of institutions and dissolution of ideas, were the first victims of their own artifices. They demanded to qualify themselves for their mystic service by fasts and exercises, by strict seclusions, by a studied excitement of the nervous system to a pitch of frenzy beyond their own control. In this ecstatic state the prophet, self-deceived, saw incommunicable visions, and imagined Divine inspirations.

We need not doubt that much of this delusion was perfectly genuine. They were given over to believe their own lies. Worn out with fastings they saw visions, drugged with poisons they dreamed dreams, unnerved by frenzy they imagined apparitions, fluttered by the pulses of spiritual pride they believed that they were workers of miracles and prophets of the future. But more conscious imposture was sure to follow: for imposture follows fanaticism as its shadow, and avenges with a righteous judgment every moral extravagance. The impostors themselves found their Nemesis in the aroused curiosity of the sceptics, and the final detection of their organized deceit. What yet remained of reason in the heathen world, first staggered, then irritated, at last aroused to strict inquiry by the audacious attempt to master it, tore the veil asunder, and exposed the empty pretension. The records yet remain; and alas! that in these days there should again arise special reason for remembering and referring to them,—records, I say, still remain of the various forms of deception then currently practised, and of the exact way in which they were effected. We are acquainted with some, at least, of the expedients employed to represent the apparition of gods and demons and the spirits of the departed to the eye of the half-delirious votary. He was bid to look into a basin filled with water, the bottom of which had been covertly replaced with glass, with an opening in the floor beneath. The form for which he enquired was revealed to him from below; or the figure was traced invisibly on the wall, and lightly touched with a combustible composition; a torch was applied, and the god or demon or spirit was suddenly displayed in fire. The ancients, it seems, could employ many of our secret agents of deceit; sympathetic ink was not unknown to their adepts and impostors. Their conjurors and jugglers were to the full as skilful as ours; and their arts were turned to account for objects far more serious than the mere buffoonery of the streets. It is well, even for our use and instruction, that those tricks were exposed at the time, and the record of them perpetuated. The phenomena of modern spiritualism, whatever their actual origin, are, I believe, an exact reproduction of the presumed wonders of the third century; of an age not unlike our own in credulity, and in incredulity, in nervous irritability, in impatience of the grave teachings of experience. For our age, as well as for his own, even the scoffer Lucian has not lived in vain. We cannot even yet afford to consign his banter to oblivion.[1]

[1] See Note B B.

I have noticed how in these performances delusion and deceit were actually intermingled. Must we make allowance for the weakness of poor human nature? Must we grant indulgence to its fond efforts to create a soul under the ribs of the spiritual death which it was daily dying? Such allowance, such indulgence, I for one dare not claim for it. I believe that the attempt was conceived in sin, as it issued in sin. God saw that it was sin; sin in its perversion of the moral law; sin in its veiling of the natural light of truth; in its conceit of human power and independence. The sin was revealed in its results. For conjuring and necromancy led promptly to a cruel fanaticism; they excited a fearful apprehension of the spiritual world, of the hideousness of the angry demons of darkness; and to the most terrible expedients for baffling or appeasing them. An atonement of blood was demanded for a reconciliation with hell. Hence the revival of human sacrifices with which many an altar was stained; still more the conviction, deliberately, entertained that it was only by the offering of man's best and dearest that the inscrutable could be discovered, and the implacable appeased. Belief in God, belief in a personal connection with God, in the possibility of personal communion with God, led the natural man directly to the fearful sense of his distance from Him, of estrangement from Him, of dread of His wrath, of despair of His mercy. The persecution of the Christians, the martyrdoms of the stake and the amphitheatre, the cry of 'the Christians to the lions,' was one vast scheme of human sacrifice for the propitiation of this averted Deity. The persecution by Nero was an atonement for the burning of the city; the persecution by Domitian for the destruction of the capitol; the persecution by Trajan for the overthrow of Antioch by an earthquake; the persecution of Aurelius for the world-wide pestilence which swept the empire with an universal disaster. Not yet satisfied, not yet relieved—nay, as dangers and distresses thicken around him, more agitated, more alarmed, more furious than ever—the heathen defies the Christian to mortal combat in the latter persecutions of Decius and Diocletian; he will sweep away the enemies of his gods in one hurricane of slaughter, or perish together with them in the impending ruin of his polity and culture.[1]

This last revelation of cruelty and fanaticism was not needed to convince us of the moral superiority of the regenerated believer over the heathen seeker after truth. Whatever be the weaknesses betrayed by the early Christians themselves, whatever ignorance or credulity, whatever superstitious fancies, whatever extravagance in act or creed, whatever disparagement has been cast on Christian faith and truth by the errors of its early disciples, on whom the shadows of an age of darkness still partially lingered; this I am bold to affirm, that morally and intellectually, in heart and understanding, the Christians of the empire are to the heathens of the empire as men of a purer blood

---

[1] See Note C C.

and a nobler spiritual lineage. In their writings, whatever errors we may note in them, we breathe a purer atmosphere; in their actions, whatever infirmities we may trace in them, we discover a higher rule. Their society is pervaded by a new and freer spirit. A new principle is developed in it. Their love indeed is but the love of the most refined of the heathens ten times refined; his sympathy infinitely expanded: but their faith, their belief in the being and providence of God —in the love and goodness of God—in the reality of sin and human corruption, mingled with the assurance of God's reconciliation to sinners—in the one sufficient atonement by the blood of a divine victim—is a new principle, a new germ of religious life, the token of a genuine revelation. The fashion of the ancient world is perishing; and the modern world, with a philosophy and morality, a faith and practice of its own, is shaping itself out of chaos. Again the Spirit of God is moving upon the face of the waters: again the voice of the watchman on the hills is heard replying to the challenge, 'What of the night?' the genesis of a new heaven and a new earth is commencing, with the new Adam for their Lord, with the Gospel for the bow of His covenant, with the new Jerusalem for their metropolis, and the kingdom of God for their final inheritance. Even from the bosom of an effete and dying society a new life is springing, in which the signs of health and vigour, of truth and soundness, are the more plainly revealed from the very abomination of corruption which is manifested around it.

LECTURE VII.

THE DOCTRINES OF CHRISTIANITY RESPOND TO THE QUESTIONS OF THE HEATHENS.

ST. MATTHEW XXVIII. 19.

The name of the Father, and of the Son, and of the Holy Ghost.

WE have marked the breaking down of the ancient mythology of the Pagans, and again of the political religion which replaced it; the diffusion among them of larger and more liberal conceptions of the nature of man, and of his relation to God; the awakening of their conscience to a sense of sin, and the consequent straitening of the bands of human sympathy among them; their yearning for access to God and communion with him in prayer, their fuller acknowledgment of His Being and Providence, however disfigured it became by the extravagance of mystical devotion in the more refined, of gross superstition in the vulgar; with a resort to magical arts, with self-abandonment to the grossest spiritual terrors, culminating in panic, despair, and bloodshed. Many a mind was now ripe for conversion to the true God, to the religion which teaches the equality of men in His sight, which proclaims the abolition of exclusive spiritual privileges, and merges the city upon earth in the city of God in heaven; which finally leads the sinner to the one Being who can forgive sin, bids him seek God in the prayer of an enlightened faith, entreat for reconciliation with Him, and accept the doctrine of the divine Atonement, Mediation, and Redemption.

While thousands day by day were going through this spiritual process and attaining to this blessed conversion, it is remarkable how meagre are the records of their experience which have been transmitted to us. We would give much for a genuine and full account of the heathen pilgrim's progress ' from this world to that which is to come.' One partial glimpse at such progress, and I believe one only, is afforded us in a work called 'The Clementines,' which pretends to narrate the conversion of a certain Roman named Clemens; and which, though itself a fiction, is clearly a fiction drawn from real life in the age before us. It represents the mental condition of a youth, devout and pious by nature, harassed by intellectual doubts, unsettled by the strife of conflicting opinions, longing for the truth, and painfully seeking it, till led at length, after many a pang of disappointment, to the only sure refuge and haven of the soul.

'From my youth,' says Clemens, 'I was exercised with doubts, which had found an entrance, I know not how, into my soul—" Will my being end with death? and will none hereafter remember me, when infinite time shall whelm all things in oblivion? .... When was the world created, and what was there before the world? If it has existed always, will it continue to exist for ever? If it had a beginning, will it likewise have an end? And after the end of the world, what then? The silence of the grave? or something else, some other thing of which we can form no notion?" Haunted by such thoughts as these, which came I know not whence, I was sorely troubled in spirit. I grew pale, and wasted away: when I strove to drive them from me, they returned again and again with renewed and increased violence, so that I suffered greatly. I knew not that in these very thoughts I enjoyed a friendly companion, guiding me to eternal life, nor allowing me to rest till I found it. Then, indeed, I learned to pity the wretched men whom, in my ignorance, I had deemed the happiest. .... But, while thus perplexed and worried, I ran to the schools of the philosophers, hoping to find a foundation on which I could rest in safety. But nought could I see but the building up and tearing down of theories; nought but endless dispute and contradiction: sometimes, for example, the demonstration triumphed of the soul's immortality, and then again of its mortality. When the one prevailed I was happy; when the other I was dispirited. Thus was I tossed to and fro by contending arguments, and forced to the conclusion that things appear not as they really are, but only as they are represented. I grew dizzier than ever, and sighed from my heart for deliverance.'

Thus distressed, the devotee of Truth would seek relief and conviction elsewhere. He would visit Egypt, the land of mysteries and portents, and extort from a necromancer the apparition of a departed spirit. Could such a being be presented to him, he would know for certain the existence of a spiritual world, the immortality of souls. No reasoning, no logical demonstration would thenceforth shake his abiding conviction. But a wiser man dissuaded him from this vain endeavour, and from seeking God's truth by arts which God has forbidden; from sacrificing peace of conscience for peace of the understanding. The Providence of God led him at this crisis to the preaching of the Christians, and among them he found in a legitimate way the assurance of peace which he had fruitlessly sought amid the wanton fancies of the heathen.[1]

That assurance and peace were founded on the belief in certain positive dogmas, which themselves exactly fulfilled the conditions of faith which the heathen had longed for. The creed of the Church— the creed transmitted from the first preaching of the Apostles—implied in the sacred records of the Scripture canon—stamped with the seal of Divine inspiration; the creed maintained by bishops, confessors, and martyrs, through three centuries of trial, and held by a firm concurrent tradition in the east and the west, the

---

[1] See Note D D.

north and the south; the creed, finally, drawn out in the confession of the Nicene fathers, and ratified by the Spirit of God, presiding at a general council of the Church;—this creed, in its three great divisions, the name of the Father, the Son, and the Holy Ghost, replied to the questions of the heathen, solved his doubts, showed to him the nature of God, of sin, of redemption, and the fact of a future judgment and final retribution. It laid before him the scheme of Divine providence, for the salvation of a lost world. It vindicated God's ways to man. Not answering every importunate question of human curiosity, it might satisfy at least every legitimate interest. It might fill him with faith in the Author of his being, and persuade him that with Him all things are possible, that to His all-knowledge and all-wisdom may be safely left every question yet unanswered.

I. The creed opens with the assertion of the being of God, of one Supreme and only God, supreme over all powers and dominions, either in heaven or earth, supreme over the abstract conception of a law of fate, or necessity. He is the Father or Author of all being; He is the Maker of heaven and earth, and of all things that they contain, visible or invisible. He is not, as the heathen had imagined, merely the disposer and arranger, but the Maker and Creator. 'Look upon the heaven and the earth, and all that is therein, and consider that God made them of things that were not.'[1]

---

[1] 2 Macc. vii. 28.

Such was the gloss of the later Jewish Church upon the less explicit statement of the book of Genesis; and such was the conviction of the Christian Church, deduced from the undoubting ascription of omnipotence to God in the apostolic preaching, from the immeasurable eminence in which He is placed in the minds of Christ's disciples above all being and matter, existing before it, and outside of it, and independent of it;—as when it is said of Him in Revelations: 'Thou hast created all things, and for Thy pleasure they are and were created.'[1]

Again, there is no conflict between Him and mind; no rival will, no concurrent principle of action. The evil in the world and the power of evil, however real and personal, is only a perversion, a corruption of the good which He originally created. It exists only by His sufferance, and for His designs, under such limits as He has put upon it. The dualism, or double principle of the philosophers, a reality to them, is a mere expression, an accommodation to human thought, among Christians. It is enough for the believer to know that his life below is a state of trial, and that evil is permitted for the perfecting of glory.

Further, God is Providence, and supports and sustains all things by the hand of His power. He orders their coming in and their going out: He keeps them in their appointed channel; He leads every thought and action of man to the end designated in His eternal mind: He

[1] Rev. iv. 11.

is a personal, living, and ruling Providence. He numbers every hair of our heads; to Him are known the motions of the stars and the measure of the sea-sands: not a soul is born or dies without His counting it; not a sparrow falls to the ground without His noticing it. Words fail us, imagination itself faints in the attempt to realize the infinite foresight and oversight of Providence, as intellectually accepted by the Christian believer. The heathen disputant Celsus might pretend that to suppose there was one and the same God of the diverse nations of Europe, Asia, and Libya was incredible and absurd; but to the Christian, to limit this infinite solicitude of the Almighty to the concerns of a single tribe or nation, to confine infinite Providence to the fortunes of Greece or Rome, to draw a fence of human interests and prejudices round His ever outflowing acts of consideration and mercy, and make God the God of one people—a mere provincial idol—would be the height of folly or of blasphemy. The Creed of Nicæa threw boldly into the world this first fundamental conception of a true divinity; and deep was the satisfaction with which it was received by the vexed, the wavering, the terrified schools of disenchanted heathenism.

II. But again, the God of the Christian is distinct from any abstract law and principle of nature. Our Theism must not be confounded with the Pantheism of the Platonists and Stoics. 'Jupiter,' said the Stoics, 'is whatever we see, by whatsoever we are moved or influenced.' 'God is the world, and the world is God.'

'God is all matter, and all mind.' The last utterance of heathen science was the declaration of the naturalist Pliny, after casting his eye over creation, and scanning, with all the lights of accumulated experience, the height and depth and breadth of the universe; that 'the world—this heaven, as we also call it—which embraces all things in its vast circumference, may be truly regarded as itself a Deity, immense, eternal, never made, and never to perish.'[1] Hence followed the inevitable deduction, missed only by those whose common sense was too strong for their logic, that all weakness and infirmity,—man himself with all his sin and corruption,—all nature brute and inanimate, the slave of man, and of creatures inferior to man,—all, all is God. Evil is God; Sin is God. This is Pantheism, twin-brother of Atheism. This is the end to which the Theism of the heathen inevitably tends: to which the Theism of the Christian would tend, and too often is found to tend, unless counteracted by the conviction, real and vital, of God's personality as revealed in Scripture. But for this revelation of God's personality, announced distinctly and characteristically in the incarnation of Jesus Christ, the religion of the Christian would have run just the same vicious course as all human creeds and philosophies before it; no purity of morals, no holiness of ideas, no conviction of miraculous gifts, no assurance of an indwelling Spirit would have saved it; for all these elements may be found in more or less force among the heathen systems; the salt of

---

[1] See Note E E.

Christianity has been the dogmatic belief in the incarnation of the Divine; in the personal manifestation of God; in Jesus Christ, the Son of God, Himself God issuing from God, and returning to Him.

'I believe,' says the Creed, 'in Jesus Christ the Son of God.' The fatherhood of God extends over all mankind, claiming them all as His children, as all equal in His sight, all heirs of His promise, all partakers of His blessing. But this sonship is illustrated by the peculiar relation in which the divine Son is said to stand to the divine Father. 'When the fulness of time was come, God sent forth His Son . . . that we might receive the adoption of sons. And because ye are sons, God sent forth the Spirit of His Son into your hearts, crying, Abba, Father. Wherefore thou art no more a servant, but a son; and if a son, then an heir of God through Christ.'[1] This revelation of the sonship of Christ seals to us the great and fruitful truth of our common descent from God, and of the place we hold in the divine economy. 'Come out from among them, and be ye separate, saith the Lord . . . and I will be a Father unto you, and ye shall be my sons and daughters, saith the Lord Almighty.'[2] The fond notions of the heathens, and of the Jews also, of a federal compact between God and a peculiar people, are for ever extinguished. The principle which separates Christianity from all previous forms of religion, the principle of its universality, is finally established. There can henceforth be no return to Heathenism or Judaism.

---

[1] Gal. iv. 4–6.   [2] 2 Cor. vi. 17, 18.

Any system which is evolved out of Christianity, or raised upon it, such as the Mahommedan, must accept this principle as its own foundation. The enthusiast of Mecca was compelled to claim for his own inventions the same foundation as that which Jesus Christ had first assumed for God's own truth. The lurking heathenism in the corrupt heart even of baptized Christians, struggles here and there against it, and seeks to set up a local divinity in the persons of tutelary saints; but the heart of Christianity ever protests against this corruption; and the votary of the intrusive shrine in the corners of the temple is still fain to colour his pagan superstition with fallacious glosses; he acknowledges even by his evasions that God is one, the Father of all, that all men are equally His sons, and equally under His sole undisputed guardianship.

Further, it was 'for us men, and for our salvation,' that God 'came down from heaven;' came down into the world, in the person of the incarnate Son. God saw that sin was in the world. He knew, long before man had made the discovery, the sin which, as we have seen, became revealed in the fulness of time to the conscience of the heathen world. He had prepared even from the beginning the means of a reconciliation with Him whose eyes are too pure to behold iniquity. Man was uneasy, terrified, stricken with despair, and with good reason; his sin was greater than in the depth of his own self-accusation he had imagined; the power of sin and the devil, the author of sin, was more engrossing, more constraining; the destined retribution for sin was heavier than any human terrors had conceived of it. The consciousness of sin was the lurid reflection upon the heart of the perils and sufferings of the world about it; but man in his most dread alarm had not apprehended the horrors of the future sufferings, the sufferings of another world, which, when once revealed by God's certain word, would strike despair into the soul of the sinner. Man demanded sacrifices, the blood of animals, of men, of the true believers, to avert a temporal retribution for the sins of which he accused himself;—what would he have demanded—what hecatomb of victims would have seemed to him sufficient to avert the spiritual punishment, the death of the soul, the abandonment to hell, to the blackness of darkness for ever—had he been fully aware of the estrangement in which he lay from God, of the blank hopelessness of his condition, as an outcast from the divine presence! But Christ Jesus came down from heaven, dwelt upon earth, died upon the cross, was buried and rose, and again ascended for the salvation of man; the all-sufficient sacrifice was accomplished; man was redeemed from the power of the evil one; his soul was restored in the divine image; he was assured of acceptance with God, and eternal happiness in the bosom of his Father. Such had been the terror of the heathen conscience, and lo! such again was the teaching of the Christian Creed.[1] Such was the teaching of the divine records. For it was not a mere

[1] See Note F F.

conjecture of devotees and philosophers. It was not the invention of sage and godly speculation. It was not the augury of a Plato, the yearning of an Aurelius; it was not the cheerful hope of a Plutarch, or the pious fiction of the schools of Alexandria. Such hopes, such fictions we have noted and lamented in the restless perturbations of the heathen mind; but we have seen that they led—that they could lead—to nothing but fond and ghastly extravagances. And why? Because they had no basis of fact to rest upon; no touchstone of experience to be tried by; no record of history to be traced to. Christianity is history. It is a religion which teaches by examples; a revelation stamped with the seal of accredited fact. This it is, or it is nothing. But this, I say, it is. And so the creed emphatically proclaims of it. When we recite the solemn words—Christ 'for us men and for our salvation came down from heaven . . . was made man . . . was crucified under Pontius Pilate, suffered and was buried, and the third day rose again . . . and ascended into heaven,'—we appeal to recorded facts, witnessed by men upon earth, and attested as things most surely known and believed among them. We appeal, now as ever, to a Book, to a standing and abiding testimony, open to all readers, addressed to all hearers, upon which sixty generations of men have successively passed their judgments. We appeal to the long experience of mankind, who have weighed and pondered the records of this Book of books, each according to his own light and intellectual leanings: who have pressed it to their hearts in faith, or criticized it with all the powers of the understanding; have sometimes worshipped it as an idol; sometimes inquired of it as an oracle; have again sifted it as the pleader sifts the testimony at the bar, and cross-examined it with heat and acrimony, as seeking to catch it tripping, and extort from it evidence against itself. And this is the result: the testimony to the truth of our record is admitted to be more complete, more varied, more consistent than to any series of events announced in the secular history of antiquity. No mere man, king or statesman or warrior of old, is so fully pourtrayed to us in the incidents of his career, as Jesus Christ in the narrative of the Gospels. No writings on a common subject leave so little room for questioning their general agreement on all points of interest as the Gospels and Epistles; the fidelity of none is more strikingly attested by fresh discoveries even from day to day of their minute accuracy in detail. They claim and they sustain the test of genuine history. No other account of their origin, however often put forward, has ever long maintained itself against them; but one theory overthrows another, each generation launches its own extravagance, and each gives way to a successor. The infidel makes no real progress, but returns from age to age upon his own footsteps. Voltaire's theory of imposture is supplanted by Strauss's theory of the myth; and lo! in thirty years Strauss's theory of the myth is replaced by Renan's theory of imposture.

This Jesus Christ, thus declared, and thus proved to the conviction of the heathen, has ascended into Heaven. He has gone back to the Father, has quitted the world which He visited once for all. No; not once for all only : He will come again once more ; a second advent remains for us. He will come—not as a Teacher or a Saviour, but as a Judge; for to Him the Father hath committed the judgment of the world, and in the fulness of time He will determine the future state and destiny of His creatures. He will come to make a final separation between the good and the evil, the penitent and impenitent, the Church and the World. There will be no respect of persons then ; the heathen notions of merit and works will be utterly disregarded ; the philosophic dream of an aristocracy of souls, a spiritual claim to immortality confined to a few favourites of God, to those who can claim affinity to the Divine, to those who are themselves God-like, will be finally dissolved. Jesus Christ will know His own by another test—by the test of faith, fruitful in holy practice. The systems of the ancients will sink into the obscurity they justly merit; man will breathe again, relieved from the incubus of terror they had cast upon him ; he will breathe freely in the joyful anticipation of a righteous judgment, according to the blessed revelation of the Holy One and the Just.

III. But when shall all this be ? There was a time, in the first flush of Christian faith, when the Second

Coming was daily, nay hourly, expected; when the believers looked little to the future, which seemed to be about so suddenly to close upon them, and fancied that the ministry of Jesus Christ had been but the beginning of the end. But time went on; there was no sign of His appearing. Jerusalem was overthrown. In one sense He then appeared; His judgment was made manifest upon Israel; His Gospel was established on the abolition of the law; Christianity was shifted from its Jewish foundations, and the Gentiles were admitted to the promises of God. Still the end was not yet. 'I am with you,' He had said on His departure, ' even unto the end of the world.' From day to day this saying assumed a deeper significance. ' I will not leave you comfortless; I will send you the Holy Ghost to comfort you.' From age to age this promise demanded its confirmation. And so, in the fulness of time, the Church of Christ came forward with the third great article of its creed: 'I believe in the Holy Ghost, the Lord and Giver of life; who proceedeth from the Father and the Son; who with the Father and the Son is worshipped and glorified; who spake by the prophets.' And thence it went on to proclaim the existence of the Church as of Divine appointment,—with all the graces and privileges which are divinely vouchsafed to it,—as the pillar and ground of truth, as the eternal witness to the faith, as having the spirit of knowledge, and the promise that Jesus Christ will be for ever with it.

Here, then, was a substitute for the visible presence

of Christ upon earth. Here was an answer to the question, When will He appear? and how shall His Church continue without Him? His visible presence is not required. His appearance may be indefinitely delayed. His faithful disciples shall ever have the witness of His presence in their hearts by the indwelling of the Holy Spirit. The world shall ever have the witness of His existence in Heaven in the visible Church which He has founded and protects and keeps for His own for ever. The saints of God shall ever have the assurance of His power throughout the history of religion, in the record of the Divine operations contained in the Holy Scripture: for He 'spake by the prophets.' The Bible assures us that the Holy Spirit of God has from the first inspired and fashioned this record of His revelation of Himself; the manner, the extent of this inspiration is a mystery to which the human mind has no key; the operations of the Holy Spirit are manifold and diverse; they act more or less upon all men; they tend to a Divine conclusion in all their manifestations; but we know not the how or the when, the whence or the whither. They are compared to the wind, invisible and unsearchable, which bloweth where it listeth.

But so it was, that when the heathen who had sought in vain for a basis for his faith in the traditions and speculations of old, turned to the Church of Christ, and asked for the proofs and sanctions of its teachings, he was directed to a Holy Book, a book of vast antiquity, of high pretensions to authority—a book which gave a plain and intelligible account of God's dealings with the world—which pointed to the tokens of His providence running through it—which evinced design from one end to the other—which bespoke a unity of purpose, and in the highest sense a unity of authorship —which revealed a purer conception of God than any known before, a higher law, a holier idea of religion— which sometimes in history, sometimes in prophecy, sometimes in the character of individual men, again in the waxing and waning fortunes of a people, betrayed a thread of continuity, a sequence, an appointment, such as men had yearned for and vainly imagined in human affairs, but had never been able fully to realize.

The City of God took the place of the city of man, and overlapped it on every side; more ancient, more extensive, and more enduring. The last and fondest, as we have seen, of the heathen religions, had been the belief in the divinity of Rome, of the Roman Empire, of the Roman fortunes. Through many an age of victory and triumph this faith had grown and flourished, while still implicit and unavowed. It was in the decline of the Pagan city that men seemed most fully to realize its divinity, and cling to it most passionately. Long did they struggle against defeats and disgraces, against misgiving and despair. The faith of Christ was already enthroned in the East; half the empire had been torn away from the city of the heathen. Still the trembling votary fastened upon what remained—still refused to listen to the creed of Nicæa, proclaiming the Church of the Holy Spirit as the true city of the

Christians. Then at last in the fulness of time came the assault of Alaric and the Goths; the crumbling of the walls, the conflagration in the streets; the abomination of desolation stood in the holy place of heathendom; the temples fell, the idols were broken, the spell of ages was dissolved; the Romans ceased to be a nation, and Rome the national deity had no more worshippers for ever.

That was the moment to make a blessed impression upon the mind of the heathen. Conversion was at hand. The hour had come, and the man was not wanting; the man who should interpret and apply, under God's providence, the teachings of the Holy Spirit in Scripture. The manifestation of the City of God by Augustine, the explanation of God's divine appointments from the creation to the redemption of man, was a full and final appeal to the conscience of the inquiring heathens, the stricken and despairing votaries of the discredited city of the Romans. The manifestation of the Holy Spirit of God working through all time, by revelations to the patriarchs, kings, and prophets of old, to the disciples of Jesus Christ in the latter days;—the manifestation of a church or spiritual society, revealed to Abraham at Haran, latent in Egypt, wandering in the desert, militant in Canaan, triumphant in Jerusalem, captive in Babylon, oppressed under the Syrians and the Romans; sustained by heavenly food, by visions and inspirations, by miracles and portents, by God's effective stay on the right hand and on the left;—of a church revived and sanctified by the special revelation and ministry of Jesus, refined and purified, and brought ever nearer—aye, into actual union with God; expanded (once more) by communication to the Gentiles, preached to all the world, established in the high places and the low places of the earth, tried by malice and envy, purged by suffering, confirmed and rooted by the storms of persecution, protected through every trial, and against all the powers of earth and hell, by a heavenly arm which no believer could fail to recognise;—this manifestation, I say, crowned as it was by a visible completion under the first of the Christian emperors, when the Sancta Sophia, the Holy Wisdom of God, was enshrined in the metropolitan temple of the empire—this manifestation established to the full belief and satisfaction of men the existence of a city of God upon earth.

And finally, he was encouraged to believe that this church or city upon earth was but the type and shadow of the universal city of God in heaven, to which it led, and in which it became absorbed and mingled. The things that are seen became to his imagination shapes and patterns of the holier things that shall hereafter be revealed. Such from the first was the mind of Scripture, the sense of the divine revelation. When the Psalmist proclaimed triumphantly of the city of the children of Israel, 'Glorious things are spoken of thee, O city of God,' the Christian believes that he had a further spiritual meaning, and that the holy city on the hill of Zion was a type of the Church of the faithful of all ages, transfigured into an abode 'incorruptible and undefiled, reserved in heaven' for them. And yet the two cities are so closely joined together that he could hardly separate one from the other in idea or in language. 'We are come,' he would say in impetuous anticipation, ' we are come unto Mount Zion, and unto the city of the living God, the heavenly Jerusalem, and to an innumerable company of angels, to the general assembly and church of the firstborn which are in heaven, and to God the Judge of all, and to the spirits of just men made perfect, and to Jesus the mediator of the new covenant, and to the blood of sprinkling, that speaketh better things than that of Abel.'[1]

And there, according to the preaching of his great teacher Augustine,—in that abode of beatified spirits, the spirits of the just made perfect in life everlasting,— 'there will true honour be denied to none deserving it, accorded to none undeserving. There will be true peace, where none will suffer harm either from himself or from others. The reward of righteousness will be He who Himself imparted righteousness, and who promised Himself, than whom there can be no gift better or greater.'

For what else has He said by His prophet : 'I will be to them a God, and they shall be to me a people:' what else but this : 'I will be that whereby they shall be satisfied ; I will be all things that men righteously desire ; life and health, and food and abundance, glory

---

[1] Heb. xii. 22–24.

and honour, and peace and all things?' For so is that rightly understood of the apostle; 'that God may be all in all.' He will be the end of all our desires, who will be seen Himself without end, will be loved without satiety, will be praised without weariness. This affection, this business, this function of our being will be common to us all, like life itself everlasting.'[1]

[1] See Note G G.

LECTURE VIII.

THE GODLY EXAMPLE OF THE CHRISTIANS COMPLETES THE CONVERSION OF THE EMPIRE.

ACTS XVII. 6.

These that have turned the world upside down are come hither also.

I SHOWED in the last Lecture how the dogmas of the Christian Church, set forth by the council of Nicæa, replied to the most urgent questions of the heathen on spiritual matters, and offered to them assurance and repose from intellectual perplexity.

What then remained that they should not be converted and baptized into the faith of Christ? Their old gods had failed them, and lo! a new divinity was presented and recommended to them. There remained that which must always remain at the bottom of all religious questions, that condition of full belief and acceptance which no reasonableness of doctrine, no harmony of system, no holiness of moral precept can alone fulfil;—the tender and yearning soul of the devout inquirer still requires the satisfaction of his heart and conscience; he demands to follow the doctrines in their results, to scan the precepts in their effects, to observe the religion in action; to know how the professed revelation of God's will works practically in the world. He wants to trace the operation of inspired truth upon the heart and soul of the believer, and above all upon His own soul by personal experience. He must know and feel the beauty of true holiness, and learn where to find it, and how to attach it to himself as an eternal possession. He must comprehend the spirit of that saying of the Apostle: 'Whosoever shall confess that Jesus Christ is the Son of God, God dwelleth in him, and he in God.'[1]

On bringing to a close the partial survey we have taken of the conversion of the Empire to Christ, we must now glance at the aspect of Christian society, as it presented itself to the view of the still dubious and hesitating heathen. The men who had turned the world upside down had come to him, had found him out, wherever he was, in the stronghold of his religion, of his philosophy, of his pride, of his indifference. They had come to him, and their importunity allowed him no rest. Who and what manner of men were they?

Now, we read in the 17th chapter of the Acts of the Apostles, that when Paul and Silas crossed over from Asia into Europe, and preached the Gospel in Thes-

---

[1] 1 John iv. 15.

salonica, the first great city on this side of the Hellespont—and when some of those which consorted with them believed—the Jews there residing, moved with envy, gathered a company, made a tumult, drew some of the brethren before the heathen rulers, crying, 'These that have turned the world upside down are come hither also. And these,' they continued, 'all do contrary to the decrees of Cæsar, saying that there is another king, one Jesus.'

To those who look back upon the history of Christianity, what irony appears in this passage! How peevish an exaggeration seems this cry in the mouth of those who uttered it! How little had the preachers of the Gospel yet done! How far were they from turning the world upside down—from overthrowing the beliefs of the time, from upsetting the deep-rooted system of religious domination; from unhinging the conscience of the heathen world, even of that Eastern world, the world of ancient creeds and philosophies, from whence they had come 'hither,' to the West, to make their first assault on the stedfast politics of Europe. What had they accomplished hitherto? In a few cities of Asia they had impugned the national belief of a handful of Jewish residents. In Jerusalem, the home of the Jewish people and the Jewish creed, their Founder had suffered death for His temerity, their preaching had been forbidden, they had been imprisoned, scourged, threatened with death, one or more of their number had been stoned or beheaded; their doctrines were scorned, their manners and practices maligned. Such success as they obtained was limited to alarming the consciences of a few only, and those mostly of the lower sort, among the Jews, and casting into the minds of speculative thinkers some germ of doubt and suspicion of the will of Jehovah to save Israel from her sins, and restore her political independence. They had scattered here and there the seeds of a spiritual interpretation of prophecy, and had led one man or another to look for a spiritual realization of their long-treasured promises of a new heaven and a new earth, and a king from the loins of David, namely one Jesus, a Saviour and Redeemer of souls.

This was all they had yet effected, as far as human vision could penetrate! And how had they been requited? Wherever they had presented themselves with the words of love and wisdom, they had been met with insult and violence by the Jewish residents in heathen cities; the feelings of the natives had been prejudiced against them, they had been overborne with clamour, the arm of the magistrate had been invoked to punish them for the tumults insolently raised by their opponents. They had been driven from one city to flee to the next. Never, surely, was there a charge more grossly belied by the fact than this, at this time made against them, that they had turned the world upside down. They had only cast off its dust from their feet. Nor more true was the further charge, more insidious, more invidious, appended to it, that they ' did contrary to the decrees of Cæsar, saying that there was another king, one Jesus.'

Yet there was something strangely prophetic in these charges. Far as they were from the truth at the time, an era was coming when they might truly be alleged. At the era of the council of Nicæa it was indeed true that the Christians had, to use a figure well understood, 'turned the world upside down;' that they had proclaimed another king, another polity, a temporal rule under a new sanction; that the whole framework of the heathen state was overthrown through their preaching, and a new city established, the law of which was God's law, the faith of which was God's truth, the chief of which received his unction from the Holy One, and bowed his knee to Jesus, as King of kings and Lord of lords.

What manner of men, then, it might fairly now be asked, were these who had thus turned the world upside down? What was the law and rule of life through which they had done such great things?

It was none other but this, as declared of old by the Apostle:

'This I say therefore, and testify in the Lord, that ye henceforth walk not as other Gentiles walk, in the vanity of their mind, having the understanding darkened, being alienated from the life of God through the ignorance that is in them, because of the blindness of their heart: who being past feeling have given themselves over unto lasciviousness, to work all uncleanness with greediness. But ye have not so learned Christ; if so be that ye have been taught by Him, as the truth is in Jesus: that ye put off concerning the former

conversation the old man, which is corrupt according to the deceitful lusts; and be renewed in the spirit of your mind; and that ye put on the new man, which after God is created in righteousness and true holiness.'
. . . . And so after practical exhortations to divers acts of holy living—'Be ye kind one to another, forgiving one another, even as God for Christ's sake hath forgiven you.'[1]

And how were the Christians seen to carry out this divine morality? The Apologists may answer; Justin and Tertullian and the rest; who writing on the spur of actual exigency, replied to the current calumnies of the day, and retorted upon the slanderers of the Christian Church with truths manifest to all, and which could not be gainsaid. The lives of the believers were for the most part exemplary amidst the seething corruption of the times. The heathens, whose conscience, as we have seen, was roused to feel the enormity of their own conduct, and of the familiar vices which had become ingrained in them, but who had not courage or constancy to reform themselves, to expel the devil who had taken possession of their own hearts, might behold in the Christians the example and pattern which they sighed for. They remarked among them sobriety in the midst of moral and sensual intoxication; chastity in the midst of flagrant and allowed licentiousness; good faith, where to betray a trust and deny a deposit was the rule and habit of society; forbearance, where

[1] Ephes. iv. 17-24, 32.

hate and vengeance were commonly approved and sanctioned; kindness and charity one towards another; almsgiving and collecting for the necessities of the saints; tending in sickness, even to the foundation of charitable hospitals, an institution unknown to the selfishness of the heathens; redeeming of captives; burying of the dead; courage in the midst of pestilence and contagion; the fostering care of the community extended to the infants and the aged; regard for the sanctity of human life, as the image of the source and parent of all life; love to man as the child of God the Father. And more particularly they might remark that parental affection, too often violated in those selfish days, which shrank with horror from the custom of exposing children, and devoted itself with resolution and industry to the task of providing for the pledge of God's love in marriage, instead of fleeing basely from the burden imposed by it. And further, the heathen might remark with admiration the firmness of the brethren in relinquishing many modes of profitable employment which were deemed incompatible with the Christian profession; their boldness in the confession of their faith in the face of the persecutors; in refusing compliance with the forms and usages of the heathen religion, with the demand to sacrifice to idols, to swear by the name of the Emperor, to wear the chaplet of the triumphant soldier, to bear the banner of the Pagan army. And finally, they might regard with awe the patience of the Christian martyrs; their constancy under torments, their self-devotion unto death, their implicit reliance on the spiritual promises of their

Master, who seemed even in death and torments to impart to them a portion of His own divine endurance.[1]

Such was the outward bearing of the individual Christian, such the character of his society, patent to the observation of the incredulous world around it.

And such the heathen, proud and incredulous as he was, himself acknowledged it, in the well-known letter of Pliny,—the first Christian apology, as it has been called; when with every wish to find reasonable ground for the complaints advanced against the Christians, he could on the strictest inquiry discover none; when the slanders of the wicked resolved themselves on examination into a confession of their innocence, and the curse was changed into a blessing. They used, it was found, to meet together on certain days; they joined in a hymn of praise to Christ their God; they bound one another, not to the commission of any crime, but to refrain from theft, from adultery, to keep their promises and hold their pledges sacred; they partook of a simple meal in common, a meal of charity and sobriety. And hence the crowning eulogium which another heathen was constrained to pass upon them: 'See how these Christians love one another.'

Nor were these outward tokens of purity and holiness merely casual and variable. The heathen indeed might judge them by the signs which were apparent only, by outward phenomena; but the Christian knew the law by which these phenomena were regulated. The Christian could appeal to rules

[1] See Note I I.

and public institutions, which became a standing guarantee of the fixedness of these practical graces. The institution of baptism was a pledge, given in the face of the Church, given before jealous witnesses, that the believer once initiated, once received, should keep to the uttermost every promise then made by him. Baptism was a sacrament, a vow pledged to the highest authority, to God Himself through His appointed ministers; a vow such as the Roman felt the full force of, which brought to his imagination the holiest sanctions of his own religious ritual. Giving his hand to the bishop or minister, the candidate for admission to the Christian covenant declared aloud his renunciation of the devil, the world, and the flesh; his abjuration of all heathen ceremonies, of the idols and demons of the heathen hierarchy. He separated himself from the kingdom of the Evil One, and came over to the dominion of Christ; he swore to be His soldier and servant, as the Roman legionary swore obedience to his military chief. He swore to abandon, with God's grace, the lusts of the rebellious flesh, to lead a holy and a Christian life, after the rule of the Church and the Gospels, after the teaching of the Apostles, after the pattern of Christ Himself. He presented his forehead to the laver of regeneration; he bowed under the sign of the cross; he rose again in newness of life, in the assurance of a special grace imparted by the Holy Spirit of God, by which every moral stain was purged away, and remission of his sins had been granted to him. All this he said, he promised, he imagined, he felt, in the face of the assembled believers, with the full assurance of excommunication here, if he should fail to keep his vow, and of final perdition hereafter.

And further, he acknowledged that to will and to do all these things required not only grace and strength imparted at the moment, but constant refreshment and renewal from a divine source of strength and vigour. The law and system of his Church informed him where to look for this support, and how to secure it. The Word of God was given him to study, access to God was given him in prayer, he might open his heart to his Maker and receive Him therein as to a private shrine and a special sanctuary. But no private communion with the Invisible, no mystical union with Him, no ascetic devotion, no seclusion from the world could release him from the duty of using and applying to his own particular case the public and general means of grace by seeking Christ in His own temple, at His own altar, in the elements of an eucharistic meal at which His presence was specially vouchsafed, in the midst of the congregation of believers like himself. The Christian then believed—and we believe it now—that at such eucharistic communions a special virtue and grace were imparted to the faithful communicant. He believed in the presence of Jesus Christ in His temple, upon His altar, in the elements of bread and wine. And even the heathen, who cared not perhaps to inquire into the idea of the Christian mysteries,—who would hesitate no doubt to accept the Christian rule and theory—could not fail to see in this belief thus publicly avowed—in the vows of holiness by which it was accompanied thus publicly ratified—in this sacramental act of faith and obedience, so congenial to its own spiritual aspirations, thus from age to age continued and repeated—an assurance that the obligations thereby imposed were not lightly undertaken, and would by none be lightly disregarded.

The sacraments, then, of the Christian Church were a pledge to the heathen of the sincerity and trustworthiness of the Christian votaries. When the heathen beheld or heard speak of them he began to know something of the men who had turned the world upside down, who had put faith in the place of materialism, hope in the place of desperation, love in the place of selfish and sensual corruption—and how they had done so, and why they had done so. He felt, moreover, the assurance that they would persevere, and continue to do so more and more unto the end.

The core of their whole system was plainly the belief in Christ's personality. This it was that gave strength, cohesion, and permanence to the whole fabric of Christian faith and practice. In Holy Scripture the believer read of the Lord Jesus as the author and finisher of his faith; in every office of the Church he recognised Him as the great object of his worship; every sermon spoke of Him, every hymn was addressed to Him, every prayer was made through Him. He was the Way, and the Truth, and the Life. He was a perfect model of holy living; a perfect example of all goodness. The Christian could turn from the abstract conception of virtue recommended by the cold rhetoric of the philosophers, to the incarnation of all virtue in the life and practice of the blessed Jesus. And when he was dazzled by such brilliancy, when he fainted in spirit at the contemplation of so inimitable a pattern, when his head swam with sickness at the thought of his own weakness and insufficiency, he was invited to come week by week, day by day, to the commemoration of the one sufficient sacrifice, to the holy communion of the faithful with one another, and with Him of whom they all spiritually partook and were strengthened. In their hearts this Jesus the Redeemer, with His Spirit the Sanctifier, was gloriously enthroned. They acknowledged by this act of obedience the kingship and rule which He exercised over them. They believed that He had all authority over men's souls given to Him of the Father. They called Him their king, and themselves His people. Of His kingdom there should be no end: of the glory which they should inherit in communion with Him in heaven, far above all the powers and principalities of the Gentile world, there should be no limit in time or eternity,—no defect in its circle, no shadow on its brightness.

They knew, and therefore they believed. They did not need the upsetting of the domination of the world to convince them of their future rule and glory with Him. To the last moment,—to the day of the battle of the

Milvian bridge and the whelming of their last persecutor in the waters,—to the eve of the Decree of of Milan, and the establishment of their Church in security and honour,—they dreamt not of the fall of the heathen empire upon earth; and when it came, their first thought was that the frame of human society was loosened, and about to fall utterly in pieces. To the last they expected no conversion of Cæsar unto Christ; no setting up of a Christian emperor over the nations of the world. 'God,' said Tertullian, 'would long since have converted Cæsar to His faith, if the world could have existed without the Cæsar, or Christians could have been Cæsars themselves.'[1] The heathens themselves were not more perplexed by the conversion of Constantine than the Christians. The Church was taken by surprise,—it was put out in its calculations,—confined in its prospects,—baffled, I believe, in some of its dearest and most spiritual anticipations. This event threw back the near-expected millennium into the illimitable future. The political establishment of the Church of Christ proved no unmixed good to the faith of Christ; and doubtless there were many good Christians who regarded it with pious apprehension. So far were the believers from wilfully setting up another Cæsar in Jesus.

Nevertheless the time had come for the public confession in the world of the Lord Jesus Christ whom Pilate had crucified. God's designs were to be

---

[1] Tertullian, *Apol.* c. 21.

accomplished, and His ways are not as our ways, nor can His ends be measured by our notions of expediency or fitness. The confession of Christ's spiritual kingship was to be extended to the acknowledgment of His pre-eminence over the kings and rulers of this world also. The believers had passed from city to city, preaching the eternal kingdom of the anointed Son of God. They had been misunderstood, slandered, persecuted; they had been accused of turning the world upside down, with all its political combinations; of rejecting the laws of the empire, and setting up another ruler in the place of Cæsar; while in fact the vital principle of their faith had resided in the stedfastness with which they clung to a purely spiritual idea, and shrank from mingling it with any temporal alloy. This self-denial, this simplicity of purpose had now reaped its reward. The graces of the Christian had shone brighter from the effort. The slanders of the heathen had been converted into actual truth. At the meeting of the fathers of the church at Nicæa the heathen were for the first time solemnly invited to see the men who had thus turned the world upside down, and had set up by the hands of their champion Constantine another law, another rule, a new order of political life. We have traced through various channels the preparation for the Gospel which had been long in progress in the minds of the heathen: the disruption of their old creeds and intellectual bonds—the extinction of their familiar prejudices—the awakening of many new moral senses, the sense of spiritual equality, the sense of sin, of a need for a Redeemer, of a fearful and desperate apprehension of their lost and hapless condition. Again we have seen how the dogmas of the Christian creed, now at last discovered to them, might precisely meet the demands of the latest heathen speculation; and to-day we have observed, still further, how the character of the Christian life and conduct might reassure them in their last moments of hesitation, and complete the golden proof of the descent of Christianity from God. Thus they were prepared on all sides. Gently the Holy Spirit had trained and manipulated them, and they stood like spirits imprisoned waiting for the word of God to set them free. A word, a touch, an invisible impulse, a breath of sympathy from the source of life everlasting, might kindle their imaginations as with fire, and set their hearts aglow with holy flame. And the awful suspense of that central moment, the solemn issues pending, the suddenness with which the blessed movement should be at last communicated, and the confession of Christ imperiously extorted—the final triumph of faith over the sluggish scruples of the understanding—all this is indicated to my mind by a striking incident recorded at the time, by a story of individual conversion which betokens, as it were, in a single typical instance, the operation of the Holy Spirit diffused at one moment in the hearts of millions.

'Hearken to me, O philosopher,' said a Christian divine to one who hovered, wondering and perplexed, about the footsteps of the fathers as they marched triumphantly to the council; 'hearken in the name of

Jesus Christ. There is one only God, Creator of the heavens and the earth, and of all things visible and invisible. He has made everything by the power of His Word, and established all by the sanctity of His Spirit. This Word is He whom we call the Son of God; who taking pity on the errors of men, and their way of life, like that of the beasts which perish, has deigned to be born of a woman, to dwell among us, and to die for us. He will come again as a Judge of all their deeds upon earth, as a Punisher and a Rewarder. Behold simply the sum of our belief. Seek not with pain and anxiety for the proof of things which faith only can realize, nor for the reason of their existence. Say only, Wilt thou believe? The philosopher trembled and stammered, "I believe."'[1]

And so it was with the heathens generally. The case of this individual inquirer is a type of the heathen society, gasping for spiritual life. In this story we read, as in a myth, the conversion of the Roman Empire. Argument and conjecture, testimony and proof, had been accumulated from generation to generation; the decision of mankind was trembling in the balance. Then came the last touching appeal to the court of final resort, to the heart, to the source of all spiritual faith. God was in it; the world believed; the Roman Empire was converted.

Nor is the history of this splendid conversion without its application to ourselves. It is, as I have shown,

---

[1] See Note K K.

on a grand and general scale, the history of many an
individual conversion. It shows how God even now
works on the heart of the natural man; for every man
is by nature a heathen. Every man has his innate
pride, his fancied claims upon God, his complacent
self-reliance in spiritual things; every man fashions a
God or Idol of his own, after his own heart, and
adapted to his own conceit. Every man has an
inveterate hankering after material things, and rises
with pain and weariness to the conception of the
spiritual; can hardly retain his hold of it, if he has in
any wise attained to it. But let fear or sorrow awaken
the sense of sin in him, a sense by God's mercy not
difficult to awaken in most men, and the whole man is
changed. Alarm and agony take possession of him, he
will do anything, he imagines anything, that may seem
to offer a prospect of salvation. He rushes to the
extreme of superstition and fanaticism, to wild and
gloomy practices, to magical arts, to purifications by
blood, to self-torture and immolation. To restore the
balance of his mind he requires the stay of pure and
simple doctrine;—a knowledge of God and of the true
means of grace in Him, founded upon a historical
basis; something firm to grasp, stable to rest upon;
something to fill the heart, to feed the imagination, to
satisfy the understanding. He wants something that he
can feel, and at the same time something that he can
reason about. Christianity offers him an exercise for
the moral, the intellectual, and the spiritual faculty.
It is abundant in consolation, fruitful in argument,

overflowing in its apprehension of the divine. It is what every tender and pious soul would wish to make its own by believing. Then let him finally trace it in its results. Let him examine what it has effected on the souls of men, as far as his vision can penetrate, and this is but skin deep; what it is now doing; what it promises to do in him and in all men; what love, what holiness, what resignation, what hope it produces! The lives of Christians have been ever the last and surest argument for Christianity. This completed he conversion of the Empire: this completes day by day the conversion of the worldling and the sinner. It defies criticism; it transcends philosophy. It leads direct to the throne of God, to the source of all moral goodness and holiness, and reveals the object of our faith, the Author of every good and perfect gift, in whose image we are made, in whose righteousness we trust hereafter to be clothed. Faith in Him, thus revealed to the imagination, will calm the last fluttering tumult of the soul, and rock us asleep in the bosom of our Redeemer. And such is the blessed end to which the sacred record leads us, in words which breathe a strain of heavenly music, wafted onward from age to age, from generation to generation: 'But ye, beloved, building up yourselves on your most holy faith, praying to the Holy Ghost, keep yourselves in the love of God, looking for the mercy of our Lord Jesus Christ unto eternal life.'[1]

[1] Jude 20, 21.

NOTES.

NOTES.

Note A, page 11.

The language used by Cæsar, Cato, and Cicero, in the debate on the punishment of the Catilinarian conspirators, has drawn the marked attention of inquirers into the religious opinions of the ancients. Among others, Warburton made great use of it to enforce his opinion that the students of heathen philosophy were universally disbelievers in a future state of retribution, although from prudential motives, legislators and statesmen generally combined to uphold one. More recently, Lord Brougham, in his 'Discourse on Natural Theology,' referred to it in discussing Warburton's views on the general question, and elicited a shrewd and accurate review of the debate before us from Dr. Turton. 'I will state,' says the last-named writer, 'as briefly as possible, the circumstances of the case. The question proposed to the senate was, "What should be done, with regard to those of the agents in Catiline's conspiracy, who were in custody?" Julius Silanus, as consul elect, spoke first, and was of opinion that they should be put to death. Cæsar, who, it will be recollected, was an Epicurean, dwelt upon their deeds as crimes to which no sufferings that could be devised would be adequate; represented death as, in cases of grief and wretchedness, the termination of sorrows, not the exacerbation—all the ills of life being dissipated by that event, beyond which there was neither trouble nor joy; and recommended the severest punishment that was consistent with the continuance of life.

["Equidem sic existumo, Patres conscripti, omnes cruciatus minores quam facinora illorum esse: . . . De pœna possumus equidem dicere id quod res habet: in luctu atque miseriis mortem ærumnarum requiem non cruciatum esse: eam cuncta mortalium mala dissolvere: ultra neque curæ neque gaudii locum esse."— *Sallust, Bell. Catil.* c. 51.

'Cato, a Stoic—in a speech also given by Sallust—mentioned, with commendation of the manner and no dislike of the matter, Cæsar's dissertation on life and death; slightly observing that he supposed Cæsar to consider as false the things that were reported of the infernal regions; namely, the separation of the good from the bad, who were consigned to places abounding in everything disagreeable and horrible.

["Bene et composite C. Cæsar paulo ante in hoc ordine de vita et morte disseruit; falsa, credo, existumans, quæ de inferis memorantur; diverso itinere malos a bonis loca tetra, inculta, fœda atque formidolosa habere" (*Sallust*, c. 52). I trace the irony of the speaker in the words, "bene et composite," still more in the parenthetic "credo." Plutarch supplies other instances of what I have called Cato's humour. See in the Life chapters 12, 21, 24, and 46.]

'So far we have depended upon the authority of Sallust, and notwithstanding the "Sallustian style" [*Brougham's Discourse*, p. 286] in which he has reported the speeches of Cæsar and of Cato, there is ample reason to believe that he has accurately given the substance of what was spoken. Let us now turn to the orations of Cicero, and see what information can be gathered from that great master of the academic school, in his own style. In the course of his address he mentions the two opinions which had been delivered: the one enforcing death, the other the severest punishment in this life: the former, as demanded by the danger to which the Roman people had been exposed; the latter, as being more efficacious than death, which was not ordained for punishment at all. He goes on to describe Cæsar's plan, as subjecting those miscreants to chains and imprisonment and poverty and despair, as leaving them nothing but life—which being taken away, they would be freed from the punishment of their wickedness. So that, by way of terror to the evil, the ancients were of opinion that some punishments should be assigned to the impious in the infernal regions, conceiving that, without such punishments, death would not be an object of dread.

["Video duas adhuc esse sententias: unam D. Silani, qui censet, eos, qui hæc delere conati sunt, morte esse multandos: alteram C. Cæsaris, qui mortis pœnam removet, cæterorum suppliciorum omnes acerbitates amplectitur. . . Alter eos, qui nos omnes, qui populum Romanum vita privare conati sunt, qui delere imperium, qui populi Romani nomen exstinguere, punctum temporis frui vita et hoc communi spiritu non putat oportere. . . . Alter intelligit mortem a Dis immortalibus non esse supplicii causa constitutam; sed aut necessitatem naturæ, aut laborum ac miseriarum quietem esse. . . Itaque ut aliqua in vita formido improbis esset posita, apud inferos ejusmodi quædam illi antiqui supplicia impiis constituta esse voluerunt, quod, videlicet intelligebant, his remotis, non esse mortem ipsam pertimescendam."—*Cicero in Catil.* iv. 4. 5.]

'We see, then, how completely Sallust's account of the debate is confirmed by Cicero's oration, as preserved in his own works. . . . We see, also, with what indifference the avowal of Cæsar's Epicurean disbelief of a future retribution was treated in the Roman Senate. Considered simply as a matter of religion, it seems not to have been deemed worthy of a remark,' &c. &c.—Turton, *Natural Theology considered*, &c., 1836, p. 320, fol.

Plutarch, I may add, in stating the conflicting opinion of Cæsar and Cato, and mentioning the curious fact that Cicero had provided means of having Cato's speech taken down by reporters for dispersion among the citizens, makes no reference to the religious bearing of their arguments. This may tend to show the indifference of the audience to the expression of sceptical views on such subjects, but it can by no means invalidate the substantial correctness of Sallust's report, confirmed as it is by the comment of Cicero himself. Sallust was about twenty-three at this period, and had not yet apparently entered upon his public career or attained a seat in the Senate; but he was a party man, intimate with the public characters of the day, and an adherent of Cæsar's. Cæsar and Sallust, it may be said, were of the party of progress, and it was their policy, as well as their temper, to unsettle the foundations of national prejudice and usage: but at the same time, it will be remembered, Lucretius, the friend of Memmius, the client and poet of the nobility, flung into the world his daring manifesto of unbelief, a work which marks in itself an era in the progress of free thought and expression among the Romans. The entire denial of a Deity, a Providence, a spiritual nature in man, or a moral purpose in creation, in the rhapsody 'De Rerum Natura,' is exactly analogous to Cæsar's declaration against a future retribution; while the strange inconsistency of the poet's address to Venus, the Mother of the Romans, the Delight of gods and men, the favourite of Mars, the divine source of life, is not less analogous to the inconsistent position assumed by Cæsar as a materialist in philosophy and a minister of religion. I shall have occasion to say more, in subsequent lectures, of the opinions of the heathen at Rome on the subject of Divine retribution. Here I wish chiefly to point out the licence of speech and thought regarding it, and the indifference with which sceptical views on the subject of a future life would be regarded at least by the upper classes of the Empire.

NOTE B, page 19.

The principal texts referred to occur in the Life of Constantine by Eusebius Pamphilus (iii. 7), and the ecclesiastical histories of the same Eusebius, of Socrates (i. 11), of Sozomen (i. 18), of Rufinus, and Theodoret. I have borrowed from De Broglie's vivid grouping of the council in his *L'Eglise et l'Empire Romain* (ch. iv.).

It should be remarked that the object of the Council of Nicæa, in regard to the settling of dogma, was not to establish, as is sometimes loosely said, the doctrine of the Holy Trinity, but to determine the position of the Divine Son in the scheme of revelation. The actual symbol subscribed at Nicæa, after asserting the various articles of our 'Nicene Creed,' as far as relates to the Father and the Son, terminates with a single additional article: 'I believe in the Holy Ghost.' The articles which define the character and functions of the third person in the Trinity, and those which follow to the end of our received formula, were added towards the end of the century at the Council of Constantinople, A.D. 381; but, as forming the accredited complement of the Creed of Nicæa, and popularly considered as included in it, I have not hesitated to cite them also as a substantive portion of the symbol in question. They serve to complete and bring out in strong relief the contrast to which I point between the scepticism of the Pagan and the dogmatism of the Christian assembly.

The text of the creed, as authorized at Nicæa, is given by Socrates, *Hist. Eccl.* i. 8 :—

'Πιστεύομεν εἰς ἕνα θεὸν, πατέρα παντοκράτορα, πάντων ὁρατῶν τε καὶ ἀοράτων ποιητήν.

'Καὶ εἰς ἕνα Κύριον Ἰησοῦν Χριστὸν, τὸν υἱὸν τοῦ θεοῦ· γεννηθέντα ἐκ τοῦ πατρὸς μονογενῆ· τοῦτ' ἔστιν, ἐκ τῆς οὐσίας τοῦ πατρὸς, θεὸν ἐκ θεοῦ καὶ φῶς ἐκ φωτὸς, θεὸν ἀληθινὸν ἐκ θεοῦ ἀληθινοῦ· γεννηθέντα οὐ ποιηθέντα, ὁμοούσιον τῷ πατρί· δι' οὗ τὰ πάντα ἐγένετο, τά τε ἐν τῷ οὐρανῷ καὶ τὰ ἐν τῇ γῇ. Δι' ἡμᾶς τοὺς ἀνθρώπους καὶ διὰ τὴν ἡμετέραν σωτηρίαν κατελθόντα, καὶ σαρκωθέντα, καὶ ἐνανθρωπήσαντα· παθόντα, καὶ ἀναστάντα τῇ τρίτῃ ἡμέρᾳ, ἀνελθόντα εἰς τοὺς οὐρανοὺς, ἐρχόμενον κρῖναι ζῶντας καὶ νεκρούς.

'Καὶ εἰς τὸ ἅγιον πνεῦμα.'

To which was appended an explanatory statement, concluding with an anathema:—

'Τοὺς δὲ λέγοντας, ὅτι ἦν ποτὲ ὅτε οὐκ ἦν· καὶ πρὶν γεννηθῆναι οὐκ ἦν· καὶ ὅτι ἐξ οὐκ ὄντων ἐγένετο· ἢ ἐξ ἑτέρας ὑποστάσεως ἢ οὐσίας φάσκοντας εἶναι· ἢ κτιστὸν, ἢ τρεπτὸν, ἢ ἀλλοιωτὸν τὸν υἱὸν τοῦ θεοῦ· ἀναθεματίζει ἡ ἁγία καθολικὴ καὶ ἀποστολικὴ ἐκκλησία.'

Note C, page 25.

I distinguish here between the conception of a Future State, as pretended to be revealed in the ancient mythology, and such as the philosophers might represent to themselves from the light of reason or imagination. Undoubtedly the common sentiment of mankind demands a belief in a future Retribution, and such we find to have been the teaching of the earliest mythological systems of Paganism. Such a belief is implied repeatedly in casual expressions of Homer, and is more positively declared in his description of Elysium and Tartarus. Nevertheless, when he sets himself deliberately to give an account of the infernal regions, his views become at once confused, and his picture of the state of the blessed is little less gloomy than that of the punishment of the wicked. This gloom is evidently a reflection of his own perplexity, and the painful feelings it naturally produced. As long as the Pagans could refrain from thinking on this subject, they might acquiesce implicitly in the mythological teaching; but this otiose assent vanished immediately when they began to reflect, and to draw logical inferences from the bare outlines of their traditional creed. The poets, to whom the fantastic stories of the popular religion furnished inexhaustible attractions, continued long to foster this unreflecting belief or acquiescence, and the common language of the people would still longer retain the tone of ages of a more real faith; but the philosophers meanwhile discarded without reserve the fables of the ancient mythology, and generally lost their grasp altogether of the idea which lay at the bottom of them. The positive side of their tenets on the subject of a future life will be referred to in another place. I believe there will be no question as to the truth of the statement in the text of the general unbelief of the educated people in Greece and Rome. The well-known passage in which Juvenal is often supposed to rebuke the discredit into which the mythological creed had fallen, seems to me, on the contrary, to show that in his view and that of the classes he addressed, not only the ancient

Hades was a fable, but the ground-idea of a future retribution was equally baseless. See *Sat.* ii. 149 :

> 'Esse aliquid manes, et subterranea regna,
> Et contum et Stygio ranas sub gurgite nigras,
> Atque una transire vadum tot millia cymba,
> Nec pueri credunt, nisi qui nondum ære lavantur :
> Sed tu vera puta : Curius quid sentit et ambo
> Scipiadæ,' &c.

'Puta,' I conceive, both from the common use of the expression, and from the analogy of the writer's teaching elsewhere, can only mean, 'But suppose them true!' Juvenal not only rejects the superstition of the vulgar, but is at a loss to refer to any more hopeful ground from reason or revelation for inculcating a religious belief in a future retribution at all. Throughout his moral teaching he is consistent in confining his views to temporal rewards and punishments only.

'Dans les classes cultivées les mythes du Tartare et de l'Élysée étaient traités de fables absurdes; un matérialisme grossier né de l'Épicurisme, ou bien une résignation orgueilleuse à l'anéantissement produite par le Panthéisme stoïcien, parfois un rêve platonicien ou plutôt oriental de métempsycose, telles étaient les croyances prédominantes parmis les païens éclairés.'—Pressensé, *Hist. des Trois Premiers Siècles de l'Église Chrétienne*, 2e série, i. 111.

Note D, Page 27.

The ceremony of lustrating the city by a procession of the priests of the four great colleges (quatuor summa vel amplissima collegia), namely, the Pontifices, Augures, Quindecimviri, and Septemviri or Epulones, to whom, in the Imperial times, were added the Augustales, occurs frequently in the early history of Rome, on the occasion of disasters to be expiated or averted. The Supplication was a solemnity of similar import, and of still more frequent occurrence : in the one the procession made a circuit of the space to which the lustration or expiation was to be applied; in the other the images of certain deities were carried from shrine to shrine, with hymns, sacrifices, and other formalities. Both these ceremonies were resorted to under the empire, as we read in Tacitus, *Annal.* iii. 64; xiii. 24; *Hist.* i. 87; iv. 53.

I refer in the text to a lustration of the city which seems to have taken place in the culminating period of Roman irreligion, on the alarm at Cæsar's crossing the Rubicon. The historian, Appian (*Bell. Civ.* ii. 36), says simply: εὐχαὶ δὲ, ὡς ἐπὶ φοβεροῖς, προυγράφοντο. I see no reason to doubt that Lucan follows a genuine tradition when he paraphrases this statement with a rhetorical description of a lustration of the city, such as he may himself have witnessed about an hundred years later, A.D. 56, in the reign of Nero. (Tac. *Ann.* xiii. 24). 'Urbem Princeps lustravit ex responso haruspicum, quod Jovis ac Minervæ ædes' (the Capitol) ' de cœlo tactæ.' Lucan's representation of the ceremony which took place on such solemn occasions is ample and vivid, *Pharsalia*, i. 592, foll.

> 'Mox jubet et totam pavidis a civibus Urbem
> Ambiri, et festo purgantes mœnia lustro
> Longa per extremos pomœria cingere fines
> Pontifices, sacri quibus est permissa potestas.
> Turba minor ritu sequitur succincta Gabino,
> Vestalemque chorum ducit vittata sacerdos,
> Trojanam soli cui fas vidisse Minervam.
> Tum qui fata deûm secretaque carmina servant,
> Et lotam parvo revocant Almone Cybeben;
> Et doctus volucres Augur servare sinistras;
> Septemvirque epulis festis, Titiique sodales;
> Et Salius læto portans ancilia collo;
> Et tollens apicem generoso vertice Flamen.'

It may be interesting to compare this poetic description with the prose narration of what was doubtless a very similar solemnity by Tacitus, *Hist.* iv. 53 (A.D. 70).

'Curam restituendi Capitolii in L. Vestinum confert. . . . Undecimo calendas Junias, serena luce, spatium omne, quod templo dicabatur, evinctum vittis coronisque. Ingressi milites, quis fausta nomina, felicibus ramis: dein virgines Vestales, cum pueris puellisque patrimis matrimisque, aqua vivis e fontibus amnibusque hausta perluere. Tum Helvidius Priscus prætor, præeunte Plautio Æliano pontifice, lustrata suovetaurilibus area et super cæspitem redditis extis, Jovem, Junonem, Minervam præsidesque imperii deos precatus, uti cœpta prosperarent, sedesque suas pietate hominum inchoatas divina ope attollerent, vittas quis ligatus lapis innexique funes erant contigit. Simul ceteri magistratus et sacerdotes et senatus et eques et magna pars populi, studio lætitiaque connixi, saxum ingens traxere; passimque injectæ fundamentis argenti aurique stipes, et metallorum primitiæ nullis fornacibus victæ, sed ut gignuntur.'

Note E, Page 39.

Lactantius, *Institutionum divin.*, vii. 6 :—

'Nunc totam rationem brevi circumscriptione signemus. Idcirco mundus factus est, ut nascamur: ideo nascimur, ut agnoscamus factorem mundi ac nostri Deum: ideo agnoscimus, ut colamus; ideo colimus, ut immortalitatem pro laborum mercede capiamus, quoniam maximis laboribus cultus Dei constat: ideo præmio immortalitatis adficimur, ut similes angelis effecti, summo patri ac domino in perpetuum serviamus, et simus æternum Deo regnum. Hæc summa rerum est, hoc arcanum Dei, hoc mysterium mundi, a quo sunt alieni, qui, sequentes præsentem voluptatem, terrestribus et fragilibus se bonis addixerunt, et animas ad cœlestia genitas suavitatibus mortiferis, tanquam luto cœnove demerserunt. Quæramus nunc vicissim, an in cultu Deorum ratio ulla subsistat: qui si multi sunt, si ideo tantum ab hominibus coluntur, ut præstent illis opes, victorias, honores, quæque alia non nisi ad præsens valent; si sine causa gignimur; si in hominibus procreandis providentia nulla versatur; si casu nobismetipsis ac voluptatis nostræ gratia nascimur; si nihil post mortem sumus: quid potest esse tam supervacuum, tam inane, tam vanum, quam humana res, et quam mundus ipse;

—qui, quum sit incredibili magnitudine, tam mirabili ratione constructus, tamen rebus ineptis vacet? Cur enim ventorum spiritus citent nubes, cur emicent fulgura, tonitrua mugiant, imbres cadant, ut fruges terra producat, ut varios fœtus alat; cur denique omnis natura rerum laboret, ne quid desit earum rerum, quibus vita hominis sustinetur, si est inanis, si ad nihilum interimus, si nihil est in nobis majoris emolumenti Deo? Quod si est dictu nefas, nec putandum est fieri posse, ut non ob aliquam maximam rationem fuerit constitutum quod videas maxima ratione constare; quæ potest esse ratio in his erroribus pravarum religionum, et in hac persuasione philosophorum, qua putant animas interire? Profecto nulla.'

Note F, Page 43.

M. Denis, in his *Histoire des Théories et Idées Morales dans l'Antiquité* (i. p. 149), thus describes the spiritual deity conceived by Plato:—

(1.) 'Au-dessus du monde sensible, l'esprit conçoit nécessairement un autre monde, celui des intelligibles ou des Idées, et au sommet du monde des Idées brille d'une éternelle splendure l'Idée du bien, d'où toutes les autres émanent. Le bien, dit Platon, est fort au-dessus de l'essence en perfection et en dignité; le bien n'est point la vérité ni l'intelligence: il en est le père. De même que le soleil, qui est l'image visible du bien, règne sur ce monde qu'il éclaire et qu'il vivifie: de même le bien, dont le soleil n'est que l'ouvrage, règne sur le monde intelligible, qu'il enfante en vertu de son inépuisable fécondité. Le bien, c'est Dieu même dans ce qu'il a de plus essentiel. C'est vers cette perfection souveraine que la raison s'élance; c'est à cette beauté infinie que l'amour aspire. "Beauté merveilleuse," s'écrie Platon, "beauté éternelle, incréée, impérissable, exempte d'accroissement et de diminution; ... beauté qui n'a rien de sensible, ni de corporel, comme des mains ou un visage; qui ne réside pas dans un être différent d'elle-même, dans la terre, dans le ciel, ou dans toute autre chose, mais qui existe éternellement et absolument en elle-même et par elle-même; beauté de laquelle toutes les autres beautés participent, sans que leur naissance ou leur destruction lui apporte la moindre diminution ou le moindre accroissement, et la modifie en quoi que ce soit," ' &c. Compare among many other passages *Convivium*, p. 211; *Timæus*, 28, 29, 30, 37.

(2.) Of God's Providence. Denis, p. 150 :—' Si telle est la nature de Dieu, on peut juger de son action sur l'univers. C'est lui qui a fait ce bel ordre visible que nous appelons le monde. . . . Il l'a donc fait selon son intelligence et selon sa bonté; l'œil toujours fixé sur les idées ou sur le modèle éternel et immuable, il a partout introduit l'ordre, la mesure, le nombre et l'harmonie. . . . Si Dieu conserve, soutient et gouverne ce monde, peut-on croire qu'il ne s'inquiète pas de la partie la plus divine de son ouvrage, de celle qui certainement vient de lui quant à sa substance, lors même que tout le reste ne viendrait pas? Non. . . . Sage simplement par rapport aux objets sensibles, Dieu est juste par rapport aux esprits. Nous avons déjà vu comment il est le principe de la justice est de la loi. Mais se pourrait-il qu'il négligeât ceux qui se conforment à ses décrets éternels, et qui, en obéissant à la justice, s'efforcent de lui ressembler? Quiconque est juste doit être heureux, . . . mais en voyant des hommes violents et impies s'élever de la plus basse condition jusqu'aux plus hautes dignités et même jusqu'à la tyrannie, ne voulant pas accuser Dieu de ces désordres, nous en venons à penser qu'à la vérité Dieu existe, mais qu'il dédaigne de s'occuper des affaires humaines. Les apparences nous deçoivent, et nous ne voyons pas quel terrible tribut ces hommes heureux doivent un jour payer à l'ordre général.'—Plato, *Leges*, p. 716; comp. pp. 889, 906; *Meno*, pp. 99, 100.

(3.) Plato seems to have augured the possibility of a future state of retribution, rather than to have insisted on it as a certain or probable fact. When he says, as in the 'Laws,' p. 716, that divine justice always follows those who fall short of the divine law, he may regard punishments in this life rather than in another. The use he makes of the mythological fables of Elysium and Tartarus seems to imply a consciousness that he could not appeal to the reason of mankind on the subject, and must content himself with working on their feelings.

'Quoi qu'il en soit,' says M. Denis, p. 160, 'il est évident que l'immortalité de l'âme est nécessaire à sa morale. Aussi ses dialogues sont-ils pleins d'allusions aux biens et aux maux que la justice de Dieu réserve à nos vertus ou à nos vices. "Lorsque l'âme," dit-il dans les 'Lois,' "à fait des progrès marqués, soit dans le bien, soit dans le mal, par une volonté ferme et soutenue; si c'est dans le bien et qu'elle se soit attachée à la divine vertu jusqu'à en devenir divine comme elle, alors elle reçoit de grandes distinctions, et du lieu qu'elle occupe, elle passe dans une autre demeure toute sainte et bienheureuse; si elle a vécu dans le vice, elle va habiter une demeure conforme à son état. Ni toi, ni qui que ce soit, ne pourra jamais se vanter de s'être soustrait à cet ordre fait pour être observé plus inviolablement qu'aucun autre, et qu'il faut infiniment respecter. Tu ne lui échapperas jamais, quand tu serais assez petit pour pénétrer jusqu'aux abîmes de la terre, ni quand tu serais assez grand pour t'élever jusqu'au ciel." Il est impossible d'affirmer plus fortement cette vérité; mais Platon ne la traite guère, en général, que comme une ample matière à de beaux mythes poétiques.'

(3.) On the duty of Repentance. Denis, p. 104:—'Ne considérez, toutefois, que le fond des idées, et vous verrez que Platon a le premier établi la nécessité morale de la pénitence, dont le christianisme a fait depuis un de ses dogmes. Il faut que nous soyons punis de nos fautes; et ce n'est pas moins notre intérêt que notre devoir de courir au devant de la justice irritée, de nous exposer à ses reproches et à ses châtiments, de rétablir par la pénitence la santé de l'âme corrompue par le péché : voilà ce que prêche le christianisme; voilà ce que Platon enseignait quatre siècles avant Christ. Mais la vérité, telle que le philosophe la présente, ne sait point se prêter à notre faiblesse et compâtir à notre néant. . . Le dirai-je? Émanation du plus pur spiritualisme, cette vérité conserve encore, au moins dans l'expression de Platon, quelque chose du matérialisme des anciens âges. Le philosophe semble plus regarder aux peines physiques qu'à la contrition du cœur, qui seule constitue la vraie pénitence. On dirait qu'il craignait de n'être point compris des esprits matériels de son temps. Mais, sous quelque forme qu'elle se présente, la vérité est la vérité, et l'on ne saurait trop admirer de rencontrer au sortir de la Sophistique, et dans la corruption des Grecs, une morale si hardie, si profonde, et si austère.'

In the *Gorgias* (p. 480) Plato enjoins the criminal to accuse himself to the judge:—

' Ἐὰν δέ γε ἀδικήσῃ ἢ αὐτὸς ἢ ἄλλος τις ὧν ἂν κήδηται, αὐτὸν ἑκόντα ἰέναι ἐκεῖσε, ὅπου ὡς τάχιστα δώσει δίκην, παρὰ τὸν δικαστήν, ὥσπερ παρὰ τὸν ἰατρόν, σπεύδοντα ὅπως μὴ ἐγχρονισθὲν τὸ νόσημα τῆς ἀδικίας ὕπουλον τὴν ψυχὴν ποιήσει καὶ ἀνίατον.'

(4.) Under the name of Justice, Plato enjoins the practice of love and charity towards our neighbours in terms which deserve to be placed alongside of our Christian teaching. Denis, p. 99:—'Platon rejette toutes les définitions de la justice, qui avaient cours dans la philosophie grecque; non seulement celle des Sophistes qui mettaient la justice dans le droit du plus fort, mais encore cette définition en apparence si raisonnable, qu'il faut rendre à chacun ce qui lui est dû. Elle lui paraît digne non d'un sage, mais d'un Périandre, d'un Xerxès, ou de tout autre tyran. Avec quelle force il montre qu'elle revient à dire qu'il faut faire du bien à ses amis, du mal à ses ennemis! Veut-on dire simplement qu'il faut faire du bien aux bons et du mal aux méchants? Et quoi! est-il d'un juste de faire du mal à un homme quel qu'il soit? N'est-ce donc pas une nécessité que ceux à qui l'on fait du mal.deviennent pires par cela même? L'homme juste ne doit-il pas, au contraire, servir jusqu'à ses ennemis, et ramener les méchants au bien par sa vertu?' Comp. *Republ.*, i. pp. 331–336, and other places.

Note G, Page 44.

M. Denis, i. 144:—'On aimerait que Platon fût allé plus loin, et qu'au lieu de s'arrêter à la Grèce, sa pensée se fût étendue à l'humanité. Mais s'il déclare que les Grecs sont naturellement amis, et qu'ils sont unis par la fraternité du sang, il déclare aussi qu'ils sont naturellement étrangers et ennemis à l'égard des barbares. Sans partager absolument les préjugés de ses compatriotes à l'égard des étrangers, tout en soutenant que le roi de Perse est au moins aussi noble que le plus noble des Grecs, que les Egyptiens sont les plus sages des mortels, et qu'on trouve aussi des hommes vraiment divins chez les barbares, il accepte pourtant la division grecque de notre espèce en deux parties naturellement hostiles ; et si l'on rencontre chez lui l'amour non de telle ou telle cité, mais de la patrie, il est impossible d'y trouver l'amour de l'humanité.' Compare the *Republic*, v. p. 470 :—

' Φημὶ γὰρ τὸ μὲν ʽΕλληνικὸν γένος αὐτὸ αὑτῷ οἰκεῖον εἶναι καὶ ξυγγενὲς, τῷ δὲ βαρβαρικῷ ὀθνεῖόν τε καὶ ἀλλότριον. . . . ῞Ελληνας μὲν ἄρα βαρβάροις, καὶ βαρβάρους῞Ελλησι πολεμεῖν μαχομένους τε φήσομεν, καὶ πολεμίους φύσει εἶναι. . . ῞Ελληνας δὲ῞Ελλησιν ὅταν τι τοιοῦτο δρῶσι, φύσει μὲν φίλους εἶναι, νοσεῖν δὲ ἐν τῷ τοιούτῳ τὴν ʽΕλλάδα καὶ στασιάζειν.'

And further, i. 373 :—

'Platon, non plus qu'Aristote, ne conçoit de république que s'il l'enferme dans une certaine enceinte ; il lui faut pour cela un lieu convenable et de son choix ; il veut qu'il n'y ait dans son État imaginaire que dix mille citoyens comme à Sparte.'

Note H, Page 45.

The views of Aristotle with regard to slavery are thus summed up by Wallon, *Hist. de l'Esclavage dans l'Antiquité*, i. 372 foll. :—

'L'État, selon la définition d'Aristote, est une société composée de telle sorte qu'elle trouve en elle de quoi suffire à toutes les nécessités de la vie . . . Ainsi va se marquer, dans la masse des hommes qui le composent nécessairement, une ligne de partage nettement tracée. D'un côté, le citoyen accomplissant à lui seul la destination de la cité, tendant au bonheur par la vertu au sein du loisir; et de l'autre, des hommes dont le seul but paraît être de rendre aux citoyens ces loisirs possibles: pour l'agriculture et l'industrie, des laboureurs et des artisans, pour le service privé des esclaves.

'Cette organisation nécessaire à l'État ainsi conçue, Aristote la retrouve jusque dans la famille, jusque dans la nature même de l'homme. Car l'homme est né sociable. Il n'est donc complet que dans l'association domestique; et cette association comprend trois êtres: l'homme qui commande la famille, la femme qui la perpétue, et l'esclave qui la sert. Supprimez une de ces trois lignes d'un triangle, et le triangle n'est plus; de même l'esclave est en quelque sorte un troisième côté de l'homme; supprimez-le, et vous n'avez plus l'homme; l'homme en société, c'est à dire, l'homme vrai. Mais la relation d'esclave à maître ne se trouve pas seulement dans la constitution de l'homme sociable, dans la famille, Aristote la découvre jusque dans le fond même de l'homme individu: c'est le rapport du corps à l'âme. L'esclave est un corps, et l'idée finit par en passer dans le langage: on l'appela purement et simplement corps, σῶμα.'

For the essential difference between the master and the slave, as Aristotle conceived it, see the whole of the second chapter of the first book of the *Politica*. Compare, for instance:—

'Φύσει μὲν οὖν διώρισται τὸ θῆλυ καὶ τὸ δοῦλον . . . οὕτω γὰρ ἂν ἀποτελοῖτο κάλλιστα τῶν ὀργάνων ἕκαστον, μὴ πολλοῖς ἔργοις ἀλλ' ἑνὶ δουλεῦον. Ἐν δὲ τοῖς βαρβάροις τὸ θῆλυ καὶ δοῦλον τὴν αὐτὴν ἔχει τάξιν· αἴτιον δέ, ὅτι τὸ φύσει ἄρχον οὐκ ἔχουσιν, ἀλλὰ γίγνεται ἡ κοινωνία αὐτῶν δούλης καὶ δούλου. Διό φασιν οἱ ποιηταί· Βαρβάρων δ' Ἕλληνας ἄρχειν εἰκός· ὡς ταὐτὸ φύσει βάρβαρον καὶ δοῦλον ὄν.

''Ἀνάγκη γὰρ εἶναί τινας φάναι τοὺς μὲν πανταχοῦ δούλους, τοὺς δ' οὐδαμοῦ . . . ἀξιοῦσι γὰρ, ὥσπερ ἐξ ἀνθρώπου ἄνθρωπον καὶ ἐκ θηρίων γενέσθαι θηρίον, οὕτω καὶ ἐξ ἀγαθῶν ἀγαθόν. . . . "Ὅτι μὲν οὖν ἔχει τινὰ λόγον ἡ ἀμφισβήτησις, καί εἰσιν οἱ μὲν φύσει δοῦλοι, οἱ δ᾽ ἐλεύθεροι, δῆλον.'

The inextricable difficulties in which this theory involved him must appear at first sight, and are well stated by Wallon:—'Mais, en admettant qu'il y ait un esclavage naturel, de quel appui serait-il à l'esclavage comme il est constitué dans la société?' &c.

M. Troplong (*De l'Influence du Christianisme sur le Droit Romain*, i. ch. iv.—a book of which I shall have to speak again) thus compares the views of Plato and Aristotle on the subject of slavery:—'Platon disait : "Si un citoyen tue son esclave, la loi déclare le meurtrier exempt de peine, pourvu qu'il se purifie par des expiations ; mais si un esclave tue son maître, on lui fait subir tous les traitements qu'on juge à propos, pourvu qu'on ne lui laisse pas la vie." Aristote allait plus loin, s'il est possible, dans sa théorie de l'esclavage. "Il y a peu de différence dans les services que l'homme tire de l'esclave et de l'animal. *La nature même le veut*, puisqu'elle fait les corps des hommes libres différents de ceux des esclaves ; donnant aux uns la force qui convient à leur destination, et aux autres une stature droite et élevée." Puis l'illustre philosophe conclut ainsi :—"Il est donc évident que les uns *sont naturellement libres, et les autres naturellement esclaves*, et que, pour ces derniers, l'esclavage est aussi utile qu'il est juste." (*Politic.* i. 2.) Ainsi l'esclavage est de droit naturel ; il trouve sa légitimité dans la justice et la nature : telle est la doctrine qu'Aristote expose sans objection.'

Note I, Page 48.

Plutarch (or Pseudo-Plutarch), *De Alexandri M. Virtute aut Fortuna*, i. 6 : —

'Οὐ γὰρ, ὡς Ἀριστοτέλης συνεβούλευεν αὐτῷ, τοῖς μὲν Ἕλλησιν ἡγεμονικῶς, τοῖς δὲ βαρβάροις δεσποτικῶς χρώμενος· καὶ τῶν μὲν ὡς φίλων καὶ οἰκείων ἐπιμελούμενος, τοῖς δὲ, ὡς ζῴοις ἢ φυτοῖς, προσφερόμενος, πολεμοποιῶν φυγῶν ἐνέπλησε καὶ στασέων ὑπούλων τὴν ἡγεμονίαν, ἀλλὰ κοινὸς ἥκειν θεόθεν ἁρμοστὴς καὶ διαλλακτὴς τῶν ὅλων νομίζων, οὓς τῷ λόγῳ μὴ συνῆγε, τοῖς ὅπλοις βιαζόμενος, εἰς τὸ αὐτὸ συνενεγκὼν τὰ πανταχόθεν, ὥσπερ ἐν κρατῆρι φιλοτησίῳ, μίξας τοὺς βίους καὶ τὰ ἤθη, καὶ τοὺς γάμους καὶ διαίτας, πατρίδα μὲν τὴν οἰκουμένην προσέταξεν ἡγεῖσθαι πάντας, ἀκρόπολιν δὲ καὶ φρουρὰν τὸ στρατόπεδον, συγγενεῖς δὲ τοὺς ἀγαθούς, ἀλλοφύλους δὲ τοὺς πονηρούς· τὸ δὲ Ἑλληνικὸν καὶ βαρβαρικὸν μὴ χλαμύδι, μηδὲ πέλτῃ, μηδὲ ἀκινάκῃ, μηδὲ κάνδυϊ διορίζειν, ἀλλὰ τὸ μὲν Ἑλληνικὸν ἀρετῇ, τὸ δὲ βαρβαρικὸν κακίᾳ τεκμαίρεσθαι· κοινὰς δὲ τὰς ἐσθῆτας ἡγεῖσθαι καὶ τραπέζας, καὶ γάμους καὶ διαίτας, δι' αἵματος καὶ τέκνων ἀνακεραννυμένους.'

If this treatise is not by Plutarch himself, it breathes the spirit of his age and of his views of history. It regards the character of Alexander's conquest from the point of a much later generation, and of a liberal and humane philosophy. It judges of Alexander's policy from a comprehensive view of the effects it produced, and ascribes, fondly perhaps, to the man, a deliberate intention of which he may have had no conception. The earlier historians of Alexander, and Livy, who acutely criticizes his military character, indulged apparently in no such imaginations regarding him. Whether they were right or wrong in describing him as a mere conqueror need not be considered here. In any case the effect of his conquest was the same, and we may acknowledge our obligation to the author of the treatise before us, for calling attention to it in his own fashion.

Note J, Page 51.

I transcribe a passage from Denis (*Idées Morales*, &c., i. 369), in which he signalizes the effect of the Macedonian conquest on the speculations of Greek philosophy, and especially of the Stoic :—

'Alexandre avait essayé de faire un seul peuple des Grecs et des barbares, et de les unir dans une vaste communauté de droits, d'intérêts, de langage, et de civilisation. Le Stoïcisme semble avoir hérité de l'esprit universel qui animait le héros dans sa conquête. Je le sais, l'idée seule de l'honnête pouvait conduire un esprit juste et rigoureux à concevoir l'unité du genre humain, et tous les devoirs ou les droits qui en dérivent. Car lorsqu'on n'apprécie les hommes que par leur capacité naturelle pour la vertu, toutes les distinctions et toutes les inégalités disparaissent : il n'y a plus de Grecs ni de barbares, de maîtres ni d'esclaves ; il n'y a que des êtres raisonnables qui, possédant tous la liberté à un égal degré, sont tous soumis à la même loi universelle. Mais pourquoi Zénon, qui n'était peut-être qu'un esprit médiocre, a-t-il eu des vues plus larges et plus humaines que les grands esprits qui l'avaient précédé ? C'est que, pour tirer les conséquences du principe moral, il n'avait pas besoin de faire violence à ses préjugés, ni de s'élever beaucoup au-dessus de la réalité : il lui suffisait, au contraire, d'ouvrir les yeux et de regarder les faits.

'A cette époque, un Grec retrouvait partout la Grèce, sur les côtes de l'Italie méridionale, en Sicile, à Pergame, à Alexandrie, à Séleucie, à Babylone, dans une partie de l'Europe, et presque dans toute l'Asie jusqu'aux bords du Gange et de l'Indus. Il pouvait donc se croire à juste titre non plus citoyen de Sparte ou d'Athènes, mais citoyen de l'univers. La vanité pouvait encore le séparer du barbare ; mais les haines et les animosités, qui entretenaient auparavant les préjugés nationaux, s'éteignaient de plus en plus dans un commerce et des relations de tous les jours. On vit bientôt, jusque dans les écoles des philosophes, une image de cette société mêlée qui venait de toutes les contrées de la terre. Comme toutes les conditions se rencontraient dans le Portique et que, selon le mot de Timon, " une nuée de *Penestes* ou de serfs et de gueux," tels que le manœuvre Cléanthe et l'esclave Persée, s'y pressaient à côté des citoyens les plus riches et les mieux nés : de même on voyait à côté des vrais Grecs une foule d'hommes de toute nation, partis de Tyr, de Carthage, d'Alexandrie, ou d'Antioche pour se former dans

Athènes à la sagesse hellénique. Le fondateur du Stoïcisme n'était lui-même qu'un étranger, et ses ennemis lui reprochaient sottement son origine phénicienne. Les hommes, jusqu'alors séparés les uns des autres par la distance ou par la haine, se rencontraient enfin pacifiquement et apprenaient à se connaître. La vérité et la vertu ne paraissaient plus enfermées dans les bornes d'une cité ou d'une nation ; l'on racontait mille merveilles sur les mœurs, sur les lois, sur la religion et sur la philosophie des peuples lointains, qu'avait à peine entrevues les compagnons d'Alexandre ; on allait même jusqu'à rabaisser la science des Grecs devant la sagesse de ces Indiens, dont les austérités remplissaient Zénon d'admiration, et dont le mépris pour la vie lui faisait dire qu'un Brachmane, mourant tranquillement sur le bûcher, lui en apprenait plus sur la patience et sur le courage que toutes les argumentations des philosophes. La fusion entre les idées commençait avec la fusion entre les peuples : les Grecs retrouvaient, ou croyaient retrouver, partout le berceau de leurs dieux et de leurs croyances ; et déjà le juif Aristobule, dont l'exemple devait être suivi par tant d'Orientaux, altérait et la Bible et les dogmes de la philosophie grecque, pour démontrer qu'Aristote, Platon et Pythagore n'avaient fait que piller Moïse et les prophètes. Le cosmopolitisme était partout, mais obscur et indécis encore comme les vagues pressentiments de l'instinct. Il devint une théorie aussi claire que fortement arrêtée sous les mains de Zénon et de ses disciples. Mais ce n'était, je le répète, qu'une conséquence naturelle des grands événements qui venaient de changer la face du monde. Alexandre avait voulu, dans sa gigantesque entreprise, faire du monde entier un seul empire, et malgré la mort qui vint si vite interrompre ses desseins, malgré le démembrement de sa conquête, il avait jusqu'à un certain point réussi : il avait laissé la Grèce dans l'Asie, le mouvement dans l'immobilité, la vie dans la mort, la civilisation dans la barbarie. L'audace du conquérant a passé dans les spéculations des philosophes : Zénon, lui aussi, médite une république universelle, la grande republique des intelligences, avec Dieu pour maître, et sa pensée éternelle pour conduite et pour loi.

'Que la république de Platon, ce rêve si vanté, est loin de la grandeur d'une telle conception!' As far, one might say, as in its historic development, the national Church of Judaism from the Catholic Church of Christendom.

M. Denis, after the manner of the French school of history, assumes without question Alexander's personal aims and aspirations. On this difficult subject a soberer criticism will perhaps suspend its judgment. The effect of his conquests is undeniable, whatever views or no views we may attribute to the conqueror himself. Droysen, after writing the political history of the successors of Alexander, has entered on the great subject to which it naturally leads, and in his *Geschichte des Hellenismus* promises to unfold in all their magnificence the features of the momentous social revolution which followed upon Alexander's conquests, and formed the most general preparation for the reception of Christianity.

Note K, Page 54.

I quote again from M. Denis, from whom I have borrowed this contrast between Plato (with whom I class the Stoics and others who derived from him) and the earlier philosophers (*Idées Morales*, i. p. 126):—

'Qu'on remue tant qu'on voudra les institutions et les mœurs de la Grèce, on n'y trouvera jamais la trace des spéculations presque mystiques de Platon. Même si on le compare à Xénophon et à Socrate, non plus aux idées populaires, mais aux doctrines philosophiques, quelle profonde différence! Ce qui fait le prix de la tempérance aux yeux de Socrate et de Xénophon, c'est qu'elle nous met à même d'agir virilement; ce qui en fait le prix pour Platon, c'est qu'elle nous détache du corps et de la terre. Le courage, tel que le conçoit Socrate, a pour but de nous procurer l'empire, ou tout au moins la liberté. Il n'est pour Platon que le complément de la tempérance, qui nous apprend à mourir au corps, au monde et à nous-mêmes. Je sais que Socrate, en tant que philosophe, estimait surtout dans la tempérance et le courage la liberté intérieure qu'ils nous assurent. Mais aurait-il compris, et son bon sens aurait-il approuvé ce que Platon appelle si énergiquement la méditation de la mort? Ce qu'il y avait dans Socrate de plus original après son caractère, c'étaient ses idées sur la sagesse et sur l'amour; mais qu'elles paraissent timides et terre à terre à côté de celles de son élève! Il ne suffit pas à Platon de comprendre ce qu'il y a de rationnel dans la nature de l'homme et dans celle de l'univers; il aspire à la vision face à face du divin. L'amour n'est plus pour lui cette amitié qui doit unir les hommes par les liens de la vertu et des bienfaits; c'est la passion de l'Éternel, regret d'un monde meilleur, et pressentiment de notre future immortalité. Ces idées et ces aspirations paraissent si étranges dans un Grec, qu'on croit partout y reconnaître l'inspiration de l'Orient.'

The relations of Plato with Zoroaster and the Brahmins are matters of conjecture only; but of the influence of these and other teachers upon the later Greek philosophy of Zeno and his successors there can be no question.

Note L, Page 55.

I would not be supposed to merge Judaism in the mass of national religions to which this language may be justly applied. The circumstances which render the Revelation to the Jews essentially a religion by itself, however similar in some outward features to the common type of the Heathen cults, require, and have often received, special and separate treatment. One great and vital distinction between them is that Judaism, alone as far as we learn, presents the character of an exclusive national religion, combined with the worship of one God. All Heathen nations believed in their own god or gods as peculiar to themselves, and opposed to other gods of their enemies. There are numerous traces, indeed, of a tendency among the Jews to this false but attractive conception; but it is distinctly repudiated by the real genius of the Mosaic Revelation. I find this remark in Colani's *Jésus-Christ et les Croyances Messianiques*, p. 3:—

'La grande originalité des Israélites consiste précisément en ceci, qu'ils ont cru avec une égale énergie à l'unité de l'Être divin et à sa prédilection pour leur race : il n'y a d'autre Dieu que Jéhova, et Jéhova a fait une alliance éternelle avec Jacob. La conviction étonnante qu'ont eue certains hommes d'être si bien élus du Très-Haut qu'Il n'aurait pu se passer d'eux, le peuple juif l'a eue, en tant que peuple.'

Note M, Page 59.

On the opinions of the Stoics regarding the Future Life, I refer again to Denis (*Idées Morales*, i. 359):—

'Doit-on ajouter à cette morale religieuse le dogme de l'immortalité de l'âme. Si je ne me trompe, les Stoïciens, tant ceux de la seconde époque que ceux de la première, n'ont jamais insisté fortement sur cette idée consolante. Caton se tue en lisant le Phédon de Platon, et non pas un livre de quelqu'un de ses bons amis les Stoïciens. Epictète, Marc-Aurèle et Sénèque ne parle qu'incidemment, et non pas même sans réserve, de l'immortalité. Jamais ils n'en font le but et l'encouragement de la vertu. On ne peut cependant douter qu'ils ne l'aient admise, je ne dis pas comme une opinion établie et fermement arrêtée, mais au moins comme une grande et belle espérance. Parmi les principaux représentants du Portique, Panétius est le seul qui nous soit signalé comme niant toute espèce de vie future, malgré sa prédilection pour Platon. . . . Quant aux autres Stoïciens, leurs opinions peuvent sembler étranges, mais elles indiquent évidemment la permanence possible de l'âme. "Ils avançait," nous dit Cicéron, " que les âmes continuent à exister après qu'elles sont sorties du corps, mais qu'elles ne doivent point toujours durer, nous gratifiant ainsi nou de l'immortalité, mais d'une longue vie, à peu près comme des corneilles."

Diogène nous explique ces mots de Cicéron. Selon lui, Cléanthe pensait que les âmes se conservent jusqu'à la conflagration du monde, c'est-à-dire, jusqu'au moment où l'univers rentre dans le sein de Jupiter d'où il est sorti, de sorte que toutes les âmes, celles des hommes et celles des dieux, doivent un jour se perdre et s'anéantir dans la substance de l'Être premier. Mais Chrysippe n'accordait cette permanence et cette durée qu'aux âmes des gens de bien et des sages.* Il paraît donc penser avec Platon, que l'âme n'emporte avec elle dans l'autre vie que ses actes intellectuels et moraux. L'âme survit donc au corps, du moins lorsqu'elle a été vertueuse ; et selon Chrysippe, elle conserve les vertus et les vérités dont elle s'est ornée. Mais sur quelles preuves les Stoïciens affirmaient-ils cette espèce d'immortalité ? Je n'en trouve qu'une seule ; s'il faut en croire Sénèque, nous devons regarder comme tout stoïcien l'argument du consentement unanime des peuples. . . . Si les Stoïciens se bornaient réellement à cette raison, j'en conclurais qu'ils ne voulaient pas abandonner l'immortalité de l'âme, parce qu'elle est une opinion salutaire, mais aussi qu'elle ne faisait point partie de leurs dogmes arrêtés et philosophiques. Ils ne la rattachaient pas d'ailleurs au principe moral. Car c'est pour eux une idée invariable que la vertu se suffit à elle-même, et qu'elle trouve en soi sa récompense, comme le vice renferme en soi sa propre punition. Or, si les bons avaient dû recevoir dans une autre vie le prix de leurs vertus, pourquoi

---

* [Comp. Plutarch, *De Placit. Philos.* iv. 7. 'Οἱ Στωϊκοὶ, ἐξιοῦσαν τῶν σωμάτων ὑποφέρεσθαι τὴν μὲν ἀσθενεστέραν ἅμα τοῖς συγκρίμασι γενέσθαι, ταύτην δ' εἶναι τῶν ἀπαιδεύτων· τὴν δ' ἰσχυροτέραν, οἷα ἐστὶ περὶ τοὺς σοφοὺς, καὶ μέχρι τῆς ἐκπυρώσεως.' Seneca, *Consol. ad Marc.* 26. 'Et quum tempus advenerit, quo so mundus renovaturus exstinguat: viribus ista sese suis cædent, et sidera sideribus incurrent, et omni flagrante materia, uno igne, quicquid nunc ex disposito lucet, ardebit. Nos quoque, felices animæ, et æterna sortitæ, quum Deo visum erit iterum ista moliri, labentibus cunctis, et ipsæ parva ruinæ ingentis accessio, in antiqua elementa vertemur.' Comp. also Epict. *Diss.* iii. 13. 1. Eusobii *Præpar. Evangel.* xv. 20. 'Τὸ δὲ διαμένειν τὰς ψυχὰς οὕτω λέγουσιν, ὅτι διαμένομεν ἡμεῖς ψυχαὶ γενόμενοι, τοῦ σώματος χωρισθέντος καὶ εἰς ἐλάττω μεταβαλόντος οὐσίαν τὴν τῆς ψυχῆς. Τὰς δὲ τῶν ἀφρόνων καὶ ἀλόγων ζώων ψυχὰς συναπόλλυσθαι τοῖς σώμασι.']

les méchants n'auraient-ils aussi reçu le prix de leurs actions mauvaises ? Mais ni Cléanthe, ni Chrysippe, ni leurs disciples grecs ou romains de l'époque impériale ne paraissent avoir admis cette nécessité soit de la récompense, soit de l'expiation ; . . . pour eux toute mauvaise action porte en elle-même son châtiment, et le vice ne paraît heureux qu'aux insensés. Ils ne voulaient pas d'ailleurs qu'on dirigeât les hommes par la crainte des dieux et de leurs vengeances. " Non," disait Chrysippe, " ce n'est pas un bon moyen de détourner les hommes de l'injustice que la crainte des dieux." Il ne faut donc pas traiter les hommes comme des enfants à qui l'on fait peur, et il n'y a de véritable moralité que lorsqu'on aime et qu'on embrasse la vertu pour elle-même et par raison. Voilà le motif, je n'en doute pas, pour lequel les Stoïciens parlaient si peu de l'immortalité de l'âme, et ne se riaient pas moins que les Épicuriens de tout ce qu'on débite sur les enfers. Platon aime à insister sur les croyances populaires ; il est politique autant que moraliste. Les Stoïciens ne sont plus que moralistes ; ils blâment Platon d'avoir eu recours à des fables et presqu'à une fraude, parce que le philosophe ne doit pas remplacer la vérité et la raison par l'imagination, ni la moralité par l'égoïsme et la peur.'

NOTE N, Page 60.

M. Denis, *Idées Morales*, i. 344 :—' Si la loi n'est que la droite raison, elle n'existe que pour les êtres raisonnables. D'où il suit qu'il n'y a aucun droit naturel entre les hommes et les bêtes. Mais il en existe un entre les hommes, et nul ne peut le violer sans crime et sans abjurer la nature, puisque tous participent à la raison. Or, c'est cette participation, cette sorte de parenté rationnelle, qui est le fondement de la justice et de la communauté sociale. Il y a plus : le même droit unit les hommes et les dieux, puisqu'ils ont une origine et une nature communes. Il les rattache les uns et les autres au principe de la nature et de la vérité, à Jupiter, d'où émanent toute justice et toute raison. Que si c'est la communauté de droit qui constitue l'État, il n'y a donc qu'un seul État, comme il n'y a qu'une loi universelle : c'est le monde, république des hommes et des dieux. "Il n'y a pas plus d'États distingués par nature," disait Aristote, "qu'il n'y a naturellement de maisons, d'héritages ou de boutiques de serruriers et de chirurgiens." Donc tous les États de la terre ne le sont que de nom ; le monde seul l'est de fait et de droit. Aussi les Stoïciens ne regardaient-ils pas comme des magistrats ceux qui ne doivent leurs titres et leur autorité qu'aux suffrages du sort ou de la foule. Le seul législateur, le seul magistrat, le seul juge, le seul souverain légitime est le sage. De là ce paradoxe que le sage seul est libre et citoyen, tandis que les insensés ne sont que des exilés, des étrangers et des esclaves. Il y a un grand sens sous ces étranges paroles. . . . Nous trouvons dans cette fiction une haute pensée philosophique, l'idée de la société des esprits, dont Dieu est le père et le souverain. Et quand nous voyons que le Stoïcisme admettait dans cette cité inférieure les esclaves si méprisés des anciens, nous oublions volontiers ses imaginations antiphysiques, pour saluer la première apparition du droit et de l'humanité. . . .' M. Denis adds in a note, a little farther on :—' La théorie de la loi et de la cité universelles a été donnée par quelques modernes comme appartenant surtout à Cicéron et aux Stoïciens postérieurs. C'est une des plus graves erreurs historiques. Quand je n'aurais pas les témoignages de Plutarque, de Clément d'Alexandrie, de Philon et de bien d'autres qui attribuent cette théorie au Stoïcisme en général, je saurais par Cicéron même que c'est là une théorie toute stoïcienne. Dans les Lois il avoue qu'il expose les idées du Portique. Dans les traités des Fins, des Devoirs, de la Nature des Dieux, et dans les Académiques, il donne cette théorie non pour sienne, mais comme appartenant à Zénon et Chrysippe. J'en dis autant de Sénèque, et d'Épictète, qui en parlent toujours comme d'une chose reconnue. Et n'est-il pas question de la loi unique et universelle dans l'hymne même de Cléanthe ?'

The beatification, so to say, of the true philosophers

hereafter, and the spiritual communion of the saints of Stoicism in heaven, is a well-known dogma of the school, though not altogether peculiar to it; for which it is sufficient to cite the verses of Lucan, *Pharsal.* viii. init.:—

'Quodque patet terras inter lunæque meatus
Semidei Manes habitant, quos ignea virtus,
Innocuos vitæ, patientes ætheris imi
Fecit, et æternos animam collegit in orbes.
Non illic auro positi, non thure sepulti
Perveniunt. Illic postquam se lumine vero
Implevit, stellasque vagas miratus et astra
Fixa polis, vidit quanta sub nocte jaceret
Nostra dies. . . .'

Note O, Page 62.

St. Augustin, *De vera Religione,* i. 3:—

'Si enim Plato ipse viveret, et me interrogantem non aspernaretur; vel potius, si quis ejus discipulus, eo ipso tempore quo vivebat, eum interrogaret, cum sibi ab illo persuaderetur, non corporeis oculis, sed pura mente veritatem videri: cui quæcumque anima inhæsisset, eam beatam fieri atque perfectam: ad quam percipiendam mihil magis impedire quam vitam libidinibus deditam et falsas imagines rerum sensibilium, quæ nobis ab hoc sensibili mundo per corpus impressæ, varias opiniones erroresque generarent: quamobrem sanandum esse animum ad intuendam incommutabilem rerum formam, et eodem modo semper se habentem atque undique sui similem pulcritudinem, nec distentam locis, nec tempore variatam, sed unum atque idem omni ex parte servantem, quam non crederent esse homines, cum ipsa vere summeque sit: cætera nasci, occidere, fluere, labi, et tamen in quantum sunt, ab illo æterno Deo per ejus veritatem fabricata constare: in quibus animæ tantum rationali et intellectuali datum est, ut ejus æternitatis contemplatione perfruatur, atque afficiatur orneturque ex ea, æternamque vitam possit mereri: sed dum nascentium atque transeuntium rerum amore ac dolore sauciatur, et dedita consuetudini hujus vitæ atque sensibus corporis, inanibus evanescit imaginibus, irridet eos qui dicunt esse aliquid quod nec istis videatur oculis, nec ullo phantasmate cogitetur, sed mente sola et intelligentia cerni queat:— cum hæc ergo a magistro sibi persuaderentur, si ex eo quæreret ille discipulus, utrum si quisquam existeret vir magnus atque divinus, qui talia populis persuaderet credenda saltem, si percipere non valerent, aut si qui possent percipere, non pravis opinionibus multitudinis implicati, vulgaribus obruerentur erroribus, eum divinis honoribus dignum judicaret:—responderet, credo, ille, non posse hoc ab homine fieri, nisi quem forte ipsa Dei Virtus atque Sapientia ab ipsa rerum natura exceptum, nec hominum magisterio, sed intima illuminatione ab incunabulis illustratum, tanta honestaret gratia, tanta firmitate roboraret, tanta denique majestate subveheret, ut omnia contemnendo quæ pravi homines cupiunt, et omnia perpetiendo quæ horrescunt, et omnia faciendo quæ mirantur, genus humanum ad tam salubrem fidem summo amore atque auctoritate converteret.'

Note P, Page 79.

I cannot better illustrate this subject than by extracts from Amédée Thierry's 'Tableau de l'Empire Romain,' one chapter of which (p. 273, foll.) is entitled 'Marche vers l'Unité par le Droit':—

'Où se décèle avec un surcroît d'évidence cette révolution [marche vers l'unité] dont nous retrouvons partout les vestiges, c'est dans l'histoire du droit romain. . . . On l'y suit pas à pas, depuis la grossière organisation des sujets de Romulus, jusqu'au jour où, de transformations en transformations, ce droit local, devenu une formule applicable à toutes les sociétés, et, comme on l'a dit, la raison écrite, nous annonce à son tour, par la voix de la science juridique, que la petite association des bords du Tibre est devenue aussi l'association universelle.

'Le droit primitif de Rome se montre à nous en effet avec

un caractère de rudesse tout à fait original. La famille y est constituée sur des bases sans analogie ailleurs, les jurisconsultes romains eux-mêmes nous l'affirment : ces bases sont la *puissance paternelle* et la *puissance maritale*, qui se rattache étroitement à la première.

‘Dans cette organisation l'esprit aristocratique domine, la famille a sa règle particulière, son autorité absolue. . . Le droit de propriété, de domaine, est un droit exclusif romain, au moins quant aux immeubles ; l'étranger n'y participe qu'en vertu d'un privilége spécial, comme le Latin et l'Italien. . .

‘Ce droit si fortement marqué au cachet du patriciat, le patriciat s'était réservé le privilége de l'interpréter. Il avait seul le clef de cette procédure à moitié religieuse, de ces jours fastes et néfastes, de ces gestes symboliques, de ces paroles fatales, qui dominaient la loi. Mais les mystères du sacerdoce juridique furent enfin dévoilés. . . . Le droit passe dès-lors de l'état de tradition et de doctrine occulte à l'état de science.

‘Mais tandis que, dans sa sphère propre et dans son développement normal, la jurisprudence civile éprouvait ces grands changements, il s'était ouvert en dehors d'elle une carrière de discussion bien autrement libre, un champ de progrès bien autrement vaste, par la création de la préture. . . . .

‘La préture eut pour objet l'administration de la justice. Papinien en définit les attributions principales par les trois mots, *aider, suppléer, corriger* le droit civil : aider la loi en l'interprétant quand elle était obscure ; la suppléer quand elle était muette ; la corriger quand elle choquait dans l'application le sentiment naturel d'équité, ou quand elle ne concordait plus avec les besoins contemporains et le changement des mœurs. . . . .

‘La juridiction prétorienne avait eu, dès le principe, un grand problème à résoudre, celui-ci : quel droit était applicable aux étrangers ? . . . . Or la loi romaine était, dans toute son étendue, le patrimoine du Romain ; dans certaines proportions déterminées, le privilége du Latin ou de l'Italien ; mais le provincial, mais le sujet d'un gouvernement vassal, quand ils se trouvaient à Rome, ne pouvaient invoquer aucune loi écrite. Quelle législation auraient-ils réclamée comme leur bien ? . . . .

‘ La difficulté fut tranchée comme elle devait l'être : le préteur, dans la nécessité de rendre justice sans loi préétablie, fit la loi lui-même ; son édit, interprétatif du droit civil quant au Romain, fut, quant à l'étranger, un acte législatif pur. Et lorsque le préteur des étrangers vit se presser autour de son tribunal des représentants du monde entier, Européens, Africains, Asiatiques, hommes civilisés, hommes barbares, quand il rendit des sentences qui retentissaient bientôt d'Italie en Grèce, et de Grèce en Asie, le droit prétorien prit une importance, la dignité prétorienne un éclat. . . .

‘ Cette obligation de tout construire imposait l'obligation de chercher et de connaître beaucoup. On se livre avec empressement à l'étude des législations qui régissaient les plus considérables, et les plus éclairées des nations conquises. . . .

‘ Ce ne fut même là qu'un premier degré dans le travail de la généralisation. Des données de l'expérience, l'esprit s'élança vers les spéculations abstraites. Il voulut remonter aux notions éternelles du juste et de l'injuste pour en redescendre, avec des préceptes et des règles de philosophie morale supérieures à tous les faits juridiques, au droit des gens comme au droit civil ; et le *droit naturel* se forma à l'aide de la philosophie grecque, à l'aide surtout du Stoïcisme, dont la doctrine ferme et élevée convenait bien à la gravité des lois. . . . .

‘ Grâce à cette science nouvelle, l'étranger eut sa loi qu'il put invoquer, et qui prit de jour en jour plus de stabilité dans l'édit du préteur. . . . . C'est ainsi qu'il se créa un domaine du droit des gens, qui vint se placer à côté du domaine quiritaire ; une propriété prétorienne, etc. . . . . On aperçoit d'un coup d'œil quelle altération ce mélange dut apporter dans le droit national. Le droit prétorien, devenu synonyme d'*équité*, représenta le bon sens humain et la science philosophique, en opposition à l'interprétation et à la routine du droit civil. . . . .

' C'est à partir de cette époque ' [of the edictum perpetuum of Hadrian and the edictum provinciale of M. Aurelius] ' que le droit romain, fondé sur ses deux bases, également solides désormais, la loi des Douze Tables et l'édit perpétuel, se développe avec le plus de régularité. La lutte féconde des écoles avait produit ses fruits; les idées s'étaient fixées; la conciliation du monde romain, qui marchait alors à si grands pas, accélérait la conciliation du droit civil et du droit des gens, dans les théories de la science. . . . .

' Les travaux des jurisconsultes contemporains de Septime et d'Alexandre Sévère nous montrent l'alliance du droit quiritaire et du droit universel dans son plus beau développement. A mesure qu'on s'éloigne de ce siècle, l'élément national décroît, son sens antique devient de moins en moins compris, son cachet s'efface; et dans la législation de Justinien, d'élagage en élagage, le droit romain se réduit à peu près au droit des gens. . . . .

' Au frontispice de ce grand édifice on lit des lignes telles que celles-ci : —

' " 1. Justitia est constans et perpetua voluntas jus suum cuique tribuendo. Ulpian. l. x. Dig. *de Just. et Jur.*

' " 2. Jurisprudentia est divinarum atque humanarum rerum notitia; justi atque injusti scientia. Ulpian. l. x. Dig. eod. tit.

' " 3. Veluti erga deum religio ; ut parentibus et patriæ pareamus. Pompon. l. ii. Dig. *de Just. et Jur.*

' " 4. Utpote cum jure naturali omnes liberi nascerentur . . . sed postea quam jure gentium servitus invasit. Ulpian. l. iv. Dig. *de Just. et Jur.*

' " Servitus est constitutio juris gentium qua quis dominio alieno contra naturam subjicitur. Florent. l. ix. Dig. *de Stat. hom.*

' " 5. Juris præcepta sunt hæc : Honestè vivere, alterum non lædere, suum cuique tribuere. Ulpian. l. x. Dig. *de Just. et Jur.* . . . . "

' C'est dans ce dernier état que le droit romain nous est arrivé, et qu'il à fondé les mœurs des nations modernes sorties de la société romaine. Il y tient une place immense ; et cette place s'agrandira encore à mesure que les restes de la barbarie féodale disparaîtront en Europe, et que la civilisation s'étendra. " Si les lois romaines," dit Bossuet, " ont paru si saintes que leur majesté subsiste encore, malgré la ruine de l'Empire, c'est que le bon sens, qui est le maître de la vie humaine, y règne partout, et qu'on ne voit nulle part une plus belle application des principes de l'équité naturelle." '

These extracts may suffice to indicate the nature of M. Thierry's argument, which well deserves a more complete study. It must lead to the conclusion that the expansion of Roman law was caused not by the influence of individual statesmen and legislators, in advance of their age, nor by the more general diffusion of philosophical views, nor, again, by the humanizing tendency of Christian sentiments. It was mainly at least the work of natural circumstances; it flowed from the necessity of the position of a conquering people in the centre of a great aggregation of subject communities. The attempt to trace every liberal advance in Roman ideas of law to Christian influence must be regarded as unsuccessful. The rhetoric of a writer like Chateaubriand on such a subject may be dismissed as frivolous. Hugo, in his 'History of Roman Law,' refers to a work of Rhoer directed especially to this point, which does not appear to have deserved much attention. Hugo himself considers the influence of Christianity in this matter to have been, ' on the whole less than might have been expected ' (§ 382), a phrase wanting in clearness and precision. More recently, M. Troplong has written his work ' De l'Influence du Christianisme sur le Droit Civil des Romains,' in which the subject is treated with ample learning, and with all the neatness and logical acumen of a great French scholar, except for the original confusion, as it seems to me, between cause and effect. In the main, I should contend that the expansion of Roman law led to a just appreciation of Christianity, rather than the converse.

Note Q, Page 83.

I have pointed out some particulars in which the teaching of St. Paul seems to be imbued with the ideas of Roman jurisprudence. Seeking to place before his readers the true relation in which the believer stands to God, he adopts significant illustrations from a subject familiar to himself, and familiar perhaps at the same time to those whom he immediately addresses.

1. The mission of our Lord Jesus Christ for the salvation of man is described in Scripture in two ways; sometimes as being done of His own will, sometimes as the accomplishment of a task imposed on Him by the Father. It will be found that while St. John and St. Peter represent it in the former light, St. Paul introduces the notion of the Father's will controlling Him, and insists strongly upon it. Thus we have in St. John's Gospel, xviii. 37: 'To this end was I born, and for this cause came I into the world; that I should bear witness of the truth.' 1 Epist. iii. 16: ' Because He laid down his life for us.' St. Peter, 1. iii. 18: 'Christ also hath once suffered for sins, the just for the unjust.' Comp. iv. 1. In one place St. John passes on towards the other view, where he says (1. iv. 9): ' In this was manifested the love of God towards us, because that God *sent* His only begotten Son into the world that we might live through Him.' But in St. Paul, the view of Christ's work being one of obedience to the Father becomes more prominent. Romans iii. 25: ' Whom God hath set forth to be a propitiation.' V. 19: ' As by one man's disobedience many were made sinners, so by the obedience of one shall many be made righteous.' Gal. i. 4: 'Who gave Himself for our sins, . . . according to the will of God the Father.' Phil. ii. 8: '· Who . . . humbled Himself and became obedient unto death.' Col. i. 19: 'It pleased the Father that in Him should all fulness dwell; and having made peace through the blood of His cross, by Him to reconcile all things unto Himself.' Heb. v. 8: 'Though

He were a son, yet learned He obedience by the things which He suffered.' Comp. x. 7. It is not meant that there is any real discrepancy in the two views here indicated, but that the one apostle dwells more upon the obedience of Christ, the others on the spontaneousness of His sacrifice.

But this notion of the absolute subjection of the Son to the Father agrees exactly with the well-known principle of Roman law involved in the patria potestas, or authority of the father. Down to a late period of the Empire, the law of the Twelve Tables, which gave the father power over the person and property of his son, even after he had come of age, continued, at least in theory, unabated. Gaius, under the Antonines, still speaks of it as peculiar to Roman law (*Institut.* i. 55):—' Item in potestate nostra sunt liberi nostri quos justis nuptiis procreavimus, quod jus proprium civium Romanorum est; fere enim nulli alii sunt homines, qui talem in filios suos habent potestatem, qualem nos habemus.' He adds: ' nec me præterit Galatarum gentem credere in potestate parentum liberos esse.'

It is curious at least that these Galatians should be the persons whom St. Paul addressed in the following language (Gal. iv. 1): ' Now I say that the heir, as long as he is a child, differeth nothing from a servant, though he be lord of all; but is under tutors and governors until the time appointed of the father. Even so we, when we were children, were in bondage under the elements of the world. But when the fulness of time was come, God sent forth His Son,' &c. So in Romans viii. 21, the ' bondage of corruption ' seems to allude to the subjection of the Roman son to his earthly father.

2. In the Epistle to the Galatians, iii. 15, we read : ἀδελφοὶ, κατὰ ἄνθρωπον λέγω, ὅμως ἀνθρώπου κεκυρωμένην διαθήκην οὐδεὶς ἀθετεῖ ἢ ἐπιδιατάσσεται, where the apostle declares that he is making use of an illustration from secular customs, and seems to refer to the Roman law of wills, according to which the testator, after certain formalities fulfilled, could neither revoke nor alter his disposition of his property. Thus

when we are told by Suetonius that Cæsar, and subsequently Augustus, placed their testaments in the hands of the Vestal Virgins (*Jul.* 83, *Oct.* 101), we are to understand that they thereby renounced the power of cancelling or adding a codicil to them. Comp. Schleusner in voce διαθήκη. See also the above-cited passage from the same epistle, iv. 1.

Again, in the Epistle to the Hebrews, there seems to be such a reference to the Roman law of testation, where, however, the writer apparently mixes up the ideas of a covenant and of a will. *Hebr.* ix. 15-17: καὶ διὰ τοῦτο διαθήκης καινῆς μεσίτης ἐστίν, κ. τ. λ. He had been describing Jesus Christ as the mediator or intermediate instrument of a new *covenant*, διαθήκη, as opposed to the old covenant made by God with Moses; but he goes on to introduce the idea of a *will*, suggested apparently by the death of Christ, the word διαθήκη having the double signification: ὅπου γὰρ διαθήκη, θάνατον ἀνάγκη φέρεσθαι τοῦ διαθεμένου. διαθήκη γὰρ ἐπὶ νεκροῖς βεβαία, ἐπεὶ μή ποτε ἰσχύει ὅτε ζῇ ὁ διαθέμενος; which Schleusner explains: 'ut testamentum ratum fiat necesse est ut mors testatoris probetur judicialiter. . . Sic *proferre*, ut sit *probare coram judice,* legitur apud Cic. *pro Rosc. Amer.* c. 24.' This forensic use here of the word φέρεσθαι is remarked by Hammond, and is generally admitted.

This coincidence in the use of forensic language in an acknowledged epistle of St. Paul's, and another which must at least be regarded as Pauline, is worth remarking, particularly when we consider how peculiar the forms of testamentary law were to the Romans. 'To the Romans,' says Mr. Maine, 'belongs preeminently the credit of inventing the will. . . . It is doubtful whether a true power of testation was known to any original society except the Romans. Rudimentary forms of it occur here and there, but most of them are not exempt from the suspicion of a Roman origin. The Athenian will was, no doubt, indigenous, but then, as will appear presently, it was only an inchoate testament . . . Similarly the rudimentary testament which (as I am informed) the Rabbinical Jewish law provides for, has been attributed to contact with the Romans. . . . The original institutions of Jews have provided nowhere for the privileges of testatorship.'—*Ancient Law*, p. 194, foll.

3. Upon these apparent illustrations from the Roman law I should, however, lay little stress, were they not confirmed by an unquestionable reference in the use St. Paul makes of the idea of adoption. The spiritual connection of the true disciple with God is repeatedly represented to us under the figure of sonship. This idea is brought prominently forward by St. John; as in 1 iii. 1 : ἵνα τέκνα θεοῦ κληθῶμεν, 'that we should be called,' i.e., ' should be, sons of God.' v. 9 : ὁ γεγεννημένος ἐκ τοῦ θεοῦ. v. 10 : τὰ τέκνα τοῦ θεοῦ. iv. 6 : πᾶς ὁ ἀγαπῶν ἐκ θεοῦ γεγένηται; and elsewhere. But whereas St. John always represents this idea in its simple form, St. Paul, and St. Paul only, describes this sonship more artificially as adoptive. This view is set forth in a marked manner in the Epistle to the Romans, viii. 14, foll. : ' As many as are led by the Spirit of God, they are the sons of God. For ye have not received the spirit of bondage again to fear ; but ye have received the Spirit of adoption whereby we cry Abba, Father. . . .; 21: Because the creature itself also shall be delivered from the bondage of corruption into the glorious liberty of the children of God. For we know that the whole creation groaneth and travaileth in pain together until now. And not only they, but ourselves also, which have the first fruits of the Spirit, even we ourselves groan within ourselves, waiting for the adoption, to wit, the redemption of our body." Now this illustration is not taken from any Jewish custom ; the law of Moses contains no provision for such a practice, nor is there any indication of its having obtained among the Jewish people. Adoption was an essentially Roman usage, and was intimately connected with the Roman ideas of family. The maintenance of the *sacra privata*, the domestic rites of the family, was regarded by the Romans as a matter of deep political importance, and their law accordingly described minutely the forms under which, in default of natural heirs, the paterfamilias might thus prospectively secure it. The son

was considered as the absolute property of his father from his birth to his father's decease. In order to his being adopted out of his own family into that of another man, it was necessary that he should undergo a fictitious sale. But if a son was sold by his father and recovered his liberty, he fell again under the paternal dominion, and it was not until he had thus been sold, *emancipatus,* three times, that he was finally free from this paramount authority. Accordingly the adopter required that the fiction of sale should be repeated three times before he could be received into his new family and fall under the dominion of his new father. When, however, these formalities had been complied with, the adopted son became incorporated in the family of his adopter, identified as it were with his person, made one with him; so that on the decease of the adopter he became not so much his representative as the perpetuator of his legal existence. He assumed also, on adoption, the burdens or privileges incident to the performance of the rites of his new family. He relinquished his former sacra, and attached himself to those of his new parent.

All this appears to have been in the apostle's mind when he addressed the Roman disciples in the passage before us. The Spirit of God, he says, bears witness with our spirit, confers upon us an inward persuasion, that we are now, by adoption, the children of God, whereas we were before the children of some other father, the world, or the Evil One. But we are delivered from the bondage of corruption, from the state of filial subjection to this evil parent, and admitted to the glorious liberty of the happy children of a good and gracious father, even God. He goes on to insist on the hardness of the bondage of the son of a bad father (such as the world), his sighing and groaning for the blessed change which should henceforth ensue to him; such an expectation or hope of escape as may often have been felt by the victims of the cruel law of Rome, and which is here likened to the hopes mankind might be supposed to feel of an escape at last from their bondage to the world, the flesh, and the devil. And how was this escape to be effected? God paid a price for it. As the Roman adopter paid, or made as if he paid down copper weighed in the scale, so God gave His Son as a precious sacrifice, as a ransom to the world or the Evil One, from whom He redeemed His adopted children. ' He spared not His own Son, but delivered Him up for us all.' Henceforth we become the elect, the chosen of God.

The same illustration is indicated in a passage in Galatians, iv. 3: 'When we were children we were in bondage under the elements of the world,' addicted to the sacra of our original family; 'but when the fulness of the time was come, God sent forth His Son . . . to redeem them that were under the law, that we might receive the adoption of sons. . . . Howbeit,' it continues, 'when ye knew not God,' and were not enrolled in this family, 'ye did service unto them which by nature are no gods. But now, after ye have known God . . . how turn ye again to the weak and beggarly elements,' such as the sacra of your former family, 'whereunto ye desire to be again in bondage?'

The 'adoption of children' is mentioned again in Ephesians i. 5, where it seems to point to a recognised custom. Ephesus, it may be remarked, as the capital of the province and the residence of a proconsul's court, must have been familiar with the ordinary processes of the Roman civil law.

On the word 'Adoption,' the writer of the article in Smith's 'Dictionary of the Bible' says: 'St. Paul probably alludes to the Roman custom of adoption, &c. . . The Jews themselves were unacquainted with the process of adoption; indeed, it would have been inconsistent with the regulations of the Mosaic law affecting the inheritance of property. The instances occasionally adduced as referring to the customs (Gen. xv. 8, xvi. 2, xxx. 5-9) are evidently not cases of adoption proper.'

Note R, Page 84.

There seem to be some indications in the Scripture records that St. Paul was considered, both at Rome and among the Romans and the governing class in the provinces, as a person of some social rank and distinction. The respect with which he is treated by Festus and Felix, Agrippa and Gallio, implies that the rulers in the provinces regarded him as of a somewhat different stamp from the Jews, the mere subject-provincials, with whom he had connected himself. The courteous treatment he received on his voyage to Italy, and by the chief men of the island of Melita, accords with this view of his position. The consideration extended to him, apparently beyond his expectation, at Rome; his being allowed to dwell, while awaiting the judgment which he had claimed of the emperor himself, in a private residence under the surveillance of the police, attests the same consideration. To this may be added the fact, which it seems reasonable to admit, that the place assigned him for his sojourn was within the precincts of the Imperial quarters, as they may be called, on the Palatine; and that his preaching was attended by the Greek and Jewish freedmen attached to the Imperial household. Even before his arrival at Rome the Church of Christ in the city comprised members of the upper class of freedmen, that is, the clients and dependents, often prosperous, wealthy, and accomplished, of noble Roman houses. They 'of the household of Narcissus' may have been such dependents of the celebrated favourite of Claudius, lately dead, a freedman himself, but equal in wealth and position to most of the old patrician heads of families. Names identical with those of several persons included in St. Paul's salutations to disciples at Rome, such as Tryphæna, Philologus, Amplias, Hermas, have been found among the sepulchral inscriptions in the columbaria of the Claudian Cæsars; and it is difficult to resist the conjecture that many of those whom the apostle addressed as recognised members of a circle of devout inquirers, and at last converts to the Gospel at Rome, were domestics of the Imperial palace. So a little later he himself sends from Rome the greetings of 'many of Cæsar's household.' The curiosity at Rome about Jewish opinions and customs, and the progress they had made there among the Romans themselves, as well as among resident foreigners, is strikingly witnessed in the literature of the Augustan age. The reaction against them after the great revolt in Palestine, is strongly marked in the change of tone observable in Tacitus, Juvenal, and Martial, as compared with that of Ovid and Tibullus.

Notwithstanding the persecutions under Nero and Domitian the Gospel continued, I believe, to attract notice in high quarters at Rome; and the staid, reserved, and almost tame character of Roman Christianity, compared with its more salient and vigorous features in Greece, in Africa, and in Egypt, in the first ages, may perhaps be ascribed to an early and continued connection with the court and courtly society. The curious history of Callistus, in the reign of Commodus, as detailed in the work of Hippolytus, seems to indicate a fatal degeneracy among the Roman Christians, resulting from this very connection.

Note S, Page 91.

It is common among the freethinkers of modern times to augur the constant moral advance of society, in conformity with its advance in material knowledge. Impatient at the slow progress they observe in this moral movement, they are tempted to impute it to the discouragement which the Christian teaching throws, as they say, upon it. They accuse Revelation of turning men's thoughts backward to a pretended Paradise, a past state of original bliss which can never be regained in this life. Such, they declare, is the teaching of all *mythologies*; the fancy of a golden age deteriorating to a silver, a brazen, and an iron age. On the other hand, Philosophy, they allege, has generally taken the opposite view, and, tracing mankind back to its cradle in the primeval Past, has represented it as developing, advancing, improving, from then till now, and capable of indefinite improvement in the illimitable future. Lucretius, no doubt, in a well-known passage (v. 923 sqq.), in accordance with the Epicurean denial of a Providence, does so trace the history of man to his first crude, barbarous origin, and marks the various stages of his material and moral progress. Nor is it the philosopher only who resorts to this solution. Many of the mythological legends of classical antiquity point to a belief in such a progressive development, and going much farther back than Lucretius, derive man from the first elements of nature, from animals, from birds, from trees, and from stones. I do not find, however, in Lucretius, any expectation of a continuous progress hereafter. With him morals, no doubt, as well as arts, 'ad summum venere cacumen.' The ancient philosophers held that the species had fully attained the limits of its progress. They admitted the existence of a principle of evil in the world, which leavened, and must continue to leaven, the mass to all time, and keep the moral world at least at a standstill, if it did not, according to the common persuasion of mankind, gradually corrupt and undermine it altogether. The common opinion, derived neither from philosophers nor from mythologies, but from men's personal experience, and their disappointment at the constant frustration and baffling of their own hopes and efforts, represented man as ever declining from the height to which he had by some happy providence attained, and gliding down a fatal incline to an ever worsening Future. The sentiments of Virgil and Horace, 'omnia fatis in pejus ruere;' 'ætas parentum pejor avis,' &c., seem to me fully borne out by the general feeling of antiquity at the period of its highest moral and material attainments. If, indeed, we have more sanguine aspirations in our modern schools of thought, it is to the teaching of Christianity itself that we mainly owe them. For Christianity first led men to look stedfastly to the future, and to hope for the attainment of consummate perfection hereafter through gradual, and feeble, and imperfect attempts at improvement here. The theory of Christianity is the most temperate, the most modest, and, as far as appearances have hitherto gone, the truest theory of moral development.

The later Greek philosophy is distinguished by its ever-deepening sense of the universality, and the real evil of sin. 'We have already seen,' says Döllinger (*Gentile and Jew*, ii. 153, Engl. trans.), ' what a close connection there was between the defective knowledge which the old philosophy had of human freedom and of the nature of evil, with the relation in which the Deity stood to both. These thinkers were wanting in an insight into the nature and conditions of the personality of God as well as of men; and therefore looked upon evil as partly resulting from mere defectiveness or infirmity of means of knowledge; they set it down to ignorance, and thought, accordingly, there was no other or higher remedy than philosophy. And partly from not distinguishing between the physical evil and the moral bad, they charged matter and its natural repugnance to the intellectual with being the source of the bad. Hence, the idea of sin was in fact strange to them; they had no perception how a free act of evil done by the creature bore upon divine holiness and justice. In fine, the Stoics had further obscured this important question by their theory that evil was as absolutely necessary in the order of the world as the shadow is to the light, and that all evil was equal. They raised man above all responsibility and account, and represented him as without freedom, the irresistibly determined tool of destiny. Even the Emperor Marcus Aurelius, with his mild temperament, found a complete justification herein for the greatest criminal. A man of a certain nature can do nothing else but act viciously. To make him responsible for his actions would be on a par with punishing another for having bad breath, or bidding a fig-tree bear anything besides figs. It was utterly impossible for vicious men to act otherwise than we see them act, and to demand impossibilities is folly.

'This view of evil was expressly combated by Platonists like Plutarch. Evil had not come into the world like an episode, pleasant and acceptable to the Deity; it filled every human thing. The whole of life, equally stained from its opening to its concluding scene, was a mass of errors and misfortune, and in no part pure and blameless. "No one," he said, "is sober enough for virtue; but we all of us are unseemly and in unblest confusion." This severe notion of evil, its universality in the life of man, and the deep roots it had struck in his nature, is a characteristic of thinkers of this period. We meet with similar expressions in Seneca, to the effect that not a man will be found who does not sin, has not sinned, and will not continue sinning to his dying hour. Galen, a physician, and at the same time one of the acutest of the philosophers of this latter time, went farther still. He declared the dispositions of children to evil to be in excess, and thought that only by little and little the disposition to good got the upper hand, the more the intelligent soul got the mastery over the two others, for he adopted with Plato a "threefold division of the soul."

'The solution of the problem of the origin of evil appeared all the more difficult now. All did not accept the comfortable expedient of Platonists like Celsus, of its having sprung from matter in existence from eternity; or, like Plutarch, who accepted an evil and eternal world-soul, and an unintelligent element of essential evil in the soul of man. Maximus of Tyre, therefore, thought that Alexander, instead of consulting the oracle of Ammon about the sources of the Nile, should rather have put a question of importance to humanity generally, namely, that of the origin of evil. He then made an attempt of his own at a solution, which only ended again in placing the seat and fount of all evil in matter. (M. Anton., *Medit.* ix. 1; x. 30; viii. 14; v. 28. Plutarch, *Adv. Stoic.* 14. Senec. *de Clement.* i. 6. Maximus Tyr. *Diss.* xli. p. 487 seq.)'

Note T, Page 94.

After describing the rebellious attitude of the Stoic philosophy towards the Cæsars, and the measures of the government to control it, M. Denis says (*Idées Morales*, vol. ii. p. 62 foll.:—'Le Stoïcisme grandit dans cette lutte de l'esprit contre la force brutale. Il devint une foi ardente et vigoureuse, une sorte de religion des grandes âmes, qui eut ses dévots et ses martyrs. . . . . De là les caractères nouveaux du Stoïcisme ; le ton de la prédication remplaçant la discussion philosophique, une science jusqu'alors inconnue de la vie, et un art singulier de démêler les plus obscurs sophismes du vice et de la faiblesse, mais par-dessus une austère tendresse pour l'humanité. Le philosophe n'est plus un logicien qui dispute, ni un beau parleur, qui cherche les applaudissements. C'est un maître qui enseigne ; c'est un censeur public, chargé du soin des consciences ; c'est un témoin de Dieu, qui ne doit aux hommes que la vérité. . . . Il ne faut pas chercher dans ces philosophes de profonds et subtils raisonnements, mais des conseils affectueux ou sévères, des remontrances, des exhortations, et d'instantes prières de se convertir à la vertu et à la loi de Dieu. . .'

Note U, Page 97.

Epictet. *Dissertat.* iv. c. 8 : Ἄνθρωπε, χειμάσκησον πρῶτον· ἰδοῦ σου τὴν ὁρμήν . . . ἀγνοεῖσθαι μελέτησον πρῶτον τίς εἶ· σαυτῷ φιλοσόφησον ὀλίγον χρόνον. Οὕτω καρπὸς γίνεται· κατορυγῆναι δεῖ ἐπί τινα χρόνον τὸ σπέρμα, κρυφθῆναι, κατὰ μικρὸν αὐξηθῆναι, ἵνα τελεσφορηθῇ . . . τοιοῦτον εἶ καὶ σὺ φυτάριον. Θᾶττον τοῦ δέοντος ἤνθηκας, ἀποκαύσει σε ὁ χειμών. κ. τ. λ. . . . c. 10. Ἀγαθὸς ὢν ἀποθάνῃ, γενναίαν πρᾶξιν ἐπιτελῶν· ἐπεὶ γὰρ δεῖ πάντως ἀποθανεῖν, ἀνάγκη τί ποτε ποιοῦντα εὑρεθῆναι . . . τί οὖν θέλεις ποιῶν εὑρεθῆναι ὑπὸ τοῦ θανάτου ; Ἐγὼ μὲν, τὸ ἐμὸν μέρος, ἔργον τί ποτ' ἀνθρωπικὸν, εὐεργετικὸν, κοινωφελὲς, γενναῖον. . . . c. 12.

Τί οὖν; δυνατὸν ἀναμάρτητον ἤδη εἶναι; 'Αμήχανον· ἀλλ'
ἐκεῖνο δυνατὸν, πρὸς τὸ μὴ ἁμαρτάνειν τετάσθαι διηνεκῶς.
. . . Νῦν δ' ὅταν εἴπῃς, Ἀπ' αὔριον προσέξω· ἴσθι ὅτι
τοῦτο λέγεις, Σήμερον ἔσομαι ἀναίσχυντος, ἄκαιρος, ταπεινός.
. . . Βλέπε, ὅσα κακὰ σεαυτῷ ἐπιτρέπεις. κ. τ. λ.

Seneca, *Epist.* xciv. 52: Nonne apparet nobis opus esse
aliquo advocato, qui contra populi præcepta præcipiat?
Nulla ad nostras aures vox impune perfertur: nocent qui
optant, nocent qui exsecrantur. Nam et horum imprecatio
falsos nobis metus inserit, et illorum amor male docet bene
optando . . . Non licet, inquam, ire recta via: trahunt in
pravum parentes, trahunt servi: nemo errat uni sibi, sed dementiam spargit in proximos, accipitque invicem. Et ideo
in singulis vitia populorum sunt, quia illa populus dedit.
Dum facit quisque pejorem, factus est. Didicit deteriora,
deinde docuit; effectaque est ingens illa nequitia, congesto in
unum, quod cuique pessimum scitur. Sit ergo aliquis custos,
et aurem subinde pervellat, abigatque rumores, et reclamet
populis laudantibus. Erras enim si existimas nobiscum
vitia nasci; supervenerunt, ingesta sunt. Itaque monitio-
nibus crebris opiniones quæ nos circumsonant compescamus.
Nulli nos vitio natura conciliat; nos illa integros ac liberos
genuit . . . . . Itaque si in medio urbium fremitu collocati
sumus, stet ad latus monitor, et contra laudatores ingentium
patrimoniorum laudet parvo divitem, et usu opes metientem,
&c.

M. Antoninus, *Meditat.* vi. 30: Ὅρα μὴ ἀποκαισαρωθῇς,
μὴ βαφῇς· γίνεται γάρ· τήρησον οὖν σεαυτὸν ἁπλοῦν,
ἀγαθὸν, ἀκέραιον, σεμνὸν, ἄκομψον, τοῦ δικαίου φίλον, θεοσεβῆ,
εὐμενῆ, φιλόστοργον, ἐρρωμένον πρὸς τὰ πρέποντα ἔργα.
ἀγώνισαι, ἵνα τοιοῦτος συμμείνῃς, οἷον σε ἠθέλησε ποιῆσαι
φιλοσοφία. αἰδοῦ θεούς, σώζε ἀνθρώπους. βραχὺς ὁ βίος.
εἷς καρπὸς τῆς ἐπιγείου ζωῆς, διάθεσις ὁσία, καὶ πράξεις
κοινωνικαί. πάντα,ὡς 'Αντωνίνου μαθητής. . . . . κ. τ. λ.

Plutarch, *De cohibenda ira*, 2, reports the saying of
Musonius Rufus: Καὶ μὴν ὧν γε μεμνήμεθα Μουσωνίου καλῶν
ἕν ἐστιν . . . τὸ δεῖν ἀεὶ θεραπευομένους βιοῦν τοὺς σώζεσθαι

μέλλοντας. Οὐ γὰρ ὡς ἐλλέβορον, οἴμαι, δεῖ θεραπεύσαντα συνεκφέρειν τῷ νοσήματι τὸν λόγον, ἀλλ' ἐμμένοντα τῇ ψυχῇ, συνέχειν τὰς κρίσεις καὶ φυλάσσειν. κ. τ. λ.

The gravity of this sage's teaching is further indicated by Aulus Gellius, *Noct. Att.* v. 1: Musonium philosophum solitum dicere accepimus: Quum philosophus, inquit, hortatur, monet, suadet, objurgat, aliudve quid disciplinarum disserit; tum, qui audiunt, si summo et soluto pectore obvias vulgatasque laudes effutiunt, si clamitant etiam, si vocum ejus festivitatibus, si modulis verborum, si quibusdam quasi frequentamentis orationis moventur, exagitantur et gestiunt; tum scias et qui dicit et qui audit frustra esse: neque illic philosophum loqui, sed tibicinem canere. Animus is, inquit, audientis philosophum, si, quæ dicuntur, utilia ac salubria sunt, et errorum atque vitiorum medicinas ferunt, laxamentum atque otium prolixe profuseque laudandi non habet: quisquis ille est qui audit, nisi ille est plane deperditus, inter ipsam philosophi orationem et perhorrescat necesse est, et pudeat tacitus, et pœniteat et gaudeat et admiretur: (seqq.)

Note V, Page 99.

Seneca, *Epist.* xlviii. 6, 7, 8: Vis scire quid philosophia promittat generi humano? Consilium. Alium mors vocat, alium paupertas urit, alium divitiæ vel alienæ torquent, vel suæ: ille malam fortunam horret, hic se felicitati suæ subducere cupit: hunc homines male habent, illum Dii. Quid mihi lusoria ista proponis? Non est jocandi locus; ad miseros advocatus es. Opem te laturum naufragis, captis, ægris, egentibus, intentæ securi subjectum præstantibus caput pollicitus es: quo diverteris? quid agis? hic cum quo ludis, timet. Succurre: quid quod laqueati despondent: in pœnis omnes undique ad te manus tendunt, perditæ vitæ, periturææque auxilium aliquod implorant, in te spes opesque sunt. Rogant ut ex tanta illos volutatione extrahas, ut disjectis et errantibus clarum veritatis lumen ostendas. Dic, quid. Natura necessarium fecerit, quid supervacuum, quam faciles leges posuerit; quam jucunda sit vita, quam expedita, illas sequentibus; quam acerba et implicita eorum, qui opinioni plus quam naturæ crediderunt.

Note W, Page 102.

Döllinger, *Gentile and Jew*, ii. 148 (Engl. transl.):—
'Since the middle of the first century after Christ, a growing prominence was observable in the return to a more believing disposition. One feels that a great change has taken place in the intellectual atmosphere when one compares Polybius, Strabo, Diodorus, and Dionysius with Plutarch, Aristides, Maximus of Tyre, and Dion Chrysostom.'

M. Martha has given a sketch of the Sophists of the second century, and of the character and teaching of Dion Chrysostom as their representative, from which I quote a paragraph in illustration of the views advanced in the text (*Revue Contemporaine*, tome xxxi. p. 246. 1857):—

'Parmi ces orateurs qui remplissaient le monde de leur parole et de leur gloire, il en est un petit nombre qui ont fait de l'éloquence un noble usage en répandant partout les préceptes de la morale. Il faut remarquer ici qu'aux plus tristes époques de l'histoire ancienne, c'est la philosophie seule qui soutient encore les esprits, les âmes, et résiste à cette lente dégradation morale qui menace de tout envahir. Pendant que la politique est impuissante, que les princes ne peuvent rien ou ne tentent rien pour relever les mœurs, pendant que le monde se plonge de plus en plus dans la corruption ou s'amuse à des futilités sophistiques, quelques philosophes, à la faveur de ces usages qui permettaient au premier venu de prendre la parole dans les assemblées, se glissent au milieu de la foule tumultueuse et font entendre, non sans péril parfois, quelques leçons de sagesse. C'est la philosophie qui est la dernière gardienne de la raison et de la dignité dans les sociétés antiques. Elle survit aux lois, aux institutions, aux mœurs; elle échappe même à la tyrannie, parce qu'elle peut se réfugier dans l'invisible sanctuaire d'un cœur honnête. La matière ne lui manque jamais, puisque, l'âme humaine étant le sujet de ses études, elle porte avec soi l'objet de ses méditations. Bien plus, le malheur du temps ne fait souvent que raviver sa force, la corruption des mœurs l'irrite, la dégradation des caractères l'anime d'une ardeur plus généreuse, et la vue de la servilité lui fait sentir tout le prix de la liberté intérieure. Aussi ne faut-il s'étonner si les dernières paroles sensées, raisonnables, éloquentes, sortent de la bouche des philosophes.

'Cependant il faut reconnaître que l'enseignement philosophique était bien déchu. Il s'est fait simple et modeste, et, renonçant aux grandes idées et aux problèmes savants qu'il agitait autrefois, il ne donne plus que des préceptes de conduite. Ce n'est plus le temps où de puissantes écoles établissaient, chacune à sa manière, les règles de la morale, et fondaient de vastes systèmes dont les principes et les conséquences étaient défendus avec une sorte de foi jalouse. Les hautes études de la philosophie se sont affaiblies ; on n'aime plus les recherches abstraites ni les déductions rigoureuses, et même on peut dire que les disciples ne comprennent plus la parole du maître. Les doctrines rivales de Platon, d'Aristote, de Zénon, d'Épicure, qui alors se partagent les esprits, se sont fait tant d'emprunts et de concessions réciproques qu'on a de la peine à distinguer, dans les ouvrages du temps, ce qui appartient aux unes et aux autres. Les philosophes se disent encore de telle ou telle école, ils en portent le nom et souvent le costume, mais ils ne s'apercoivent pas qu'ils sont infidèles à la doctrine qu'ils enseignent. Celui-ci se croit Stoïcien et adopte les idées de Platon sur l'âme et l'immortalité ; celui-là, voulant s'éloigner un peu des sévérités du Portique, glisse à son insu dans les molles délices d'Épicure. Tous ces compromis et ces transactions entre les diverses écoles amènent le discrédit de la philosophie dogmatique. Quand les doctrines ne s'affirment pas fortement elles-mêmes, quand elles ne sont pas exclusives, quand elles pactisent avec l'ennemi, elles ne peuvent plus compter sur des adeptes dévoués. Aussi, soit affaiblissement général des études, soit indifférence, soit tolérance excessive, presque tous les bons esprits de ce siècle s'abstiennent de traiter les hautes questions de la métaphysique et de la morale, ou s'ils les tentent quelquefois, ils confondent tous les systèmes, et ne laissent voir trop souvent que leur légèreté et leur ignorance. La philosophie aspire à devenir populaire, elle s'abaisse, elle se fait toute à tous, et pour être comprise et acceptée, elle puise ses idées non plus à la source élevée du dogme, mais dans le réservoir commun qu'on appelle le bon sens public; elle se rapproche de plus en plus de la pratique, et se contente de donner des prescriptions salutaires et incontestables, qu'elle rédige en maximes et qu'elle décore d'ornements littéraires. De là une nouvelle espèce d'éloquence qui n'est pas sans portée ni sans mérite, celle de ces orateurs philosophes qu'on appelle aussi des sophistes, et qui seraient dignes d'un nom plus honorable.'

Of these preaching philosophers, the most eminent are Apollonius of Tyana, and Dion Chrysostom. The career of the latter, as an itinerant preacher of moral truths, may be traced in his own genuine writings. We may infer nearly the same of Apollonius from various sources, but his reputed biography by Philostratus is a work of more than a century later, and is evidently fabricated for a polemical purpose. It represents its hero as a heathen counterpart to Christ, and is valuable to us, as showing the impression made upon the heathen mind by the portraiture of our Lord, and after Him of His Apostles, as 'going about doing good.' The points of evident imitation of the Gospel history in the 'Life of Apollonius' are given in full detail by M. Pressensé, *Hist. des Trois Premiers Siècles*, 2e partie, tome ii. p. 145 foll. The Lives of the Sophists by Philostratus and Eunapius discover to us a whole class of such itinerant preachers among the heathen philosophers of the second century. Others of a similar school of moral teaching fixed themselves in the great universities of the empire, or passed their lives in private retirement. The expression quoted in the text was that of Demonax, commemorated by Lucian :—'Αθηναίων δὲ σκεπτομένων κατὰ ζῆλον τὸν πρὸς Κορινθίους καταστήσασθαι θέαν μονομάχων, προσελθὼν εἰς αὐτούς, μὴ πρότερον, ἔφη, ταῦτα, ὦ' Αθηναῖοι ψηφίσεσθε, ἂν μὴ τοῦ ἐλέου τὸν βωμὸν καθέλητε. A similar sarcasm is attributed also to Apollonius. The sentiment was perhaps common to many. Demonax is said also to have quelled a tumult in Athens by the authority of his presence. Στάσεως δέ ποτε 'Αθήνῃσι γενομένης εἰσῆλθεν εἰς τὴν ἐκκλησίαν, καὶ φανεὶς μόνον σιωπᾶν ἐποίησεν αὐτούς· ὁ δὲ, ἰδὼν ἤδη μετεγνωκότας, οὐδὲν εἰπὼν καὶ αὐτὶς ἀπηλλάγη.—Lucian, *Demonax*, 57, 64.

Note X, Page 104.

Denis, *Idées Morales*, ii. p. 154:—' Le Stoïcisme ne s'arrêtait point là: à la théorie de la justice universelle, ou de l'égalité des hommes et de l'unité de notre espèce, il ajoutait celle de l'universelle charité.' The writer proceeds to give a full exposition of this thesis, pp. 154-190. The doctrines and practice of Pagan philanthropy, at their best and highest, fall far below the standard of the teaching and the practice of Christian communities. Nevertheless, they deserve to be noted in token of the purifying effect of that consciousness of moral infirmity which entered, as I believe, so deeply into the minds of the heathen, in the second and third centuries. Cicero's slight mention of his father's death in a letter to Atticus—' Pater nobis decessit A.D. viii. Kal. Dec.'(*Ad. Att.* i. 6)—is often quoted as an instance of the hardness of feeling engendered by habit and system among the Pagans in the palmiest days of their philosophy. Considering how scanty are the traces of more humane sentiment in respect of natural ties among the Romans of that age, we may be justified in so quoting it. But it is interesting to contrast with it the tribute of refined and cultivated affection which Statius, a hundred and fifty years later, pays to his deceased parent :—

> Quid referam expositos servato pondere mores;
> Quæ pietas, quam vile lucrum ; quæ cura pudoris,
> Quantus amor recti; rursusque, ubi dulce remitti,
> Gratia quæ vultus, animo quam nulla senectus?

The poet continues, indeed, to expatiate on the theme with a too elaborate rhetoric, which has cast suspicion on the genuineness of his feelings. But, however this may be, it is not to the feelings of Statius himself, but to the feelings of the age, which demanded or encouraged such a manifestation, that I principally look. Comp. Statius, *Sylv.* iii. 3, 12, and foll.

There is another passage in Cicero's letters, often cited, in which he checks himself for the sorrow he cannot help experiencing on the death of a confidential and favourite slave, the companion of his studies, and partaker in his philosophical speculations; and this is contrasted with the more natural and liberal flow of sentiment in which the younger Pliny allows himself to indulge on a somewhat similar loss. But Statius, again, with deeper and kindlier feeling, allows to the favourite slave of his friend a place in Elysium, and is not ashamed to suggest that he may there watch over the interests of his master surviving him on earth. How great a step in humanity has been made from the cold exclusiveness of the Platonists and the Stoics, even in the most genial of their respective representatives, a Virgil and a Lucan!

Statius, *Sylv.* ii. 6 :—

> Sæpe ille volentem
> Castigabat herum, studioque altisque juvabat
> Consiliis . . . . . Subit illo pios, carpitque quietem
> Elysiam . . . . .
> Pone, precor, questus ; alium tibi fata Philetum,
> Forsan et ipse dabit ; moresque habitusque decoros
> Monstrabit gaudens, similemque docebit amorem.

Note Y, Page 115.

Seneca, as quoted by St. Augustine, *De Civ. Dei*, vi. 11, had said of the Jews: Cum interim usque eo sceleratissimæ gentis consuetudo convaluit, ut per omnes jam terras recepta sit, victi victoribus leges dederunt. He was speaking, it seems, of the *sacramenta*, or mysterious rites and customs of this people; and from the context it appears plainly that he had more particularly in view the Jewish observation of the Sabbath. We learn from Ovid and Tibullus how much remark this usage had excited among the Romans, and with what favour it was regarded by them. The socialist Proudhon has written a book to recommend it on purely economical grounds, and I can easily imagine a practical people, like the Romans, being struck with the good policy of such an institution. At a later period, when the Jews had fallen out of favour at Rome, their Sabbaths are made the subject of scorn and ridicule.

Note Z, Page 117.

Denis, *Idées Morales*, ii. 234 foll.:—'Mais ce qui nous semble nouveau, ce qu'on ne retrouverait pas au même degré dans Chrysippe, dans Cléanthe, ni dans Platon, c'est la pensée toujours présente de la Providence, et de la bonté divine, c'est le sentiment de ferveur et de foi, qui anime des âmes fortes et tendres, telles qu'Épictète et Marc-Aurèle. Dieu n'est pas seulement pour les sages de l'empire l'auteur et le maître de l'univers, la loi qui conduit toutes choses au bien, la sagesse qui a tout fait avec nombre, poids et mesure : c'est avant tout un père bienveillant, un ami toujours sûr et fidèle, le refuge et la consolation qui ne manquent jamais à l'honnête homme. "Qu'aurais-je à faire," dit Marc-Aurèle, "d'un monde sans providence et sans dieux?" Dieu est bon ; il a donc ordonné toutes choses selon sa bonté, et par conséquent dans l'intérêt dernier de la vertu. . . .

" Traitez-moi, Seigneur, à votre volonté, s'écrie Épictète, conduisez-moi où il vous plaira, couvrez-moi de l'habit que vous voudrez, je suis résigné à vos lois, et votre volonté est la mienne. En toutes choses je célébrerai vos œuvres et vos bienfaits, et je serai votre témoin auprès des mortels, en leur montrant ce que c'est qu'un homme véritable." . . Cette humilité de Marc-Aurèle et d'Épictète est toute morale. Elle n'a rien de ce sentiment servile et superstitieux, qui nous fait voir dans un accident un coup de la Providence, et qui prête à Dieu je ne sais quelle jalousie par laquelle il se plaît à renverser ce qui s'élève, à exalter ce qui s'abaisse. . . . Si nous sommes si faibles, il semble naturel que nous priions Dieu, soit pour le remercier du bien que nous pouvons avoir fait, soit pour le demander un surcroît de force et de courage. " Ou les dieux ne peuvent rien," dit Marc-Aurèle, " ou ils peuvent quelque chose. S'ils ne peuvent rien, pourquoi les prier ? Et s'ils ont quelque pouvoir, pourquoi, au lieu de leur demander de te donner quelque chose ou de mettre fin à telle autre, ne les pries-tu pas de te délivrer de tes craintes, de tes désirs et de tes troubles d'esprit ? " On a raison de dire que Dieu entend et exauce les prières de l'âme raisonnable, même quand elles demeurent sans voix. . . " Mais qui l'a dit que les dieux ne viennent pas à notre secours même dans les choses qui dépendent de nous ? Commence seulement à leur demander ces sortes de secours, et tu verras. Celui-ci prie pour obtenir les faveurs de sa maîtresse, et toi, prie pour n'avoir jamais de tels désirs. Celui-ci prie pour être délivré de tel fardeau ; et toi, prie d'être assez fort pour n'avoir pas besoin de cette délivrance." Une telle prière ne ressemble pas à celles de la foule, qui paraît marchander avec Dieu, et lui reprocher d'être un mauvais débiteur, en disant : Si jamais j'ai fait fumer l'encens dans tes temples, donne-moi telle ou telle chose en revanche. Maxime de Tyr la définit très-bien : c'est une conversation fortifiante avec Dieu ; c'est un témoignage que l'âme se rend de sa vertu en remerciant celui qui nous l'a inspirée ; c'est un encouragement que se donne la vertu, en demandant à Dieu des biens que, par sa faveur, elle trouve et puise en elle-même. Les entretiens d'Épictète sont pleins de prières de cette sorte, communications intimes et familières avec Dieu, effusions d'une âme pieuse devant son maître et son père, actes de foi et de reconnaissance envers la suprême bonté. . . . Au lieu de s'échapper en frivoles sarcasmes, comme Lucien, en invectives incensées, comme Lucain, ou bien en paroles amères, comme Tacite, qui ne reconnaît guère la providence de Dieu qu'à ses coups et à ses vengeances, le pauvre Épictète, l'ancien esclave d'Épaphrodite, ne sait que bénir celui qui l'a si rudement éprouvé ; et je ne connais rien qui peigne mieux l'état de son âme, et les besoins religieux des esprits d'élite au commencement de notre ère, que ce penchant à la prière et à l'adoration.'

M. Denis refers to a variety of passages in Epictetus, M. Aurelius, and others. He omits one example of the prayers of the heathen, perhaps because it belongs properly to a later period, though evidently formed on their model. The commentary of Simplicius on the 'Conversations of Epictetus' thus concludes :—

Ἱκετεύω σε, δεσπότα, ὁ πατὴρ καὶ ἡγεμὼν τοῦ ἐν ἡμῖν λόγου, ὑπομνησθῆναι μὲν ἡμᾶς τῆς ἑαυτῶν εὐγενείας, ἧς ἠξιώθημεν παρὰ σοῦ· συμπρᾶξαι δὲ ὡς αὐτοκινήτοις ἡμῖν, πρός τε κάθαρσιν τὴν ἀπὸ τοῦ σώματος καὶ τῶν ἀλόγων παθῶν, καὶ πρὸς τὸ ὑπερέχειν καὶ ἄρχειν αὐτῶν, καὶ ὡς ὀργάνοις κεχρῆσθαι κατὰ τὸν προσήκοντα τρόπον. συμπράττειν τε καὶ πρὸς διόρθωσιν ἀκριβῆ τοῦ ἐν ἡμῖν λόγου, καὶ ἕνωσιν αὐτοῦ πρὸς τὰ ὄντως ὄντα, διὰ τοῦ τῆς ἀληθείας φωτός. καὶ τὸ τρίτον καὶ σωτήριον· ἱκετεύω, ἀφελεῖν τελέως τὴν ἀχλὺν τῶν ψυχικῶν ἡμῶν ὀμμάτων, Ὄφρ' εὖ γινώσκωμεν (κατὰ τὸν Ὅμηρον) ἢ μὲν θεὸν ἠδὲ καὶ ἄνδρα.

Note A A, Page 120.

De Broglie, *L'Église et l'Empire Romain*, iii. 165:—
'L'école d'Alexandrie ne faisait pas seulement descendre l'âme humaine, par une suite de chutes nécessaires, des

hauteurs de l'Être absolu : elle lui enseignait aussi y remonter par l'étude et par la vertu. . . . Aussi n'est-ce par aucune faculté humaine que l'homme, dans le système néoplatonicien, se met en communication avec cette suprême forme de l'Être divin : c'est au contraire par une faculté supérieure à lui, qui l'enlève à son essence, le transfigure et l'absorbe. Ce que la raison ne peut lui faire connaître, l'extase le lui révèle. Sous le nom d'extase, l'école néoplatonicienne entend non une faculté, mais un état de l'âme. C'est l'être individuel qui disparaît et se perd dans la contemplation de l'Être infini dont il est sorti autrefois, auquel il doit retourner un jour. Un vif amour de la vérité, une soif de la posséder, suppriment pour un moment, dès ici-bas, les limites de la nature finie, et lui permettent de s'abreuver et de se fondre dans la source même de son être. Ce n'est point alors l'âme qui connaît Dieu, c'est Dieu qui descend en elle : il n'y a pas deux êtres, l'un connaissant, l'autre connu ; il n'y a plus, pour parler le langage technique, un sujet et un objet de la connaissance ; l'homme ne connaît pas Dieu, il est fait Dieu pour un instant : l'éclair de l'extase, en le touchant, l'a déifié. . . Cette théorie de l'extase est le sommet de toute la doctrine néoplatonicienne. L'extase est le terme dernier de toute connaissance, et le couronnement de la vertu parfaite. C'est par un patient amour du vrai, par une constante pratique du bien ; c'est par la mortification des sens, le détachement des passions, c'est par le mépris du corps et de la terre, que le sage Plotin doit mériter cette anticipation de l'immortalité divine. C'est en cessant d'être homme qu'il peut se rendre digne de devenir Dieu. Des pratiques austères renouvelées de Pythagore, excitées peut-être encore par l'émulation des exemples chrétiens, avaient seules révélé à Plotin l'existence de cet état surnaturel. Porphyre en traçait le tableau dans son traité *De l'Abstinence*, et empruntant presque les paroles de l'Esprit-Saint, il engageait les hommes à purifier leur corps, comme le temple où doit descendre la gloire de Dieu. Sa lettre à sa femme Marcelle respire le même enthousiasme d'austérité. Son dégoût des choses de la terre était même poussé si loin, qu'il fallait l'intervention de Plotin pour le détourner du suicide. Et lui-même cependant, malgré tant d'efforts, n'avait goûté que rarement les douceurs de l'extase. "Pour moi," dit-il, en racontant les merveilles de la vie de son maître, "je n'ai été uni qu'une seule fois à Dieu, à l'âge de quarante-huit ans." '

M. Pressensé, in his *History of the First Three Centuries* (partie ii. tom. 2, p. 62), after a lucid exposition of the doctrine of the New Platonists, thus sums up his comparison between it and the Christian:—

'Le Christianisme, par l'humilité et la mortification, conduit à la plénitude de la vie, et sa morale se résume dans cette parole du Christ : "*Si quelqu'un perd sa vie, il la retrouvera.*" Le néoplatonisme, par l'ascétisme et l'extase, veut amener l'homme à l'anéantissement, car le dernier terme du progrès, selon lui, c'est de perdre toute conscience de soi, c'est d'être semblable à celui qui n'est pas, c'est donc de ne pas être. Lui aussi dit à l'homme : "Écoute-moi et tu seras comme un dieu;" mais ce dieu auquel il faut ressembler, c'est l'abstraction pure, c'est le non-être, c'est le néant imparfaitement dissimulé par un langage brillant, poétique. . . . Ainsi finit la noble philosophie grecque ; elle va se perdre dans la Nirvana du boudhisme ; elle pousse l'idée orientale jusqu'aux dernières conséquences, jusqu'au suicide moral que les sombres forêts de l'Inde semblaient devoir seules abriter.

'La philosophie de la nature a parcouru le même cycle que la religion de la nature ; elles arrivent l'une et l'autre au même terme, c'est à dire, à l'anéantissement, tant il est vrai qu'en s'enfermant dans le monde inférieur, en cherchant la vie dans la nature, on s'éloigne de la source véritable de l'être. Le principe de la nature est au-dessus d'elle et en dehors d'elle; elle ne se suffit pas à elle-même, et quiconque ne s'élève pas à la région plus haute où réside le principe de toute vie, ne rencontre en bas que la mort, et ne s'arrête sur cette pente que quand il est arrivé au néant. Le naturalisme s'ensevelit nécessairement, comme religion et comme philosophie, dans le monde inférieur, où il croyait trouver une vie suffisante.'

Note B B, Page 125.

The pretensions of the sorcerers are exposed in detail by Lucian in his account of Alexander of Abonoteichus, the Pseudomantis, as he calls him. After referring to this celebrated exposure, Döllinger (*Gentile and Jew*, ii. 199) continues:—

'The apparition of Hecate was equally efficacious. Believers were told to throw themselves prostrate on the ground at the first sight of fire. The goddess of the highways and roads, the Gorgo or Mormo wandering among the graves at night, was then invoked in verse, after which a heron or vulture was let loose, with lighted tow attached to her feet, the flame of which frightening the bird, it flew wildly about the room, and as the fire flashed here and there, the prostrate suppliants were convinced that they were eye-witnesses of a great prodigy. Similar artifices were employed to make the moon and stars appear on the ceiling of a room, and to produce the effects of an earthquake. To make an inscription show itself on the liver of a victim, the haruspex wrote the words previously with sympathetic ink on the palm of his hand, which he pressed on the liver long enough to leave the impression behind. And so the Neo-Platonists contrived to cheat the Emperor Julian when Maximus conducted him into the subterranean vaults of a temple of Hecate, and caused him to see an apparition of fire.'

The subject of the prevalence of imposture and credulity at this time in the Roman world is well reviewed by Denis, *Idées Morales*, &c. ii. 277 sqq. :—

'Non-seulement ils sentaient le besoin d'une règle et d'une discipline, mais ils étaient comme enveloppés d'un atmosphère de crédulité et de superstitions. C'est le temps, en effet, de l'astrologie, de la magie, et de mille croyances étranges sur Dieu, sur les démons, sur l'âme et sur l'autre monde, qui de toutes parts débordaient de l'Orient sur l'Occident. Les enfants perdus du Portique et de l'Académie et leurs adeptes de haut rang voulaient à toute force pénétrer l'avenir, soit en lisant dans les astres, soit en mettant en communication avec les esprits, tandis que le petit peuple courait aux cultes étrangers. En vain les Césars, à qui les sciences occultes inspiraient une féroce terreur, et qui, selon le mot de Lucain, "défendaient aux dieux de parler," sévissaient contre les imposteurs et leurs dupes, et faisaient détruire publiquement par le feu les livres de magie, déporter ceux qui en possédaient, brûler vifs les charlatans de la Perse et de la Chaldée, exposer aux bêtes ou mettre en croix les malheureux qui avaient la sottise de les consulter. En vain les hommes de sens soutenaient que tout l'art des devins n'est qu'une imposture pour soutirer de l'argent aux imbéciles; qu'il n'y a point de rélation entre une constellation et le sort si divers de tant d'hommes nés dans le même instant; que les dieux ne peuvent être soumis à la puissance et à la volonté des mortels; qu'il faudrait être d'une nature surhumaine et porter en soi quelque image de la divinité pour avoir le droit de proclamer les volontés et les ordres de Dieu. Il se trouvait toujours des hommes, ou avides, ou impatients de la destinée, qui avaient besoin d'être trompés, et Tacite pouvait dire de l'astrologie qu'elle serait toujours chassée de Rome et qu'elle y régnerait toujours. Les Grecs étaient encore plus entêtés de la magie, qui leur était venue de l'Asie et de l'Égypte. Tout leur paraissait rempli de démons bons ou mauvais, et comme les dieux étaient plus nombreux que les hommes dans certains cantons de l'Achaïe, les miracles y étaient aussi moins rares que les faits naturels. Il faut voir dans Lucien jusqu'où était poussée la crédulité. Là c'est un magicien qui vole dans l'air, qui passe au travers du feu, qui attire ou qui chasse les démons, qui guérit les malades ou qui ressuscite les morts. Ailleurs c'est un Babylonien qui rassemble, à l'aide de quelques mots sacrés, tous les serpents d'un pays, et qui les extermine de son souffle. Des malheureux sont fustigés toutes les nuits par de mauvais génies. Des statues marchent, parlent et mangent. On ne prononce qu'avec un respect plein de terreur les noms des morts, en ajoutant quelque formule qui pût leur plaire, comme le *Bienheureux* ou le *Saint.* Malheur à vous, si vous paraissiez incrédule à tant de contes ou de sottes superstitions ! Vous étiez un impie, et il n'eût pas tenu aux imposteurs ou à ceux qu'ils trompaient, que vous ne fussiez lapidé. A force de ne rien croire, on en était venu à ne plus croire que l'impossible et l'absurde. Je ne connaîtrais rien de plus triste que ce retour des peuples à l'enfance par la décrépitude de la pensée, si je ne faisais réflexion que la vie germe toujours à côté de la mort, et que ces déplorables extravaganes, étaient le symptôme d'un besoin profond et irrésistible. Épicure et les sceptiques avaient fait tous leurs efforts pour chasser le divin des esprits ; et ils ne paraissaient avoir que trop réussi. Mais le divin y rentrait avec violence et par toutes les voies, au risque d'y porter le trouble et la démence.'

Note C C, Page 127.

The burning of Rome under Nero was imputed, as we know, by popular hatred, to the Christians, and the first persecution followed in consequence. No such connection was imagined between the burning of the Capitol in the civil wars and the hated sectaries, nor can we trace the partial persecution of the Christians by Domitian to any popular apprehension of the anger of the gods. Nevertheless the character of this emperor and his superstitious belief in his own divine appointment as the guardian and restorer of the national religion, makes it probable that he was not uninfluenced by such a consideration. The trial of Ignatius under Trajan at Antioch, and the Christian martyrdoms that followed, agree with the date of the great earthquake by which the Syrian capital was partially overthrown, and it is impossible to overlook the apparent connection between this event and the persecution which immediately ensued. The same may be said of the great calamities of the empire and the persecutions under M. Aurelius. These calamities were redoubled under Decius and Gallus, and the fury of persecution simultaneously increased. Diocletian for a long time resisted the importunities of his colleague Galerius to renew the same policy with greater energy than ever; and was at last determined to it by the event, probably accidental, though imputed to Galerius himself by Lactantius, of a conflagration in his own palace. Lactant., *De Mort. Persecut.* c. 15. That the persecutions were repeatedly excited by the superstitious terrors of the populace is the constant assertion of the Christian writers.

See the classical passage in Tertull. *Apoll.* c. 40:—

Existimant omnis publicæ cladis, omnis popularis incommodi Christianos esse causam. Si Tiberis ascendit in mœnia, si Nilus non ascendit in arva, si cœlum stetit, si terra movit, si fames, si lues, statim—Christianos ad leonem!

Comp. Cyprian, *Epist.* lxxv., where he attributes an outburst of persecution in some parts of Asia Minor to the occurrence of destructive earthquakes: ut per Cappadociam et per Pontum quædam etiam civitates in profundum receptæ dirupti soli hiatu devorarentur, ut ex hoc persecutio quoque gravis adversus nos Christiani nominis fieret. See also Origen, *Comm. in Matthæum*, iii. p. 859, ed. Delarue.

Cyprian, *Ad Demetr.* c. 3. Dixisti per nos fieri, et quod nobis debeant imputari omnia ista quibus nunc mundus quatitur et urgetur, quod dii vestri a nobis non colantur. The motive and principle of these wild and sanguinary impulses lie deep in human nature, and deserve attentive consideration.

The sense of a personal relation to the Deity is assuredly an earlier development of the religious instinct than that of a public and national relation to Him. The instinct which prompts man to offer sacrifice to God was first directed to the attainment of favour for himself, or pardon and protection; and at a later period extended to the attempt to conciliate God to his country, and to its public interests. Human sacrifices may be traced back to the earlier period ; in the earliest accounts we have of them, they seem to have been offerings of individual worshippers, as when the parent offers his child, the master his slave, and the choicest victims are immolated at the tomb of the departed chieftain. They mark in such cases the extreme point to which the hopes, the terrors, or the remorse of the individual might impel him. We may conjecture that these terrible offerings were first introduced into both Greek and Roman usage with such a view to private and personal interests. But both in Greece and Rome the political instinct became early predominant, and gradually overrode all merely personal views of religion. Human sacrifices were consecrated in both the great nations of classical antiquity to the special object of procuring divine protection for the State. With this object they were publicly sanctioned and regularly practised in early times both in Greece and Rome. But the national instinct of religion, and national devotion to religious usage, were never so strong as the personal. Men could not feel the same intense, absorbing interest in the safety of the State, as in their own personal safety. They could not continue so ruthlessly to trample upon the natural feelings of humanity for the one object, as they might have done for the other. Hence it would appear that, when the idea of the need of human sacrifices was thus far dissociated from the personal interests of the offerer, the advance of civilization and cultivated feelings led the Greeks, and especially the Ionians and Athenians, the most cultivated among them, to discountenance, to modify, and finally to reject them generally as an instrument of public utility. The influence of Grecian habits and teaching operated strongly upon the Romans, and gradually tempered the gloomier instincts of that people also. Possibly the national successes and the established security of the State against the most urgent calamities of war and conquest, aided powerfully in producing this change of sentiment.

From the year B.C. 95, the era of her most triumphant prosperity, the laws of Rome expressly forbade human sacrifice. Her writers generally speak of it with horror. They felt no need of it, and they were free to regard it with the detestation which human nature properly entertains for it. They declare that no such usage exists at Rome; that it is abhorrent from Roman manners and morality; the chiefs of the Empire take measures to check it in their remoter and less civilized provinces. So strong is the protest of Roman civilization against it, that, on a superficial view of the facts, it has been often asserted that human sacrifice was actually abolished for centuries under the sway of the Roman Emperors.

Such, however, was far from the case. Even in the State-ritual of Rome some traces of the practice still continued to linger. Even on public occasions, and for national objects, human sacrifices were from time to time offered. In cases of political urgency, the 'Gaul and the Greek' were still buried solemnly in the forum.

Still worse, the practice creeps back again for private and personal objects, and is associated with magical ceremonies. When the State is merged in the ruler, it is difficult to distinguish the personal from the public interest; but it was probably more for their own sakes than for the sake of the commonwealth, that irregular sacrifices of this kind were perpetrated by Julius Cæsar, by Augustus, by Tiberius, and Nero, and after them still more frequently and without disguise by most of the succeeding emperors. Trajan himself sacrificed a beautiful woman after the earthquake at Antioch, as a propitiation, we may suppose, for the safety of that city. The self-devotion of Antinous for Hadrian is an instance of quasi-sacrifice. The significance of the rite, as the voluntary offering of the best and dearest, seems to come back upon the conscience of mankind as a revived revelation of man's relation to God. The rhetorician Aristides believes himself to be saved from imminent peril of death by the self-immolation of his brother Hermias, and in a fresh access of his disease persuades his sister Philumene to devote herself for him also. The influence of the earlier and healthier teaching of the Greek philosophers and philanthropists had now become weaker; at the same time the barbarous ideas of Asia and Africa were making themselves more powerfully felt. The calamities of the State seemed to demand greater and more striking efforts to appease the manifest wrath of Heaven. Along with the increase of other wild and gloomy superstitions, human sacrifices became more and more common, and ceased to be regarded with the horror they naturally inspire.

Undoubtedly various feelings entered into the demand for the persecution of the Christians. The magistrate regarded them as transgressors of a principle in public law, as evil-doers, as fosterers of treason and sedition; and was disposed to punish them accordingly. But the people generally, and sometimes the rulers themselves, yielded to a superstitious impulse in ascribing to their rejection of sacrifice and of idol-worship every public calamity, which testified, as they supposed, to the wrath of the offended deities. The execution of the Christians was thus popularly regarded as a means of propitiation. This idea was sanctioned and fostered apparently by the most usual manner of these executions; for the shows of the amphitheatre had sprung out of the primitive custom of sacrificing human victims at the altar of a god or the tomb of a deceased hero. Even to the time of Constantine, it is said, a vestige of this idea was preserved in the annual immolation of a gladiator on the Alban mount to Jupiter Latiaris.

For a succinct but full discussion of the subject of human sacrifice, with a copious citation of authorities, I would willingly refer the reader to a tract lately printed, but not yet published, by Sir John Acton. The writer extends his historical review to modern times, and connects with it the notorious persecution of reputed witchcraft. The other equal and parallel disgrace of Christianity, the Romish Inquisition, he regards too leniently as a merely political tribunal. I believe that in both cases the popular feeling which supported and impelled the action of the magistrate was the same: but this too was a mixed feeling. First, as in the case of the Imperial persecutions, there was the superstitious anxiety to propitiate the wrath of an offended deity, the same anxiety that has lain at the bottom of human sacrifice at all times; but, secondly, there was the notion, peculiar, so far as appears, to Christianity, and which may serve in a very slight degree to relieve the horror of these Christian persecutions, that the sacrifice is required for the sufferer's own sake, or if too late to save his own soul, may at least secure the survivors from the contagion of his fatal impiety.

NOTE D D, Page 132.

Neander, *Church History*, i. p. 43 (Engl. transl.): —
' On every side was evinced the need of a revelation from heaven, such as would give inquiring minds that assurance of peace which they were unable to find in the jarring systems of the old philosophy, and in the artificial life of the reawakened old religion. That zealous champion of the latter, Porphyry, alludes himself to the deep-felt necessity; which he proposed to supply, leaning on the authority of divine responses, by his "Collection of Ancient Oracles." On this point he says: " The utility of such a collection will best be understood by those who have felt the painful craving after truth, and have sometimes wished it might be their lot to witness some appearance of the gods, so as to be relieved from their doubts by information not to be disputed."' (See Euseb., *Præp. Evang.* iv. 7.)

The life of such a person, from his youth up harassed with doubts, unsettled by the strife of opposite opinions, ardently longing after the truth, and conducted at length, through this protracted period of dissatisfied craving, to Christianity, is delineated by the author of a sort of romance (partly philosophical and in part religious), who belonged to the second or the third century. This work is called *The*

Clementines, and, though fiction, is clearly a fiction drawn from real life; and we may safely avail ourselves of it, as presenting a true and characteristic sketch, which might doubtless apply to many an inquiring spirit belonging to those times. It commences thus:—

Ego, Clemens, in urbe Roma natus, ex prima ætate pudicitiæ studium gessi; dum me animi intentio velut vinculis quibusdam solicitudinis et mœroris innexum teneret. Inerat mihi cogitatio incertum sane unde initium sumpserit, crebro enim ad memoriam meam conditionem mortalitatis adducens, simulque discutiens: utrumne sit mihi aliqua vita post mortem, an nihil omnino sim futurus; si non fuerim antequam nascerer; vel si nulla prorsus vitæ hujus erit post obitum recordatio; et ita immensitas temporis cuncta oblivioni et silentio dabit, &c.

The work, which runs to as many as ten books, and expatiates in a number of worthless stories about St. Peter at Rome, and Simon Magus, and others, is printed in Coteler's *Patres Apostolici*, i. 493, under the title of 'Recognitionum S. Clementis libri x.' It was attributed in early times to St. Clement, the disciple of Paul and author of the Epistles to the Corinthians. The work is fully analysed by Neander in the second volume of his History, p. 25 foll. Similarly, in the conversation between Justin Martyr and his unknown interlocutor, the heathen philosopher is forced to admit the vanity of his masters' reasonings on the nature of God and the soul, and to seek speculative truth in the revelations made through the Hebrew prophets: ἐγένοντό τινες πρὸ πολλοῦ χρόνου πάντων τούτων τῶν νομιζομένων φιλοσόφων παλαιότεροι, μακάριοι καὶ δίκαιοι καὶ θεοφιλεῖς, θείῳ πνεύματι λαλήσαντες καὶ τὰ μέλλοντα θεσπίσαντες, ἃ δὴ νῦν γίνεται· προφήτας δὲ αὐτοὺς καλοῦσιν. Οὗτοι μόνοι τὸ ἀληθὲς καὶ εἶδον καὶ ἐξεῖπον ἀνθρώποις, μήτ' εὐλαβηθέντες, μήτε δυσωπηθέντες τινά, μὴ ἡττημένοι δόξης, ἀλλὰ μόνα ταῦτα εἰπόντες ἃ ἤκουσαν καὶ ἃ εἶδον ἁγίῳ πληρωθέντες πνεύματι.—Justin M., *Dial. cum Tryph.* c 7.

The 'Confessions' of St. Augustine, in which he gives a full account of the intellectual and moral perplexities which led him to renounce irreligion and heresy, and embrace a saving faith, is of a later date, and belongs properly to the post-Nicene period. See the seventh book particularly.

His first and greatest difficulty was the Origin of Evil (*Confess.* vii. 3):—Sed rursus dicebam, Quis fecit me? nonne Deus meus, non tantum bonus, sed ipsum bonum? Unde igitur mihi male velle et bene nolle, ut esset cur juste pœnas luerem? Quis in me hoc posuit, et insevit mihi plantarium amaritudinis, cum totus fierem a dulcissimo Deo meo? Si Diabolus auctor, unde ipse Diabolus? . . . (c. 5.) Et quærebam, unde malum: et male quærebam : et in ipsa inquisitione mea non videbam malum. . . . (c. 6.) Jam etiam mathematicorum fallaces divinationes et impia deliramenta rejeceram. . . (c. 7.) Jam itaque me, adjutor meus, illis vinculis solveras, et quærebam unde malum, et non erat exitus. . . . (c. 13.) Et primo volens ostendere mihi, quam resistas superbis, humilibus autem des gratiam, et quanta misericordia tua demonstrata sit hominibus via humilitatis, *quod Verbum tuum caro factum est, et habitavit inter homines*, procurasti mihi per quendam hominem immanissimo typho turgidum, quosdam Platonicorum libros . . . et ibi legi, non quidem his verbis, sed hoc idem omnino multis et multiplicibus suaderi rationibus; quod in principio erat Verbum, et Verbum erat apud Deum, et Deus erat Verbum: hoc erat in principio apud Deum; omnia per eum facta sunt. . . . (c. 14.) Item ibi legi quia Deus Verbum, non ex carne, non ex sanguine, non ex voluntate viri, neque ex voluntate carnis, sed ex Deo natus est. Sed quia Verbum *caro factum est, et habitavit in nobis*, non ibi legi. . . . Quod exin ante omnia tempora, et supra omnia tempora incommutabiliter manet unigenitus Filius tuus coæternus tibi, et quia de plenitudine ejus accipiunt animæ ut beatæ sunt, et quia participatione manentis in se sapientiæ renovantur ut sapientes sint : est ibi. Quod autem secundum tempus *pro impiis mortuus est*; et Filio unico tuo non pepercisti, sed *pro nobis omnibus tradi-*

disti eum: non est ibi. Abscondisti enim hæc a sapientibus, et revelâsti ea parvulis. . . . (c. 10.) Et inde admonitus redire ad memetipsum, intravi in intima mea duce te; et potui quoniam factus es adjutor meus: seqq.

Of the process of thought by which such inquirers were led to Christianity, Neander says (*Hist. of the Church*, iii. 135):—' Many educated Pagans were conducted to the Faith, not at once, by means of some sudden excitement, but after they had been led by particular providences, by the great multitude of Christians around them, to entertain doubts of the Pagan religion they had received from their ancestors, and to enter upon a serious examination of the several systems of religion within their reach. They read the Holy Scriptures and the writings of the Christian Fathers; they proposed their doubts and their difficulties to Christian friends, and finally made up their minds to go to the bishop. Many came, by slow degrees, through many intervening steps, to Christianity; and the Neo-Platonic religious idealism formed one stage in particular by which they were brought nearer to Christian ideas, as is seen in the examples of a Synesius and an Augustine. This system made them familiar with the doctrine of a Triad. Although this doctrine, in its speculative tendency, was altogether different from the Christian doctrine, which is in its essence practical throughout; yet they were thereby made attentive to Christian ideas. They were conducted still nearer to practical Christianity by the doctrine that man needed to be redeemed and purified from the might of the ὕλη, which not only fettered and clogged, but corrupted that element of his soul which stands related to God. It is true, they believed only in a general redeeming power of God, which was imparted to individuals in proportion to their worth; or the communication of which was connected with various religious institutions under different forms. . . . Yet when those to whom Christianity appeared at first as one particular revelation of the divine, coordinate to other forms of manifestation, and not as the absolute religion of humanity, were induced to read the Holy

Scriptures, and so attend divine worship in Christian churches. . . . they might by their own study of the Scriptures, and through numberless impressions derived from the Church life, be let more deeply into the Christian truth, until at last they found the redeeming God only in Christ. . . . Thus Synesius, for example . . . thus it happened to Augustine. . . .'

Note E E, Page 136.

Plin., *Hist. Nat.*, ii. 1 :—Mundum et hoc quod nomine alio cœlum appellare libuit, cujus circumflexu teguntur omnia, numen credi par est, æternum, immensum, neque genitum neque interiturum unquam. The philosopher seems to identify the universe of things with the heavens, or vault of æther, embracing all things, by which the globe is surrounded. Cicero recites well-known passages to the same effect from Ennius and Euripides: Aspice hoc sublime candens quem invocant omnes Jovem. . . . Vides sublime fusum immoderatum æthera, qui terram tenero circumjectu amplectitur. Hunc summam habeto Divûm, hunc perhibeto Jovem. The Stoic Chrysippus had advanced the same exposition of the Godhead: Chrysippus disputavit æthera esse eum quem homines appellant Jovem. Cicero, *De Nat. Deor.*, ii. 2, 25. Lucan, following an ampler explanation of the same school, affirmed Jupiter to be not only: quodcunque vides, the whole material universe, but: quocunque moveris, the whole of our moral nature. But such authorities as these had condescended to use at least the popular name of the Supreme Deity, and to speak of Him as a personal existence. Pliny disdains this economy. After discussing various theological views, he concludes himself: Deus est mortali juvare mortalem, et hæc ad æternam gloriam via, i. e. God is the mere abstract principle of virtue; and this leads him round to the starting-point of the Pagan mythologies, the pretended deification of the wise and good among mortals: Hac proceres iêre Romani; hac nunc cœlesti passu cum liberis suis vadit maximus omnis ævi rector Vespasianus Augustus fessis rebus subveniens. Hic est vetustissimus referendi gratiam bene merentibus mos, ut tales numinibus ascribant. Quippe et omnium aliorum nomina Deorum . . . ex hominum nata sunt meritis. And hence by an easy lapse to the denial of a Providence: Irridendum vero agere curam rerum humanarum illud quicquid est summum. Such is the vicious circle described by Pantheism and Atheism.

Note F F, Page 139.

With regard to the means of obtaining peace and favour with God, the main object of our religious affections, the notion of the ancients fluctuated, much like our own, between the principles of Sanctification and Justification, of gaining the reward by personal acts or merits, or by free acceptance in consequence of some act or merit of another. Under the first head are comprised ceremonial purifications, as well as works of justice or charity; all godly living as well as righteous observance; acts of personal discipline and self-denial; means of removing inward or outward hindrances to acceptance with the Deity. Thus man is supposed to work out his own salvation, whatever aid may be given him from above, whether by the opus operatum of ritual lustrations, or by the infusion of divine grace to prevent and follow him in all his thoughts and actions. Under the second principle is comprised the notion of satisfaction to God, of reconciliation with Him, of atonement effected by a prescribed religious service, such as sacrifice; whether the offering by the worshipper of an object precious to himself, or the self-devotion of an object precious to God, for the love it bears to the worshipper.

In the early ages of Christianity we find both these ideas of religion, both these ruling principles of divine worship, recognised equally among the heathens. Lustration and Expiation, Purification and Propitiation, the Mysteries and the Sacrifices, were in perhaps equal vogue and estimation among them. By the one they hoped to wash away the stains of guilt, to elevate the moral character, to cast off the slough of human corruption, to purge the mental vision and obtain a higher and truer conception of the Divine, or nearer communion with it; to abjure our frail humanity and assume a portion at least of divine illumination, purity, and sanctity; to raise man to God. Such was the object of the Mysteries, or Initiation into the secrets of moral nature; such the promises held forth by the Hierophants of various religious systems, especially of those derived from or connected with the East, and assured through the instrumentality of occult ceremonial observances, and most potently by the use of magical arts and appliances.

But such were the aspirations, and such the resources generally of the more refined and intelligent worshippers; this notion of lustration as the one thing needful was, in a great measure, a reaction from the grosser superstitions of the vulgar; from the popular conception that God's favour was to be attained directly, and without any personal effort, by the means of offerings and sacrifice. To pour forth before the throne of grace gifts—precious gifts, gifts ever ascending in value, gifts of life, of the life of animals, and lastly of man himself, of our friends, of our offspring, of ourselves— such was the most popular, the most ancient, the most widespread notion of religious service. The idea seems to have commonly prevailed, that such sacrifice was accepted *instead* of the suffering due from the worshipper himself for his sins, or the disfavour, however caused, in which he imagined himself to stand with God. Hence, the more precious the victim to Him, the more hope that the vicarious substitute would be accepted. Of the extent to which human sacrifices were offered in the heathen world I have spoken in a previous note, and of the incradicable feeling which prompted them, and which reappeared again and again under the pressure of terror and disaster. But even in the heathen mind this idea of the value of sacrifice assumed here and there another and a higher form. Indications are not wanting in the Pagan mythology of the conception of a spontaneous offering made to God for man by a being himself partaking of the divine nature, and having, from such participation, a certain claim upon the favour and consideration of the Deity. The highest and holiest idea of sacrifice, as the offering by God Himself of something precious to Himself for the sake of man, and in order to reconcile man to Himself, is not wholly alien even from the mind of the heathens.

The Greeks and Romans might learn, on inquiry, that Christianity offered a view of religion founded, like their own, on the ideas both of purification and of propitiation. They might learn that Baptism was regarded by the Church as an initiatory rite, leading to a new life of purity and godliness, the great hindrances to which, in natural and acquired corruption, might be removed by the grace of the Holy Spirit infused into the hearts of the believers, and manifesting itself in their conversion to God, and their amendment of life and conversation.

Again, they might learn that the death of Christ upon the cross was declared to be a sacrifice, consummated once for all, the crowning sacrifice of which all earlier offerings were but types, the offering, not of man's dearest as a ransom for himself from punishment due to his own sins, but the offering of God's dearest for the sake of man, as the means discovered by the Most High to satisfy His justice, and at the same time to illustrate His love.

They might learn, further, that the Christian mind still fluctuated, like their own, between these two conceptions; that sometimes, and in some minds, the one, in some the other, gained the predominance; that, as in after times, so even then, there were some teachers who put forward the one view as the main essence of religion, some the other; that in some schools it is the life of Christ, with the lessons and example of godly practice which it has taught us; in others, the death of Christ, the cross of Christ, the atonement of Christ, that is the one great revelation of the Gospel. There is still, as there everhas been in Christianity, as there ever has been in Heathenism, Purification on one side and Propitiation on the other; Sanctification in one scale and Justification in the other.

Thus they might read in Justin Martyr that the work of Christ is victory over the power of evil spirits prevailing in us: ἀπὸ γὰρ τῶν δαιμονίων, ἃ ἔστιν ἀλλότρια τῆς εὐσεβείας τοῦ θεοῦ, οἷς πάλαι προσεκυνοῦμεν, τὸν θεὸν ἀεὶ διὰ Ἰησοῦ Χριστοῦ συντηρηθῆναι παρακαλοῦμεν, ἵνα μετὰ τὸ ἐπιστρέψαι πρὸς θεὸν ἄμωμοι ὦμεν· βοηθὸν γὰρ ἐκεῖνον καὶ λυτρώτην καλοῦμεν. By Justin, Irenæus, Tertullian, Clement, Origen, and others, it is very commonly referred to the change He effects in men's lives on earth, and the sanctifying influence of His teaching and example. Thus Irenæus, *Adv. Hær.* iii. 18: Filius hominis factus est, ut assuesceret hominem percipere Deum, et assuesceret Deum habitare in homine. In ii. 22: Omnes venit salvare .... infantes et parvulos et pueros et juvenes et seniores: ideo per omnem venit ætatem, et infantibus infans factus, sanctificans infantes, &c. Clemens Alex., *Cohort. ad Gent.*, p. 6: ταύτῃ τοι ἡμεῖς οἱ τῆς ἀνομίας υἱοί ποτε, διὰ τὴν φιλανθρωπίαν τοῦ λόγου νῦν υἱοὶ γεγόναμεν τοῦ θεοῦ. *Pædag.* i. 2, p. 100: ἔστιν οὖν ὁ παιδαγωγὸς ἡμῶν λόγος διὰ παραινέσεων θεραπευτικὸς τῶν παρὰ φύσιν τῆς ψυχῆς παθῶν ... λόγος δὲ ὁ πατρικὸς μόνος ἐστὶν ἀνθρωπίνων ἰατρὸς ἀρρωστημάτων παιώνιος καὶ ἐπῳδὸς ἅγιος νοσούσης ψυχῆς. Origen sees in the union of the divine and human in Christ's nature the commencement of a connection between man and God (*Cont. Cels.* iii. 28): ὅτι ἀπ' ἐκείνου ἤρξατο θεία καὶ ἀνθρωπίνη συνυφαίνεσθαι φύσις· ἵν' ἡ ἀνθρωπίνη τῇ πρὸς τὸ θειότερον κοινωνίᾳ γένηται θεία οὐκ ἐν μόνῳ τῷ Ἰησοῦ, ἀλλὰ καὶ πᾶσι τοῖς μετὰ τοῦ πιστεύειν ἀναλαμβάνουσι βίον, ὃν ὁ Ἰησοῦς ἐδίδαξεν. The same writer compares the death of Christ with that of Socrates, as a means of confirming the courage of his disciples. See *Contr. Cels.* ii. 14, 40.

Again, Lactantius refers the work of Christ expressly to the effect of His baptism (*Divin. Instit.* iv. 15): Tinctus est a Johanne in Jordano fluvio, ut lavacro spiritali peccata non sua, quæ utique non habebat, sed carnis quam gerebat, aboleret.

These views, however, did not necessarily exclude the other notion of the efficacy of Christ's death for man's justification. The heathens might trace in patristic teaching many distinct assertions of the remission of sins through the merit of our Lord's sacrifice. Comp. Barnabas, c. 5: Propter hoc Dominus sustinuit tradere corpus suum in exterminium, ut remissione peccatorum sanctificemur, quod est, sparsione sanguinis illius. Clemens Rom. *ad Corinth.* i. c. 7: ἀτενίσωμεν εἰς τὸ αἷμα τοῦ Χριστοῦ καὶ ἴδωμεν ὡς τίμιον τῷ θεῷ (αἷμα) αὐτοῦ, ὅτι καὶ διὰ τὴν ἡμετέραν σωτηρίαν ἐκχυθὲν παντὶ τῷ κόσμῳ μετανοίας χάριν ὑπήνεγκεν. Tertullian, *Adv. Judæos,* c. 13: Christum oportebat pro omnibus gentibus fieri sacrificium, qui tanquam ovis ad victimam ductus est. Origen, *In Levit. Hom.* 3: Ipse etiam qui in similitudinem hominum factus est, et habitu repertus ut homo, sine dubio pro peccato quod ex nobis susceperat, quia peccata nostra portavit, vitulum immaculatum, hoc est, carnem incontaminatam, obtulit hostiam Deo. Again, *In Numer. Hom.* 4: Si non fuisset peccatum, non necesse fuerat filium Dei agnum fieri, nec opus fuerat eum in carne positum jugulari . . . peccati autem necessitas propitiationem requirit, et propitiatio non fit nisi per hostiam. *In Matth.* c. 16, *tract.* 11: Homo quidem non potest dare aliquam commutationem pro anima sua, Deus autem pro animabus omnium dedit commutationem pretiosum sanguinem filii sui. Cyprian, *Ad Demetr.* c. 22: Hanc gratiam Deus impertit . . . . redimendo credentem pretio sanguinis sui, reconciliando hominem Deo patri. Lactautius in the verses ascribed to him, *De Beneficiis Christi* :—

> Quisquis ades, mediique subis in limina templi,
> Siste parum, insontemque tuo pro crimine passum
> Respice me.

These are a few only of the passages of the Fathers on this subject, collected by Grotius, *De Satisfactione Christi*, and later writers. An ample catena, embracing almost every known name among the Christian writers of the first three centuries, is given by Professor Blunt, *Lectures on the Use of the Early Fathers*, p. 518 foll. I do not, however, discover in them any expressions opposed to the distinction thus stated by Hagenbach (*History of Doctrines*, i. p. 172, Engl. trans.) in discussing the opinions of the primitive Church:—' The tendency of Christ's appearance on earth, as such, was to redeem men from sin, and to reconcile them to God, inasmuch as it destroyed the power of the devil, and restored the harmony of human nature. But, in accordance with the doctrines preached by the apostles, the sufferings and death of Christ were from the commencement thought to be of principal importance in the work of Redemption. The Fathers of the primitive Church regarded His death as a sacrifice and a ransom, and therefore ascribed to His blood the power of cleansing from sin and guilt, and attached a high importance, sometimes even a supernatural efficacy, to the sign of the Cross. . . . Yet that *theory of satisfaction* had not yet been formed which represents Christ as *satisfying* the justice of God by suffering in the room of the sinner the punishment due to him.' Nevertheless the writer admits, what appears plainly enough, that 'the design of the death of Christ was to reconcile man to God was an opinion held by more than one of the Fathers.'

On the whole, we must allow that among the Christians, as among the Heathens of the primitive age, there was much fluctuation of opinion respecting the foundation of religious feeling; that some were inclined, sometimes at least, to lean more to the purifying and elevating effect of Christ's mission, some to the propitiatory character of His sufferings. Some looked chiefly to His life, others to His death; some to what He did for men, others to what He suffered for men; some to His sanctifying influence, others to His justifying merits.

It may be conceded, perhaps, that the former, in accordance with the prevalent religious sentiment of the time, and in the absence of any ruled decision of the Church on the subject, was the more common inclination of the two. The notion of purification and exaltation of the human soul by virtue required or imparted, by the overthrow or extinction of evil powers and dispositions, was fondly entertained by the purest of the heathen philosophical systems; such was the aim of the most popular superstitious observances of the time. It is possible that the Christians themselves may have been so far affected by the habits of thought around them, as to look more to this side of Christian doctrine than to the other. Of the Nicene creed, we may observe that while proclaiming the saving efficacy of our Lord's whole career, 'Who for us men and for our salvation came down from heaven, . . was incarnate, . . and was made man, and was crucified also for us. . . He suffered and was buried, . . and rose again,' it places the death of Christ on the same line with every other leading incident in it, and does not exalt it, as later systems of theology would generally do, to the grand and cardinal place above them all. If it speaks of the sufferings of Christ, it says nothing of His Satisfaction or Atonement; the Remission of Sins it ascribes rather to His Baptism than to His Crucifixion.

Note G G, Page 149.

S. Augustin, *De Civ. Dei*, xxii. 30 : Vera ibi gloria erit, ubi laudantis nec errore quisquam, nec adulatione laudabitur: verus honor qui nulli negabitur digno, nulli deferetur indigno: sed nec ad eum ambiet ullus indignus, ubi nullus permittetur esse nisi dignus. Vera pax ibi est, ubi nihil adversi, nec a se ipso, nec ab alio quisquam patietur. Præmium virtutis erit ipse qui virtutem dedit; eique se ipsum, quo melius et majus nihil possit esse, promisit. Quid est enim aliud quod per Prophetam dixit, *Ero illorum Deus, et ipsi erunt mihi plebs*; nisi, Ego ero unde satientur, Ego ero quæcunque ab hominibus honestè desiderantur, et vita, et salus, et victus, et copia, et gloria, et honor, et pax, et omnia bona? Sic enim et illud recte intelligitur, quod ait Apostolus, *Ut sit*

Deus omnia in omnibus. Ipse finis erit desideriorum nostrorum, qui sine fine videbitur, sine fastidio amabitur, sine fatigatione laudabitur. Hoc munus, hic affectus, hic actus profecto erit omnibus, sicut ipsa vita æterna, communis.

Note I I, Page 157.

We may assume that the Christian apologists took care to present to their heathen readers the arguments which they knew would have the greatest force with them. That, from the superior morality of the disciples, is eloquently set forth by Justin Martyr, *Apol.* i. c. 14: . . . ὃν τρόπον καὶ ἡμεῖς μετὰ τὸ τῷ λόγῳ πεισθῆναι, ἐκείνων μὲν ἀπεστήμεν, θεῷ δὲ μόνῳ τῷ ἀγεννήτῳ διὰ τοῦ υἱοῦ ἑπόμεθα· οἱ πάλαι μὲν πορνείαις χαίροντες, νῦν δὲ σωφροσύνην μόνην ἀσπαζόμενοι· οἱ δὲ καὶ μαγικαῖς τέχναις χρώμενοι, ἀγαθῷ καὶ ἀγεννήτῳ θεῷ ἑαυτοὺς ἀνατεθεικότες· χρημάτων δὲ καὶ κτημάτων οἱ πόρους παντὸς μᾶλλον στέργοντες, νῦν καὶ ἃ ἔχομεν εἰς κοινὸν φέροντες καὶ παντὶ δεομένῳ κοινωνοῦντες· οἱ μισάλληλοι δὲ καὶ ἀλληλοφόνοι καὶ πρὸς τοὺς οὐχ ὁμοφύλους διὰ τὰ ἔθη καὶ ἑστίας κοινὰς μὴ ποιούμενοι, νῦν μετὰ τὴν ἐπιφάνειαν τοῦ Χριστοῦ ὁμοδίαιτοι γινόμενοι, καὶ ὑπὲρ τῶν ἐχθρῶν εὐχόμενοι, καὶ τοὺς ἀδίκως μισοῦντας πείθειν πειρώμενοι, ὅπως οἱ κατὰ τὰς τοῦ Χριστοῦ καλὰς ὑποθημοσύνας βιώσαντες εὐέλπιδες ὦσι σὺν ἡμῖν τῶν αὐτῶν παρὰ τοῦ πάντων δεσπόζοντος θεοῦ τυχεῖν. Compare Origen, *Contr. Celsum*, i. 67: ἐμποίει δὲ θαυμασίαν πραότητα καὶ καταστολὴν τοῦ ἤθους, καὶ φιλανθρωπίαν καὶ χρηστότητα καὶ ἡμερότητα ἐν τοῖς μὴ διὰ τὰ βιωτικὰ ἤ τινας χρείας ἀνθρωπικὰς ὑποκριναμένοις, ἀλλὰ παραδεξαμένοις γνησίως τὸν περὶ θεοῦ καὶ Χριστοῦ καὶ τῆς ἐσομένης κρίσεως λόγον.

At a later period, and under less favourable circumstances, Lactantius could advance similar pretensions, though his rhetorical style commands less of our confidence (*Instit. Div.* iii. 26): Dei autem præcepta, quia et simplicia et vera sunt, quantum valeant in animis hominum quotidiana exempla demonstrant. Da mihi virum qui sit iracundus, maledicus, effrænatus; paucissimis Dei verbis tam placidum quam ovem reddam. Da cupidum, avarum, tenacem: jam tibi eum liberalem dabo, et pecuniam suam plenis manibus largientem. Da timidum doloris ac mortis: jam cruces, et ignes, et Phalaridis taurum contemnet. Da libidinosum, adulterum, ganeonem: jam sobrium, castum, continentem videbis. Da crudelem et sanguinis appetentem: jam in veram clementiam furor ille mutabitur . . . gratis ista fiunt, facile, cito; modo pateant aures, et pectus sapientiam sitiat . . . Pauca vero Dei præcepta sic totum hominem immutant, et exposito vetere, novum reddunt, ut non cognoscas eundem esse.

On the conversion of Pagans at the sight of the Christian martyrdoms, see particularly Justin Martyr, *Apol.* ii. c. 12: καὶ γὰρ αὐτὸς ἐγώ, τοῖς Πλάτωνος χαίρων διδάγμασι, διαβαλλομένους ἀκούων Χριστιανοὺς, ὁρῶν δὲ ἀφόβους πρὸς θάνατον καὶ πάντα τὰ ἄλλα νομιζόμενα φοβερά, ἐνενόουν ἀδύνατον εἶναι ἐν κακίᾳ καὶ φιληδονίᾳ ὑπάρχειν αὐτούς. κ. τ. λ.

This passage is cited by Eusebius, *Hist. Eccl.* iv. 8. Comp. Justin M., *Apol.* i. c. 25. *Dial.* c. *Tryph.* c. 110, 119, 131. To the evidence thus afforded, the Pagans could only reply by imputing the patience of the Christians to obstinacy or madness. Tertull., *Apol.* c. 27: Quidam dementiam existimant, quod cum possimus et sacrificare in præsenti, et illæsi abire manente apud animum proposito, obstinationem saluti præferamus. c. 50: propterea desperati et perditi existimamur. In the same place: Nec quicquam tamen proficit exquisitior quæque crudelitas vestra; illecebra est magis vitæ: plures efficimur, quoties metimur a vobis: semen est sanguis Christianorum. . . Illa ipsa obstinatio, quam exprobratis, magistra est. Quis enim non contemplatione ejus concutitur ad requirendum, quid intus in re sit? Quis non, ubi requisivit, accedit? ubi accessit, pati exhortat?

Compare Epict., *Dissert.* iv. 7: εἶτα ὑπὸ μανίας μὲν δύναται τὶς οὕτω διατεθῆναι πρὸς ταῦτα, καὶ ὑπὸ ἔθους ὡς οἱ Γαλιλαῖοι, ὑπὸ λόγου δὲ καὶ ἀποδείξεως οὐδεὶς δύναται. M. Aurel., *Medit.* xi. 3: μὴ κατὰ ψιλὴν παράταξιν, ὡς οἱ Χριστιανοί.

In the Epistle to Diognetus, one of the pieces attributed

to Justin Martyr, the heathen is invited to remark, among other tokens of their moral superiority, that the Christians do not expose their infants: γαμοῦσιν. . . τεκνογονοῦσιν, ἀλλ' οὐ ῥίπτουσι τὰ γεννώμενα. Among the heathen, this abominable practice, which grew probably more and more rife with the decline of society, was the result often of misery, but more commonly of indolence and selfishness. When we remember that the Christians, who denied themselves this miserable resource, were excluded by their principles from many of the employments and avocations of their fellow-citizens, we can easily imagine how superior they must have been to the mass of those around them in self-denial, self-confidence, and energy; in all the virtues, in short, which in the long run secure success in life. I imagine that no cause contributed more to the triumph of Christianity than the moral discipline to which its disciples were necessarily subjected.

Note K K, Page 165.

The story is told by Sozomen, *Hist. Eccles.* i. 18, and is repeated by most writers on Church history as a vivid illustration of the temper of the times. Some may pay it the tribute of a passing smile, others make an open jest of it. To me it seems to have a deep and grave significance. I believe that among the most thoughtful and logical of reasoners the final movement towards conversion has often been one of sudden inexplicable impulse, and I trace in this individual instance, whether actual or mythical, a striking emblem of the way in which the last links which bound the Roman Empire to Paganism were mysteriously, providentially, perhaps I may say miraculously, snapped asunder.

LONDON
PRINTED BY SPOTTISWOODE AND CO.
NEW-STREET SQUARE

39 Paternoster Row, E.C.
London, June 1864.

GENERAL LIST OF WORKS,

NEW BOOKS AND NEW EDITIONS,

PUBLISHED BY

Messrs. LONGMAN, GREEN, LONGMAN, ROBERTS, and GREEN.

Arts, Manufactures, &c. 11	Miscellaneous and Popular Metaphysical Works 6
Astronomy, Meteorology, Popular Geography, &c. 7	Natural History and Popular Science 8
Biography and Memoirs 3	Periodical Publications 20
Chemistry, Medicine, Surgery, and the Allied Sciences 9	Poetry and the Drama 17
Commerce, Navigation, and Mercantile Affairs 19	Religious Works 13
Criticism, Philology, &c. 4	Rural Sports, &c. 18
Fine Arts and Illustrated Editions 11	Travels, Voyages, &c. 15
General and School Atlases 20	Works of Fiction 16
Historical Works 1	Works of Utility and General Information 19
Index ....21—24	

Historical Works.

The History of England from the Fall of Wolsey to the Death of Elizabeth. By JAMES ANTHONY FROUDE, M.A. late Fellow of Exeter College, Oxford.

Vols. I. to IV. the Reign of Henry VIII. Second Edition, 54s.

Vols. V. and VI. the Reigns of Edward VI. and Mary. Second Edition, 28s.

Vols. VII. and VIII. the Reign of Elizabeth, Vols. I. and II. Third Edition, 28s.

The History of England from the Accession of James II. By Lord MACAULAY. Three Editions, as follows.

LIBRARY EDITION, 5 vols. 8vo. £4.

CABINET EDITION, 8 vols. post 8vo. 48s.

PEOPLE'S EDITION, 4 vols. crown 8vo. 16s.

Revolutions in English History. By ROBERT VAUGHAN, D.D. 3 vols. 8vo. 45s.

Vol. I. Revolutions of Race, 15s.

Vol. II. Revolutions in Religion, 15s.

Vol. III. Revolutions in Government, 15s.

The History of England during the Reign of George the Third. By WILLIAM MASSEY, M.P. 4 vols. 8vo. 48s.

The Constitutional History of England, since the Accession of George III. 1760—1860. By THOMAS ERSKINE MAY, C.B. 2 vols. 8vo. 33s.

Lives of the Queens of England, from State Papers and other Documentary Sources: comprising a Domestic History of England from the Conquest to the Death of Queen Anne. By AGNES STRICKLAND. Revised Edition, with many Portraits. 8 vols. post 8vo. 60s.

Lectures on the History of England. By WILLIAM LONGMAN. VOL. I. from the Earliest Times to the Death of King Edward II. with 6 Maps, a coloured Plate, and 53 Woodcuts. 8vo. 15s.

A Chronicle of England, from B.C. 55 to A.D. 1485; written and illustrated by J. E. DOYLE. With 81 Designs engraved on Wood and printed in Colours by E. Evans. 4to. 42s.

History of Civilization. By HENRY THOMAS BUCKLE. 2 vols. £1 17s.

VOL. I. *England and France*, Fourth Edition, 21s.

VOL. II. *Spain and Scotland*, Second Edition, 16s.

Democracy in America. By ALEXIS DE TOCQUEVILLE. Translated by HENRY REEVE, with an Introductory Notice by the Translator. 2 vols. 8vo. 21s.

The Spanish Conquest in America, and its Relation to the History of Slavery and to the Government of Colonies. By ARTHUR HELPS. 4 vols. 8vo. £3. VOLS. I. & II. 28s. VOLS. III. & IV. 16s. each.

History of the Reformation in Europe in the Time of Calvin. By J. H. MERLE D'AUBIGNE, D.D. VOLS. I. and II. 8vo. 28s. and VOL. III. 12s.

Library History of France, in 5 vols. 8vo. By EYRE EVANS CROWE. VOL. I. 14s. VOL. II. 15s. VOL. III. 18s. VOL. IV. nearly ready.

Lectures on the History of France. By the late Sir JAMES STEPHEN, LL.D. 2 vols. 8vo. 24s.

The History of Greece. By C. THIRLWALL, D.D. Lord Bishop of St. David's. 8 vols. 8vo. £3; or in 8 vols. fcp. 28s.

The Tale of the Great Persian War, from the Histories of *Herodotus*. By the Rev. G. W. COX, M.A. late Scholar of Trin. Coll. Oxon. Fcp. 8vo. 7s. 6d.

Ancient History of Egypt, Assyria, and Babylonia. By the Author of 'Amy Herbert.' Fcp. 8vo. 6s.

Critical History of the Language and Literature of Ancient Greece. By WILLIAM MURE, of Caldwell. 5 vols. 8vo. £3 9s.

History of the Literature of Ancient Greece. By Professor K. O. MÜLLER. Translated by the Right Hon. Sir GEORGE CORNEWALL LEWIS, Bart. and by J. W. DONALDSON, D.D. 3 vols. 8vo. 36s.

History of the Romans under the Empire. By the Rev. CHARLES MERIVALE, B.D. 7 vols. 8vo. with Maps, £5.

The Fall of the Roman Republic: a Short History of the Last Century of the Commonwealth. By the Rev. CHARLES MERIVALE, B.D. 12mo. 7s. 6d.

Critical and Historical Essays contributed to the *Edinburgh Review*. By the Right Hon. Lord MACAULAY.

LIBRARY EDITION, 3 vols. 8vo. 36s.

TRAVELLER'S EDITION, in 1 vol. 21s.

In POCKET VOLUMES, 3 vols. fcp. 21s.

PEOPLE'S EDITION, 2 vols. crown 8vo.

The Biographical History of Philosophy, from its Origin in Greece to the Present Day. By GEORGE HENRY LEWES. Revised and enlarged Edition. 8vo. 16s.

History of the Inductive Sciences. By WILLIAM WHEWELL, D.D. F.R.S. Master of Trin. Coll. Cantab. Third Edition. 3 vols. crown 8vo. 24s.

Egypt's Place in Universal History; an Historical Investigation. By C. C. J. BUNSEN, D.D. Translated by C. H. COTTRELL, M.A. With many Illustrations. 4 vols. 8vo. £5 8s. VOL. V. is nearly ready.

Maunder's Historical Treasury; comprising a General Introductory Outline of Universal History, and a Series of Separate Histories. Fcp. 8vo. 10s.

Historical and Chronological Encyclopædia, presenting in a brief and convenient form Chronological Notices of all the Great Events of Universal History. By B. B. WOODWARD, F.S.A. Librarian to the Queen. [*In the press.*

History of Christian Missions; their Agents and their Results. By T. W. M. MARSHALL. 2 vols. 8vo. 24s.

History of the Early Church, from the First Preaching of the Gospel to the Council of Nicæa, A.D. 325. By the Author of 'Amy Herbert.' Fcp. 8vo. 4s. 6d.

History of Wesleyan Methodism. By GEORGE SMITH, F.A.S. New Edition, with Portraits, in course of publication in 31 parts, 6d. each.

History of Modern Music; a Course of Lectures delivered at the Royal Institution. By JOHN HULLAH, Professor of Vocal Music in King's College and in Queen's College, London. Post 8vo. 6s. 6d.

History of Medicine, from the Earliest Ages to the Present Time. By EDWARD MERYON, M.D. F.G.S. VOL. I. 8vo. 12s. 6d.

Biography and Memoirs.

Sir John Eliot, a Biography: 1590—1632. By JOHN FORSTER. With 2 Portraits on Steel, from the Originals at Port Eliot. 2 vols. crown 8vo. 30s.

Letters and Life of Francis Bacon, including all his Occasional Works. Collected and edited, with a Commentary, by J. SPEDDING, Trin. Coll. Cantab. VOLS. I. and II. 8vo. 24s.

Life of Robert Stephenson, F.R.S. By J. C. JEAFFRESON, Barrister-at-Law, and WILLIAM POLE, F.R.S. Memb. Inst. Civ. Eng. With 2 Portraits and many Illustrations. 2 vols. 8vo. [*Just ready.*

Life of the Duke of Wellington. By the Rev. G. R. GLEIG, M.A. Popular Edition, carefully revised; with copious Additions. Crown 8vo. 5s.

Brialmont and Gleig's Life of the Duke of Wellington. 4 vols. 8vo. with Illustrations, £2 14s.

Life of the Duke of Wellington, partly from the French of M. BRIALMONT, partly from Original Documents. By the Rev. G. R. GLEIG, M.A. 8vo. with Portrait, 15s.

Apologia pro Vita Sua: being a Reply to a Pamphlet intitled 'What then does Dr. Newman mean?' By JOHN HENRY NEWMAN, D.D. 8vo.

Father Mathew: a Biography. By JOHN FRANCIS MAGUIRE, M.P. Second Edition, with Portrait. Post 8vo. 12s. 6d.

Rome; its Rulers and its Institutions. By the same Author. New Edition in preparation.

Life of Amelia Wilhelmina Sieveking, from the German. Edited, with the Author's sanction, by CATHERINE WINKWORTH. Post 8vo. with Portrait, 12s.

Felix Mendelssohn's Letters from *Italy and Switzerland,* translated by LADY WALLACE, Third Edition, with Notice of MENDELSSOHN's Life and Works, by HENRY F. CHORLEY; and *Letters from* 1833 *to* 1847, translated by Lady WALLACE. New Edition, with Portrait. 2 vols. crown 8vo. 5s. each.

Diaries of a Lady of Quality, from 1797 to 1844. Edited, with Notes, by A. HAYWARD, Q.C. Post 8vo. 10s. 6d.

Recollections of the late William Wilberforce, M.P. for the County of York during nearly 30 Years. By J. S. HARFORD, D.C.L. F.R.S. Post 8vo. 7s.

Life and Correspondence of Theodore Parker. By JOHN WEISS. With 2 Portraits and 19 Wood Engravings. 2 vols. 8vo. 30s.

Southey's Life of Wesley. Fifth Edition. Edited by the Rev. C. C. SOUTHEY, M.A. Crown 8vo. 7s. 6d.

Thomas Moore's Memoirs, Journal, and Correspondence. Edited and abridged from the First Edition by Earl RUSSELL. Square crown 8vo. with 8 Portraits, 12s. 6d.

Memoir of the Rev. Sydney Smith. By his Daughter, Lady HOLLAND. With a Selection from his Letters, edited by Mrs. AUSTIN. 2 vols. 8vo. 28s.

Life of William Warburton, D.D. Bishop of Gloucester from 1760 to 1779. By the Rev. J. S. WATSON, M.A. 8vo. with Portrait, 18s.

Fasti Eboracenses: Lives of the Archbishops of York. By the late Rev. W. H. DIXON, M.A. Edited and enlarged by the Rev. J. RAINE, M.A. In 2 vols. VOL. I. comprising the Lives to the Death of Edward III. 8vo. 15s.

Vicissitudes of Families. By Sir BERNARD BURKE, Ulster King of Arms. FIRST, SECOND, and THIRD SERIES. 3 vols. crown 8vo. 12s. 6d. each.

Biographical Sketches. By NASSAU W. SENIOR. Post 8vo. 10s. 6d.

Essays in Ecclesiastical Biography. By the Right Hon. Sir J. STEPHEN, LL.D. Fourth Edition. 8vo. 14s.

Arago's Biographies of Distinguished Scientific Men. By FRANÇOIS ARAGO. Translated by Admiral W. H. SMYTH, F.R.S., the Rev. B. POWELL, M.A., and R. GRANT, M.A. 8vo. 18s.

Maunder's Biographical Treasury: Memoirs, Sketches, and Brief Notices of above 12,000 Eminent Persons of All Ages and Nations. Fcp. 8vo. 10s.

Criticism, Philosophy, Polity, &c.

Papinian: a Dialogue on State Affairs between a Constitutional Lawyer and a Country Gentleman about to enter Public Life. By GEORGE ATKINSON, B.A. Oxon. Serjeant-at-Law. [*Nearly ready.*

On Representative Government. By JOHN STUART MILL. Second Edition, 8vo. 9s.

Dissertations and Discussions. By the same Author. 2 vols. 8vo. 24s.

On Liberty. By the same Author. Third Edition. Post 8vo. 7s. 6d.

Principles of Political Economy. By the same. Fifth Edition. 2 vols. 8vo. 30s.

A System of Logic, Ratiocinative and Inductive. By the same. Fifth Edition. 2 vols. 8vo. 25s.

Utilitarianism. By the same. 8vo. 5s.

Lord Bacon's Works, collected and edited by R. L. ELLIS, M.A., J. SPEDDING, M.A. and D. D. HEATH. VOLS. I. to V. *Philosophical Works.* 5 vols. 8vo. £4 6s. VOLS. VI. and VII. *Literary and Professional Works.* 2 vols. £1 16s.

Bacon's Essays, with Annotations. By R. WHATELY, D.D. late Archbishop of Dublin. Sixth Edition. 8vo. 10s. 6d.

Elements of Logic. By R. WHATELY, D.D. late Archbishop of Dublin. Ninth Edition. 8vo. 10s. 6d. crown 8vo. 4s. 6d.

Elements of Rhetoric. By the same Author. Seventh Edition. 8vo. 10s. 6d. crown 8vo. 4s. 6d.

English Synonymes. Edited by Archbishop WHATELY. 5th Edition. Fcp. 8vo. 3s.

Miscellaneous Remains from the Common-place Book of the late Archbishop WHATELY. Edited by Miss WHATELY. Post 8vo. [*Just ready.*

Essays on the Administrations of Great Britain from 1783 to 1830, contributed to the *Edinburgh Review* by the Right Hon. Sir G. C. LEWIS, Bart. Edited by the Right Hon. Sir E. HEAD, Bart. 8vo. with Portrait, 15s.

By the same Author.

A Dialogue on the Best Form of Government, 4s. 6d.

Essay on the Origin and Formation of the Romance Languages, 7s. 6d.

Historical Survey of the Astronomy of the Ancients, 15s.

Inquiry into the Credibility of the Early Roman History, 2 vols. 30s.

On the Methods of Observation and Reasoning in Politics, 2 vols. 28s.

Irish Disturbances and Irish Church Question, 12s.

Remarks on the Use and Abuse of some Political Terms, 9s.

On Foreign Jurisdiction and Extradition of Criminals, 2s. 6d.

The Fables of Babrius, Greek Text with Latin Notes, PART I. 5s. 6d. PART II. 3s. 6d.

Suggestions for the Application of the Egyptological Method to Modern History, 1s.

An Outline of the Necessary Laws of Thought: a Treatise on Pure and Applied Logic. By the Most Rev. W. THOMSON, D.D. Archbishop of York. Crown 8vo. 5s. 6d.

The Elements of Logic. By THOMAS SHEDDEN, M.A. of St. Peter's Coll. Cantab. Crown 8vo. [*Just ready.*

Analysis of Mr. Mill's System of Logic. By W. STEBBING, M.A. Fellow of Worcester College, Oxford. Post 8vo. [*Just ready.*

Speeches of the Right Hon. Lord MACAULAY, corrected by Himself. 8vo. 12s.

Lord Macaulay's Speeches on Parliamentary Reform in 1831 and 1832. 16mo. 1s.

A Dictionary of the English Language. By R. G. LATHAM, M.A. M.D. F.R.S. Founded on that of Dr. JOHNSON, as edited by the Rev. H. J. TODD, with numerous Emendations and Additions. Publishing in 36 Parts, price 3s. 6d. each, to form 2 vols. 4to.

The English Language. By the same Author. Fifth Edition. 8vo. 18s.

Handbook of the English Language. By the same Author. Fourth Edition. Crown 8vo. 7s. 6d.

Elements of Comparative Philology. By the same Author. 8vo. 21s.

Thesaurus of English Words and Phrases, classified and arranged so as to facilitate the Expression of Ideas, and assist in Literary Composition. By P. M. ROGET, M.D. 14th Edition, crown 8vo. 10s. 6d.

Lectures on the Science of Language, delivered at the Royal Institution. By MAX MÜLLER, M.A. Fellow of All Souls College, Oxford. FIRST SERIES, Fourth Edition. 8vo. 12s. SECOND SERIES nearly ready.

The Debater; a Series of Complete Debates, Outlines of Debates, and Questions for Discussion. By F. ROWTON. Fcp. 8vo. 6s.

A Course of English Reading, adapted to every taste and capacity; or, How and What to Read. By the Rev. J. PYCROFT, B.A. Fcp. 8vo. 5s.

Manual of English Literature, Historical and Critical: with a Chapter on English Metres. By T. ARNOLD, B.A. Prof. of Eng. Lit. Cath. Univ. Ireland. Post 8vo. 10s. 6d.

Southey's Doctor, complete in One Volume. Edited by the Rev. J.W. WARTER, B.D. Square crown 8vo. 12s. 6d.

Historical and Critical Commentary on the Old Testament; with a New Translation. By M. M. KALISCH, Ph. D. VOL. I. *Genesis,* 8vo. 18s. or adapted for the General Reader, 12s. VOL. II. *Exodus,* 15s. or adapted for the General Reader, 12s.

A Hebrew Grammar, with Exercises. By the same. PART I. *Outlines with Exercises,* 8vo. 12s. 6d. KEY, 5s. PART II. *Exceptional Forms and Constructions,* 12s. 6d.

A New Latin-English Dictionary. By the Rev. J. T. White, M.A. of Corpus Christi College, and Rev. J. E. RIDDLE, M.A. of St. Edmund Hall, Oxford. Imperial 8vo. 42s.

A Diamond Latin-English Dictionary, or Guide to the Meaning, Quality, and Accentuation of Latin Classical Words. By the Rev. J. E. RIDDLE, M.A. 32mo. 4s.

A New English-Greek Lexicon, containing all the Greek Words used by Writers of good authority. By C. D. YONGE, B.A. Fourth Edition. 4to. 21s.

A Lexicon, English and Greek, abridged for the use of Schools from his 'English-Greek Lexicon' by the Author, C. D. YONGE, B.A. Square 12mo. [*Just ready.*

A Greek-English Lexicon. Compiled by H. G. LIDDELL, D.D. Dean of Christ Church, and R. SCOTT, D.D. Master of Balliol. Fifth Edition, crown 4to. 31s. 6d.

A Lexicon, Greek and English, abridged from LIDDELL and SCOTT's *Greek-English Lexicon.* Tenth Edition, square 12mo. 7s. 6d.

A Practical Dictionary of the French and English Languages. By L. CONTANSEAU. 7th Edition. Post 8vo. 10s. 6d.

Contanseau's Pocket Dictionary, French and English; being a close Abridgment of the above, by the same Author. 18mo. 5s. 2nd Edition.

New Practical Dictionary of the German Language; German-English, and English-German. By the Rev. W. L. BLACKLEY, M.A., and Dr. CARL MARTIN FRIEDLANDER. Post 8vo. [*In the press.*

Miscellaneous Works and Popular Metaphysics.

Recreations of a Country Parson: being a Selection of the Contributions of A. K. H. B. to *Fraser's Magazine*. SECOND SERIES. Crown 8vo. 3s. 6d.

The Commonplace Philosopher in Town and Country. By the same Author. Crown 8vo. 3s 6d.

Leisure Hours in Town; Essays Consolatory, Æsthetical, Moral, Social, and Domestic. By the same. Crown 8vo. 3s. 6d.

Friends in Council: a Series of Readings and Discourses thereon. 2 vols. fcp. 8vo. 9s.

Friends in Council, SECOND SERIES. 2 vols. post 8vo. 14s.

Essays written in the Intervals of Business. Fcp. 8vo. 2s. 6d.

Companions of My Solitude. By the same Author. Fcp. 8vo. 3s. 6d.

Lord Macaulay's Miscellaneous Writings; comprising his Contributions to KNIGHT'S *Quarterly Magazine*, Articles from the Edinburgh Review not included in his *Critical and Historical Essays*, Biographies from the *Encyclopædia Britannica*, Miscellaneous Poems and Inscriptions. 2 vols. 8vo. with Portrait, 21s.

The Rev. Sydney Smith's Miscellaneous Works; including his Contributions to the *Edinburgh Review*.

   LIBRARY EDITION. 3 vols. 8vo. 36s.

   TRAVELLER'S EDITION, in 1 vol. 21s.

   In POCKET VOLUMES. 3 vols. 21s.

   PEOPLE'S EDITION, 2 vols. crown 8vo. 8s.

Elementary Sketches of Moral Philosophy, delivered at the Royal Institution. By the same Author. Fcp. 8vo. 7s.

The Wit and Wisdom of the Rev. SYDNEY SMITH: a Selection of the most memorable Passages in his Writings and Conversation. 16mo. 7s. 6d.

From Matter to Spirit: the Result of Ten Years' Experience in Spirit Manifestations. By C. D. with a Preface by A. B. Post 8vo. 8s. 6d.

The History of the Supernatural in All Ages and Nations, and in All Churches, Christian and Pagan; demonstrating a Universal Faith. By WILLIAM HOWITT. 2 vols. post 8vo. 18s.

Chapters on Mental Physiology. By Sir HENRY HOLLAND, Bart. M.D. F.R.S. Second Edition. Post 8vo. 8s. 6d.

Essays selected from Contributions to the *Edinburgh Review*. By HENRY ROGERS. Second Edition. 3 vols. fcp. 21s.

The Eclipse of Faith; or, a Visit to a Religious Sceptic. By the same Author. Tenth Edition. Fcp. 8vo. 5s.

Defence of the Eclipse of Faith, by its Author; a Rejoinder to Dr. Newman's Reply. Third Edition. Fcp. 8vo. 3s. 6d.

Selections from the Correspondence of R. E. H. Greyson. By the same Author. Third Edition. Crown 8vo. 7s. 6d.

Fulleriana, or the Wisdom and Wit of THOMAS FULLER, with Essay on his Life and Genius. By the same Author. 16mo. 2s. 6d.

Reason and Faith, reprinted from the *Edinburgh Review*. By the same Author. Fourth Edition. Fcp. 8vo. 1s. 6d.

An Introduction to Mental Philosophy, on the Inductive Method. By J. D. MORELL, M.A. LL.D. 8vo. 12s.

Elements of Psychology, containing the Analysis of the Intellectual Powers. By the same Author. Post 8vo. 7s. 6d.

The Senses and the Intellect. By ALEXANDER BAIN, M.A. Professor of Logic in the University of Aberdeen. Second Edition. 8vo. 15s.

The Emotions and the Will, by the same Author; completing a Systematic Exposition of the Human Mind. 8vo. 15s.

On the Study of Character, including an Estimate of Phrenology. By the same Author. 8vo. 9s.

Hours with the Mystics: a Contribution to the History of Religious Opinion. By ROBERT ALFRED VAUGHAN, B.A. Second Edition. 2 vols. crown 8vo. 12s.

Psychological Inquiries, or Essays intended to illustrate the Influence of the Physical Organisation on the Mental Faculties. By Sir B. C. BRODIE, Bart. Fcp. 8vo. 5s. PART II. Essays intended to illustrate some Points in the Physical and Moral History of Man. Fcp. 8vo. 5s.

The Philosophy of Necessity; or Natural Law as applicable to Mental, Moral, and Social Science. By CHARLES BRAY. Second Edition. 8vo. 9s.

The Education of the Feelings and Affections. By the same Author. Third Edition. 8vo. 3s. 6d.

Christianity and Common Sense. By Sir WILLOUGHBY JONES, Bart. M.A. Trin. Coll. Cantab. 8vo. 6s.

Astronomy, Meteorology, Popular Geography, &c.

Outlines of Astronomy. By Sir J. F. W. HERSCHEL, Bart, M.A. Seventh Edition, revised; with Plates and Woodcuts. 8vo. 18s.

⁎ Two Plates are new in this Edition, one showing the willow-leaved structure of the SUN's photosphere, the other exhibiting a portion of the MOON's surface from a model by Mr. NASMYTH.

Arago's Popular Astronomy. Translated by Admiral W. H. SMYTH, F.R.S. and R. GRANT, M.A. With 25 Plates and 358 Woodcuts. 2 vols. 8vo. £2 5s.

Arago's Meteorological Essays, with Introduction by Baron HUMBOLDT. Translated under the superintendence of Major-General E. SABINE, R.A. 8vo. 18s.

The Weather-Book; a Manual of Practical Meteorology. By Rear-Admiral ROBERT FITZ ROY, R.N. F.R.S. Third Edition, with 16 Diagrams. 8vo. 15s.

Saxby's Weather System, or Lunar Influence on Weather. By S. M. SAXBY, R.N. Principal Instructor of Naval Engineers, H. M. Steam Reserve. Second Edition. Post 8vo. 4s.

Dove's Law of Storms considered in connexion with the ordinary Movements of the Atmosphere. Translated by R. H. SCOTT, M.A. T.C.D. 8vo. 10s. 6d.

Celestial Objects for Common Telescopes. By the Rev. T. W. WEBB, M.A. F.R.A.S. With Map of the Moon, and Woodcuts. 16mo. 7s.

Physical Geography for Schools and General Readers. By M. F. MAURY, LL.D. Author of 'Physical Geography of the Sea,' &c. [*Nearly ready.*

A Dictionary, Geographical, Statistical, and Historical, of the various Countries, Places, and principal Natural Objects in the World. By J. R. M'CULLOCH, Esq. With 6 Maps. 2 vols. 8vo. 63s.

A General Dictionary of Geography, Descriptive, Physical, Statistical, and Historical : forming a complete Gazetteer of the World. By A. KEITH JOHNSTON, F.R.S.E. 8vo. 30s.

A Manual of Geography, Physical, Industrial, and Political. By W. HUGHES, F.R.G.S. Professor of Geography in King's College, and in Queen's College, London. With 6 Maps. Fcp. 8vo. 7s. 6d.

Or in Two Parts:—PART I. Europe, 3s. 6d. PART II. Asia, Africa, America, Australasia, and Polynesia, 4s.

The Geography of British History; a Geographical Description of the British Islands at Successive Periods, from the Earliest Times to the Present Day. By the same. With 6 Maps. Fcp. 8vo. 8s. 6d.

The British Empire; a Sketch of the Geography, Growth, Natural and Political Features of the United Kingdom, its Colonies and Dependencies. By CAROLINE BRAY. With 5 Maps. Fcp. 8vo. 7s. 6d.

Colonisation and Colonies : a Series of Lectures delivered before the University of Oxford. By HERMAN MERIVALE, M.A. Professor of Political Economy. 8vo. 18s.

The Africans at Home: a popular Description of Africa and the Africans. By the Rev. R. M. MACBRAIR, M.A. Second Edition; including an Account of the Discovery of the Source of the Nile. With Map and 70 Woodcuts. Fcp. 8vo. 5s.

Maunder's Treasury of Geography, Physical, Historical, Descriptive, and Political. Completed by W. HUGHES, F.R.G.S. With 7 Maps and 16 Plates. Fcp. 8vo. 10s.

Natural History and Popular Science.

The Elements of Physics or Natural Philosophy. By NEIL ARNOTT, M.D. F.R.S. Physician Extraordinary to the Queen. Sixth Edition. PART I. 8vo. 10s. 6d.

Heat Considered as a Mode of Motion; a Course of Lectures delivered at the Royal Institution. By Professor JOHN TYNDALL, F.R.S. Crown 8vo. with Woodcuts, 12s. 6d.

Volcanos, the Character of their Phenomena, their Share in the Structure and Composition of the Surface of the Globe, &c. By G. POULETT SCROPE, M.P. F.R.S. Second Edition. 8vo. with Illustrations, 15s.

A Treatise on Electricity, in Theory and Practice. By A. DE LA RIVE, Prof. in the Academy of Geneva. Translated by C. V. WALKER, F.R.S. 3 vols. 8vo. with Woodcuts, £3 13s.

The Correlation of Physical Forces. By W. R. GROVE, Q.C. V.P.R.S. Fourth Edition. 8vo. 7s. 6d.

The Geological Magazine; or, Monthly Journal of Geology. Edited by T. RUPERT JONES, F.G.S. Professor of Geology in the R. M. College, Sandhurst; assisted by J. C. WOODWARD, F.G.S. F.Z.S. British Museum. 8vo. with Illustrations, price 1s. 6d. monthly.

A Guide to Geology. By J. PHILLIPS, M.A. Professor of Geology in the University of Oxford. Fifth Edition; with Plates and Diagrams. Fcp. 8vo. 4s.

A Glossary of Mineralogy. By H. W. BRISTOW, F.G.S. of the Geological Survey of Great Britain. With 486 Figures. Crown 8vo. 12s.

Phillips's Elementary Introduction to Mineralogy, with extensive Alterations and Additions, by H. J. BROOKE, F.R.S. and W. H. MILLER, F.G.S. Post 8vo. with Woodcuts, 18s.

Van Der Hoeven's Handbook of Zoology. Translated from the Second Dutch Edition by the Rev. W. CLARK, M.D. F.R.S. 2 vols. 8vo. with 24 Plates of Figures, 60s.

The Comparative Anatomy and Physiology of the Vertebrate Animals. By RICHARD OWEN, F.R.S. D.C.L. 2 vols. 8vo. with upwards of 1,200 Woodcuts.
[In the press.

Homes without Hands: an Account of the Habitations constructed by various Animals, classed according to their Principles of Construction. By Rev. J. G. WOOD, M.A. F.L.S. Illustrations on Wood by G. Pearson, from Drawings by F. W. Keyl and E. A. Smith. In course of publication in 20 Parts, 1s. each.

Manual of Cœlenterata. By J. REAY GREENE, B.A. M.R.I.A. Edited by the Rev. J. A. GALBRAITH, M.A. and the Rev. S. HAUGHTON, M.D. Fcp. 8vo. with 39 Woodcuts, 5s.

Manual of Protozoa; with a General Introduction on the Principles of Zoology. By the same Author and Editors. Fcp. 8vo. with 16 Woodcuts, 2s.

Manual of the Metalloids. By J. APJOHN, M.D. F.R.S. and the same Editors. Fcp. 8vo. with 38 Woodcuts, 7s. 6d.

The Alps: Sketches of Life and Nature in the Mountains. By Baron H. VON BERLEPSCH. Translated by the Rev. L. STEPHEN, M.A. With 17 Illustrations. 8vo. 15s.

The Sea and its Living Wonders.
By Dr. G. HARTWIG. Second (English) Edition. 8vo. with many Illustrations. 18s.

The Tropical World. By the same Author. With 8 Chromoxylographs and 172 Woodcuts. 8vo. 21s.

Sketches of the Natural History of Ceylon. By Sir J. EMERSON TENNENT, K.C.S. LL.D. With 82 Wood Engravings. Post 8vo. 12s. 6d.

Ceylon. By the same Author. 5th Edition; with Maps, &c. and 90 Wood Engravings. 2 vols. 8vo. £2 10s.]

Marvels and Mysteries of Instinct; or, Curiosities of Animal Life. By G. GARRATT. Third Edition. Fcp. 8vo. 7s.

Home Walks and Holiday Rambles. By the Rev. C. A. JOHNS, B.A. F.L.S. Fcp. 8vo. with 10 Illustrations, 6s.

Kirby and Spence's Introduction to Entomology, or Elements of the Natural History of Insects. Seventh Edition. Crown 8vo. 5s.

Maunder's Treasury of Natural History, or Popular Dictionary of Zoology. Revised and corrected by T. S. COBBOLD, M.D. Fcp. 8vo. with 900 Woodcuts, 10s.

The Treasury of Botany, on the Plan of Maunder's Treasury. By J. LINDLEY, M.D. and T. MOORE, F.L.S. assisted by other Practical Botanists. With 16 Plates, and many Woodcuts from designs by W. H. Fitch. Fcp. 8vo. [*In the press.*

The Rose Amateur's Guide. By THOMAS RIVERS. 8th Edition. Fcp. 8vo. 4s.

The British Flora; comprising the Phænogamous or Flowering Plants and the Ferns. By Sir W. J. HOOKER, K.H. and G. A. WALKER-ARNOTT, LL.D. 12mo. with 12 Plates, 14s. or coloured, 21s.

Bryologia Britannica; containing the Mosses of Great Britain and Ireland, arranged and described. By W. WILSON. 8vo. with 61 Plates, 42s. or coloured, £4 4s.

The Indoor Gardener. By Miss MALING. Fcp. 8vo. with coloured Frontispiece, 5s.

Loudon's Encyclopædia of Plants; comprising the Specific Character, Description, Culture, History, &c. of all the Plants found in Great Britain. With upwards of 12,000 Woodcuts. 8vo. £3 13s. 6d.

Loudon's Encyclopædia of Trees and Shrubs; containing the Hardy Trees and Shrubs of Great Britain scientifically and popularly described. With 2,000 Woodcuts. 8vo. 50s.

History of the British Freshwater Algæ. By A. H. HASSALL, M.D. With 100 Plates of Figures. 2 vols. 8vo. price £1 15s.

Maunder's Scientific and Literary Treasury; a Popular Encyclopædia of Science, Literature, and Art. Fcp. 8vo. 10s.

A Dictionary of Science, Literature, and Art; comprising the History Description, and Scientific Principles of every Branch of Human Knowledge. Edited by W. T. BRANDE, F.R.S.L. and E. Fourth Edition, revised and corrected.
[*In the press.*

Essays on Scientific and other subjects, contributed to the *Edinburgh* and *Quarterly Reviews*. By Sir H. HOLLAND, Bart, M.D. Second Edition. 8vo. 14s.

Essays from the Edinburgh and *Quarterly Reviews*; with Addresses and other Pieces. By Sir J. F. W. HERSCHEL, Bart. M.A. 8vo. 18s.

Chemistry, Medicine, Surgery, and the Allied Sciences.

A Dictionary of Chemistry and the Allied Branches of other Sciences; founded on that of the late Dr. Ure. By HENRY WATTS, F.C.S. assisted by eminent Contributors. 4 vols. 8vo. in course of publication in Monthly Parts. VOL. I. 31s. 6d. and VOL. II. 26s. are now ready.

Handbook of Chemical Analysis, adapted to the Unitary System of Notation: Based on Dr. H. Wills' *Anleitung zur chemischen Analyse*. By F. T. CONINGTON, M.A. F.C.S. Post 8vo. 7s. 6d.—TABLES OF QUALITATIVE ANALYSIS to accompany the same, 2s. 6d.

A Handbook of Volumetrical Analysis. By ROBERT H. SCOTT, M.A. T.C.D. Post 8vo. 4s. 6d.

Elements of Chemistry, Theoretical and Practical. By WILLIAM A. MILLER, M.D. LL.D. F.R.S. F.G.S. Professor of Chemistry, King's College, London. 3 vols. 8vo. £2 12s. PART I. CHEMICAL PHYSICS. Third Edition enlarged, 12s. PART II. INORGANIC CHEMISTRY. Second Edition, 20s. PART III. ORGANIC CHEMISTRY. Second Edition, 20s.

A Manual of Chemistry, Descriptive and Theoretical. By WILLIAM ODLING, M.B. F.R.S. Lecturer on Chemistry at St. Bartholomew's Hospital. PART I. 8vo. 9s.

A Manual of Chemistry, Descriptive and Theoretical, for the use of Medical Students. By the same Author. PART I. crown 8vo. with Woodcuts, 4s. 6d. PART II. (completion) *just ready*.

The Diagnosis and Treatment of the Diseases of Women; including the Diagnosis of Pregnancy. By GRAILY HEWITT, M.D. Physician to the British Lying-in Hospital. 8vo. 16s.

Lectures on the Diseases of Infancy and Childhood. By CHARLES WEST, M.D. &c. Fourth Edition, revised and enlarged. 8vo. 14s.

Exposition of the Signs and Symptoms of Pregnancy: with other Papers on subjects connected with Midwifery. By W. F. MONTGOMERY, M.A. M.D. M.R.I.A. 8vo. with Illustrations, 25s.

A System of Surgery, Theoretical and Practical. In Treatises by Various Authors, arranged and edited by T. HOLMES, M.A. Cantab. Assistant-Surgeon to St. George's Hospital. 4 vols. 8vo.

Vol. I. General Pathology. 21s.

Vol. II. Local Injuries—Diseases of the Eye. 21s.

Vol. III. Operative Surgery. Diseases of the Organs of Special Sense, Respiration, Circulation, Locomotion and Innervation. 21s.

Vol. IV. Diseases of the Alimentary Canal, of the Urino-genitary Organs, of the Thyroid, Mamma and Skin; with Appendix of Miscellaneous Subjects, and GENERAL INDEX. [*Nearly ready*.

Lectures on the Principles and Practice of Physic. By THOMAS WATSON, M.D. Physician-Extraordinary to the Queen. Fourth Edition. 2 vols. 8vo. 34s.

Lectures on Surgical Pathology. By J. PAGET, F.R.S. Surgeon-Extraordinary to the Queen. Edited by W. TURNER, M.B. 8vo. with 117 Woodcuts, 21s.

A Treatise on the Continued Fevers of Great Britain. By C. MURCHISON, M.D. Senior Physician to the London Fever Hospital. 8vo. with coloured Plates, 18s.

Demonstrations of Microscopic Anatomy; a Guide to the Examination of the Animal Tissues and Fluids in Health and Disease, for the use of the Medical and Veterinary Professions. Founded on a Course of Lectures delivered by Dr. HARLEY, Prof. in Univ. Coll. London. Edited by G. T. BROWN, late Vet. Prof. in the Royal Agric. Coll. Cirencester. 8vo. with Illustrations. [*Nearly ready*.

Anatomy, Descriptive and Surgical. By HENRY GRAY, F.R.S. With 410 Wood Engravings from Dissections. Third Edition, by T. HOLMES, M.A. Cantab. Royal 8vo. 28s.

Physiological Anatomy and Physiology of Man. By the late R. B. TODD, M.D. F.R.S. and W. BOWMAN, F.R.S. of King's College. With numerous Illustrations. VOL. II. 8vo. 25s.

A New Edition of Vol. I. revised and edited by Dr. LIONEL S. BEALE, is preparing for publication.

The Cyclopædia of Anatomy and Physiology. Edited by the late R. B. TODD, M.D. F.R.S. Assisted by nearly all the most eminent cultivators of Physiological Science of the present age. 5 vols. 8vo. with 2,853 Woodcuts, £6 6s.

A Dictionary of Practical Medicine. By J. COPLAND, M.D. F.R.S Abridged from the larger work by the Author, assisted by J. C. COPLAND. 1 vol. 8vo. [*In the press*.

Dr. Copland's Dictionary of Practical Medicine (the larger work). 3 vols. 8vo. £5 11s.

The Works of Sir B. C. Brodie, Bart. Edited by CHARLES HAWKINS, F.R.C.S.E. 2 vols. 8vo. [*In the press.*

Medical Notes and Reflections. By Sir H. HOLLAND, Bart. M.D. Third Edition. 8vo. 18s.

Hooper's Medical Dictionary, or Encyclopædia of Medical Science. Ninth Edition, brought down to the present time by ALEX. HENRY, M.D. 1 vol. 8vo. [*In the press.*

A Manual of Materia Medica and Therapeutics, abridged from Dr. PEREIRA's *Elements* by F. J. FARRE, M.D. Cantab. assisted by R. BENTLEY, M.R.C.S. and by R. WARRINGTON, F.C.S. 1 vol. 8vo. [*In October.*

Dr. Pereira's Elements of Materia Medica and Therapeutics, Third Edition, by A. S. TAYLOR, M.D. and G. O. REES, M.D. 3 vols. 8vo. with numerous Woodcuts. £3 15s.

The Fine Arts, and Illustrated Editions.

The New Testament of Our Lord and Saviour Jesus Christ, Illustrated with numerous Engravings on Wood from the OLD MASTERS. Crown 4to. price 63s. cloth, gilt top; or price £5 5s. elegantly bound in morocco. [*In October.*

Lyra Germanica; Hymns for the Sundays and Chief Festivals of the Christian Year. Translated by CATHERINE WINKWORTH; 125 Illustrations on Wood drawn by J. LEIGHTON, F.S.A. Fcp. 4to. 21s.

Cats' and Farlie's Moral Emblems; with Aphorisms, Adages, and Proverbs of all Nations : comprising 121 Illustrations on Wood by J. LEIGHTON, F.S.A. with an appropriate Text by R. PIGOT. Imperial 8vo. 31s. 6d.

Bunyan's Pilgrim's Progress : with 126 Illustrations on Steel and Wood by C. BENNETT; and a Preface by the Rev. C. KINGSLEY. Fcp. 4to. 21s.

The History of Our Lord, as exemplified in Works of Art: with that of His Types, St. John the Baptist, and other Persons of the Old and New Testament. By Mrs. JAMESON and Lady EASTLAKE. Being the Fourth and concluding SERIES of 'Sacred and Legendary Art;' with 31 Etchings and 281 Woodcuts. 2 vols. square crown 8vo. 42s.

In the same Series, by Mrs. JAMESON.

Legends of the Saints and Martyrs. Fourth Edition, with 19 Etchings and 187 Woodcuts. 2 vols. 31s. 6d.

Legends of the Monastic Orders. Third Edition, with 11 Etchings and 88 Woodcuts. 1 vol. 21s.

Legends of the Madonna. Third Edition. with 27 Etchings and 165 Woodcuts. 1 vol. 21s.

Arts, Manufactures, &c.

Encyclopædia of Architecture, Historical, Theoretical, and Practical. By JOSEPH GWILT. With more than 1,000 Woodcuts. 8vo. 42s.

Tuscan Sculpture, from its Revival to its Decline. Illustrated with Etchings and Woodcuts from Original Drawings and Photographs. By CHARLES C. PERKINS. [*In the press.*

The Engineer's Handbook; explaining the Principles which should guide the young Engineer in the Construction of Machinery. By C. S. LOWNDES. Post 8vo. 5s.

The Elements of Mechanism, for Students of Applied Mechanics. By T. M. GOODEVE, M.A. Professor of Nat. Philos. in King's Coll. Lond. With 206 Woodcuts. Post 8vo. 6s. 6d.

Ure's Dictionary of Arts, Manufactures, and Mines. Re-written and enlarged by ROBERT HUNT, F.R.S., assisted by numerous gentlemen eminent in Science and the Arts. With 2,000 Woodcuts. 3 vols. 8vo. £4.

Encyclopædia of Civil Engineering, Historical, Theoretical, and Practical. By E. CRESY, C.E. With above 3,000 Woodcuts. 8vo. 42s.

Treatise on Mills and Millwork. By W. FAIRBAIRN, C.E. F.R.S. With 18 Plates and 322 Woodcuts. 2 vols. 8vo. 32s. or each vol. separately, 16s.

Useful Information for Engineers. By the same Author. FIRST and SECOND SERIES, with many Plates and Woodcuts. 2 vols. crown 8vo. 21s. or each vol. separately, 10s. 6d.

The Application of Cast and Wrought Iron to Building Purposes. By the same Author. Third Edition, with Plates and Woodcuts. [*Nearly ready.*

The Practical Mechanic's Journal: An Illustrated Record of Mechanical and Engineering Science, and Epitome of Patent Inventions. 4to. price 1s. monthly.

The Practical Draughtsman's Book of Industrial Design. By W. JOHNSON, Assoc. Inst. C.E. With many hundred Illustrations. 4to. 28s. 6d.

The Patentee's Manual: a Treatise on the Law and Practice of Letters Patent for the use of Patentees and Inventors. By J. and J. H. JOHNSON. Post 8vo. 7s. 6d.

The Artisan Club's Treatise on the Steam Engine, in its various Applications to Mines, Mills, Steam Navigation, Railways, and Agriculture. By J. BOURNE, C.E. Fifth Edition; with 37 Plates and 546 Woodcuts. 4to. 42s.

A Catechism of the Steam Engine, in its various Applications to Mines, Mills, Steam Navigation, Railways, and Agriculture. By the same Author. With 80 Woodcuts. Fcp. 8vo. 6s.

The Story of the Guns. By Sir J. EMERSON TENNENT, K.C.S. F.R.S. With 33 Woodcuts. Post 8vo. 7s. 6d.

The Theory of War Illustrated by numerous Examples from History. By Lieut.-Col. P. L. MACDOUGALL. *Third Edition*, with 10 Plans. Post 8vo. 10s. 6d.

Collieries and Colliers; A Handbook of the Law and leading Cases relating thereto. By J. C. FOWLER, Barrister-at-Law, Stipendiary Magistrate. Fcp. 8vo. 6s.

The Art of Perfumery; the History and Theory of Odours, and the Methods of Extracting the Aromas of Plants. By Dr. PIESSE, F.C.S. Third Edition, with 53 Woodcuts. Crown 8vo. 10s. 6d.

Chemical, Natural, and Physical Magic, for Juveniles during the Holidays. By the same Author. With 30 Woodcuts. Fcp. 8vo. 3s. 6d.

The Laboratory of Chemical Wonders: A Scientific Mélange for Young People. By the same. Crown 8vo. 5s. 6d.

Talpa; or, the Chronicles of a Clay Farm. By C. W. HOSKYNS, Esq. With 24 Woodcuts from Designs by G. CRUIKSHANK. 16mo. 5s. 6d.

H.R.H. The Prince Consort's Farms: An Agricultural Memoir. By JOHN CHALMERS MORTON. Dedicated by permission to Her Majesty the QUEEN. With 40 Wood Engravings. 4to. 52s. 6d.

Handbook of Farm Labour, Steam, Water, Wind, Horse Power, Hand Power, &c. By the same Author. 16mo. 1s. 6d.

Handbook of Dairy Husbandry; comprising the General Management of a Dairy Farm, &c. By the same. 16mo. 1s. 6d.

Loudon's Encyclopædia of Agriculture: Comprising the Laying-out, Improvement, and Management of Landed Property, and the Cultivation and Economy of the Productions of Agriculture. With 1,100 Woodcuts. 8vo. 31s. 6d.

Loudon's Encyclopædia of Gardening: Comprising the Theory and Practice of Horticulture, Floriculture, Arboriculture, and Landscape Gardening. With 1,000 Woodcuts. 8vo. 31s. 6d.

Loudon's Encyclopædia of Cottage, Farm, and Villa Architecture and Furniture. With more than 2,000 Woodcuts. 8vo. 42s.

History of Windsor Great Park and Windsor Forest. By WILLIAM MENZIES, Resident Deputy Surveyor. With a Map, and 20 Photographs by the EARL of CAITHNESS and Mr. BAMBRIDGE. Imperial folio. [*Just ready.*

Bayldon's Art of Valuing Rents and Tillages, and Claims of Tenants upon Quitting Farms, both at Michaelmas and Lady-Day. 8vo. 10s. 6d.

Religious and Moral Works.

An Exposition of the 39 Articles, Historical and Doctrinal. By E. HAROLD BROWNE, D.D. Lord Bishop of Ely. Sixth Edition, 8vo. 16s.

The Pentateuch and the Elohistic Psalms, in Reply to Bishop Colenso. By the same Author. 8vo. 2s.

Examination Questions on Bishop Browne's Exposition of the Articles. By the Rev. J. GORLE, M.A. Fcp. 3s. 6d.

Five Lectures on the Character of St. Paul; being the Hulsean Lectures for 1862. By the Rev. J. S. HOWSON, D.D. Second Edition. 8vo. 9s.

A Critical and Grammatical Commentary on St. Paul's Epistles. By C. J. ELLICOTT, D.D. Lord Bishop of Gloucester and Bristol. 8vo.

Galatians, Third Edition, 8s. 6d.

Ephesians, Third Edition, 8s. 6d.

Pastoral Epistles, Second Edition, 10s. 6d.

Philippians, Colossians, and Philemon, Second Edition, 10s. 6d.

Thessalonians, Second Edition, 7s. 6d.

Historical Lectures on the Life of Our Lord Jesus Christ: being the Hulsean Lectures for 1859. By the same Author. Third Edition. 8vo. 10s. 6d.

The Destiny of the Creature; and other Sermons preached before the University of Cambridge. By the same. Post 8vo. 5s.

The Broad and the Narrow Way; Two Sermons preached before the University of Cambridge. By the same. Crown 8vo. 2s.

Rev. T. H. Horne's Introduction to the Critical Study and Knowledge of the Holy Scriptures. Eleventh Edition, corrected, and extended under careful Editorial revision. With 4 Maps and 22 Woodcuts and Facsimiles. 4 vols. 8vo. £3 13s. 6d.

Rev. T. H. Horne's Compendious Introduction to the Study of the Bible, being an Analysis of the larger work by the same Author. Re-edited by the Rev. JOHN AYRE, M.A. With Maps, &c. Post 8vo. 9s.

The Treasury of Bible Knowledge, on the plan of Maunder's Treasuries. By the Rev. JOHN AYRE, M.A. Fcp. 8vo. with Maps and Illustrations. [*In the press.*

The Greek Testament; with Notes, Grammatical and Exegetical. By the Rev. W. WEBSTER, M.A. and the Rev. W. F. WILKINSON, M.A. 2 vols. 8vo. £2 4s.

VOL. I. the Gospels and Acts, 20s.

VOL. II. the Epistles and Apocalypse, 24s.

The Four Experiments in Church and State; and the Conflicts of Churches. By Lord ROBERT MONTAGU, M.P. 8vo. 12s.

Every-day Scripture Difficulties explained and illustrated; Gospels of St. Matthew and St. Mark. By J. E. PRESCOTT, M.A. late Fellow of C. C. Coll. Cantab. 8vo. 9s.

The Pentateuch and Book of Joshua Critically Examined. By J. W. COLENSO, D.D. Lord Bishop of Natal. PART I. *the Pentateuch examined as an Historical Narrative.* 8vo. 6s. PART II. *the Age and Authorship of the Pentateuch Considered,* 7s. 6d. PART III. *the Book of Deuteronomy,* 8s. PART IV. *the First 11 Chapters of Genesis examined and separated, with Remarks on the Creation, the Fall, and the Deluge,* 10s. 6d.

The Life and Epistles of St. Paul. By W. J. CONYBEARE, M.A. late Fellow of Trin. Coll. Cantab. and J. S. HOWSON, D.D. Principal of the Collegiate Institution, Liverpool.

LIBRARY EDITION, with all the Original Illustrations, Maps, Landscapes on Steel, Woodcuts, &c. 2 vols. 4to. 48s.

INTERMEDIATE EDITION, with a Selection of Maps, Plates, and Woodcuts. 2 vols. square crown 8vo. 31s. 6d.

PEOPLE'S EDITION, revised and condensed, with 46 Illustrations and Maps. 2 vols. crown 8vo. 12s.

The Voyage and Shipwreck of St. Paul; with Dissertations on the Ships and Navigation of the Ancients. By JAMES SMITH, F.R.S. Crown 8vo. Charts, 8s. 6d.

Hippolytus and his Age; or, the Beginnings and Prospects of Christianity. By Baron BUNSEN, D.D. 2 vols. 8vo. 30s.

Outlines of the Philosophy of Universal History, applied to Language and Religion: Containing an Account of the Alphabetical Conferences. By the same Author. 2 vols. 8vo. 33s.

Analecta Ante-Nicæna. By the same Author. 3 vols. 8vo. 42s.

Theologia Germanica. Translated by SUSANNA WINKWORTH; with a Preface by the Rev. C. KINGSLEY; and a Letter by Baron BUNSEN. Fcp. 8vo. 5s.

Instructions in the Doctrine and Practice of Christianity, as an Introduction to Confirmation. By G. E. L. COTTON, D.D. Lord Bishop of Calcutta. 18mo. 2s. 6d.

Essays on Religion and Literature. By Cardinal WISEMAN, Dr. D. ROCK, F. H. LAING, and other Writers. Edited by H. E. MANNING, D.D. 8vo.

Essays and Reviews. By the Rev. W. TEMPLE, D.D. the Rev. R. WILLIAMS, B.D. the Rev. B. POWELL, M.A. the Rev. H. B. WILSON, B.D. C. W. GOODWIN, M.A. the Rev. M. PATTISON, B.D. and the Rev. B. JOWETT, M.A. 11th Edition. Fcp. 8vo. 5s.

Mosheim's Ecclesiastical History. MURDOCK and SOAMES's Translation and Notes, re-edited by the Rev. W. STUBBS, M.A. 3 vols. 8vo. 45s.

The Gentile and the Jew in the Courts of the Temple of Christ: an Introduction to the History of Christianity. From the German of Prof. DÖLLINGER, by the Rev. N. DARNELL, M.A. 2 vols. 8vo. 21s.

Physico-Prophetical Essays, on the Locality of the Eternal Inheritance, its Nature and Character; the Resurrection Body; and the Mutual Recognition of Glorified Saints. By the Rev. W. LISTER, F.G.S. Crown 8vo. 6s.

Bishop Jeremy Taylor's Entire Works: With Life by BISHOP HEBER. Revised and corrected by the Rev. C. P. EDEN, 10 vols. 8vo. £5 5s.

Passing Thoughts on Religion. By the Author of 'Amy Herbert.' 8th Edition. Fcp. 8vo. 5s.

Thoughts for the Holy Week, for Young Persons. By the same Author. 2d Edition. Fcp. 8vo. 2s.

Night Lessons from Scripture. By the same Author. 2d Edition. 32mo. 3s.

Self-examination before Confirmation. By the same Author. 32mo. 1s. 6d.

Readings for a Month Preparatory to Confirmation from Writers of the Early and English Church. By the same. Fcp. 4s.

Readings for Every Day in Lent, compiled from the Writings of Bishop JEREMY TAYLOR. By the same. Fcp. 8vo. 5s.

Preparation for the Holy Communion; the Devotions chiefly from the works of JEREMY TAYLOR. By the same. 32mo. 3s.

Morning Clouds. Second Edition. Fcp. 8vo. 5s.

The Afternoon of Life. By the same Author. Second Edition. Fcp. 5s.

Problems in Human Nature. By the same. Post 8vo. 5s.

The Wife's Manual; or, Prayers, Thoughts, and Songs on Several Occasions of a Matron's Life. By the Rev. W. CALVERT, M.A. Crown 8vo. 10s. 6d.

Spiritual Songs for the Sundays and Holidays throughout the Year. By J. S. B. MONSELL, LL.D. Vicar of Egham. Third Edition. Fcp. 8vo.

Hymnologia Christiana; or, Psalms and Hymns selected and arranged in the order of the Christian Seasons. By B. H. KENNEDY, D.D. Prebendary of Lichfield. Crown 8vo. 7s. 6d.

Lyra Domestica; Christian Songs for Domestic Edification. Translated from the *Psaltery and Harp* of C. J. P. SPITTA, and from other sources, by RICHARD MASSIE. FIRST and SECOND SERIES, fcp. 4s. 6d. each.

Lyra Sacra; Hymns, Ancient and Modern, Odes, and Fragments of Sacred Poetry. Edited by the Rev. B. W. SAVILE, M.A. Fcp. 8vo. 5s.

Lyra Germanica, translated from the German by Miss C. WINKWORTH. FIRST SERIES, Hymns for the Sundays and Chief Festivals; SECOND SERIES, the Christian Life. Fcp. 8vo. 5s. each SERIES.

Hymns from Lyra Germanica, 18mo. 1s.

Lyra Eucharistica; Hymns and Verses on the Holy Communion, Ancient and Modern; with other Poems. Edited by the Rev. ORBY SHIPLEY, M.A. Second Edition, revised and enlarged. Fcp. 8vo. [*Just ready.*

Lyra Messianica; Hymns and Verses on the Life of Christ, Ancient and Modern; with other Poems. By the same Editor. Fcp. 8vo. 7s. 6d.

Lyra Mystica; Hymns and Verses on Sacred Subjects, Ancient and Modern. Forming a companion-volume to the above, by the same Editor. Fcp. 8vo. [*Nearly ready.*

The Chorale Book for England; a complete Hymn-Book in accordance with the Services and Festivals of the Church of England: the Hymns translated by Miss C. WINKWORTH; the Tunes arranged by Prof. W. S. BENNETT and OTTO GOLDSCHMIDT. Fcp. 4to. 10s. 6d.

Congregational Edition. Fcp. 1s. 6d.

Travels, Voyages, &c.

Eastern Europe and Western Asia. Political and Social Sketches on Russia, Greece, and Syria. By HENRY A. TILLEY. With 6 Illustrations. Post 8vo. 10s. 6d.!

Explorations in South-west Africa, from Walvisch Bay to Lake Ngami. By THOMAS BAINES. 8vo. with Map and Illustrations. [*In October.*

South American Sketches; or, a Visit to Rio Janeiro, the Organ Mountains, La Plata, and the Paraná. By THOMAS W. HINCHLIFF, M.A. F.R.G.S. Post 8vo. with Illustrations, 12s. 6d.

Explorations in Labrador. By HENRY Y. HIND, M.A. F.R.G.S. With Maps and Illustrations. 2 vols. 8vo. 32s.

The Canadian Red River and Assinniboine and Saskatchewan Exploring Expeditions. By the same Author. With Maps and Illustrations. 2 vols. 8vo. 42s.

The Capital of the Tycoon; a Narrative of a 3 Years' Residence in Japan. By Sir RUTHERFORD ALCOCK, K.C.B. 2 vols. 8vo. with numerous Illustrations, 42s.

Last Winter in Rome and other Italian Cities. By C. R. WELD, Author of 'The Pyrenees, West and East,' &c. 1 vol. post 8vo. with a Portrait of 'STELLA,' and Engravings on Wood from Sketches by the Author. [*In the Autumn.*

Autumn Rambles in North Africa, including Excursions in Algeria and Tunis. By JOHN ORMSBY, Author of the 'Ascent of the Grivola,' in 'Peaks, Passes, and Glaciers.' With 9 Vignettes and 4 full-page Illustrations on Wood from Sketches by the Author. Post 8vo.

The Dolomite Mountains. Excursions through Tyrol, Carinthia, Carniola, and Friuli in 1861, 1862, and 1863. By J. GILBERT and G. C. CHURCHILL, F.R.G.S. With numerous Illustrations. Square crown 8vo. 21s.

Peaks, Passes, and Glaciers; a Series of Excursions by Members of the Alpine Club. Edited by J. BALL, M.R.I.A. Fourth Edition; Maps, Illustrations, Woodcuts. Square crown 8vo. 21s.—TRAVELLERS' EDITION, condensed, 16mo. 5s. 6d.

Second Series, edited by E. S. KENNEDY, M.A. F.R.G.S. With many Maps and Illustrations. 2 vols. square crown 8vo. 42s.

Nineteen Maps of the Alpine Districts, from the First and Second Series of *Peaks, Passes, and Glaciers.* Price 7s. 6d.

Mountaineering in 1861; a Vacation Tour. By Prof. J. TYNDALL, F.R.S. Square crown 8vo. with 2 Views, 7s. 6d.

A Summer Tour in the Grisons and Italian Valleys of the Bernina. By Mrs. HENRY FRESHFIELD. With 2 Coloured Maps and 4 Views. Post 8vo. 10s. 6d.

Alpine Byways; or, Light Leaves gathered in 1859 and 1860. By the same Authoress. Post 8vo. with Illustrations, 10s. 6d.

A Lady's Tour Round Monte Rosa; including Visits to the Italian Valleys. With Map and Illustrations. Post 8vo. 14s.

Guide to the Pyrenees, for the use of Mountaineers. By CHARLES PACKE. With Maps, &c. and a new Appendix. Fcp. 6s.

Guide to the Central Alps, including the Bernese Oberland, Eastern Switzerland, Lombardy, and Western Tyrol. By JOHN BALL, M.R.I.A. Post 8vo. with Maps. [*In June.*

Guide to the Western Alps. By the same Author. With an Article on the Geology of the Alps by M. E. DESOR. Post 8vo. with Maps, &c. 7s. 6d.

A Week at the Land's End. By J. T. BLIGHT; assisted by E. H. RODD, R. Q. COUCH, and J. RALFS. With Map and 96 Woodcuts. Fcp. 8vo. 6s. 6d.

Visits to Remarkable Places: Old Halls, Battle-Fields, and Scenes illustrative of Striking Passages in English History and Poetry. By WILLIAM HOWITT. 2 vols. square crown 8vo. with Wood Engravings, 25s.

The Rural Life of England. By the same Author. With Woodcuts by Bewick and Williams. Medium 8vo. 12s. 6d.

Works of Fiction.

Late Laurels: a Tale. By the Author of 'Wheat and Tares.' 2 vols. post 8vo. 15s.

Gryll Grange. By the Author of 'Headlong Hall.' Post 8vo. 7s. 6d.

A First Friendship. [Reprinted from *Fraser's Magazine.*] Crown 8vo. 7s. 6d.

Thalatta; or, the Great Commoner: a Political Romance. Crown 8vo. 9s.

Atherstone Priory. By L. N. COMYN. 2 vols. post 8vo.

Ellice: a Tale. By the same. Post 8vo. 9s. 6d.

The Last of the Old Squires. By the Rev. J. W. WARTER, B.D. Second Edition. Fcp. 8vo. 4s. 6d.

Tales and Stories by the Author of 'Amy Herbert,' uniform Edition, each Story or Tale in a single volume.

AMY HERBERT, 2s. 6d.	KATHARINE ASHTON, 3s. 6d.
GERTRUDE, 2s. 6d.	MARGARET PERCIVAL, 5s.
EARL'S DAUGHTER, 2s. 6d.	LANETON PARSONAGE, 4s. 6d.
EXPERIENCE OF LIFE, 2s. 6d.	URSULA, 4s. 6d.
CLEVE HALL, 3s. 6d.	
IVORS, 3s. 6d.	

A Glimpse of the World. By the Author of 'Amy Herbert.' Fcp. 8vo. 7s. 6d.

Essays on Fiction; comprising Articles on Sir W. Scott, Sir E. B. LYTTON, Colonel Senior, Mr. Thackeray, and Mrs. Beecher Stowe. Reprinted chiefly from the *Edinburgh, Quarterly,* and *Westminster Reviews;* with large Additions. By NASSAU W. SENIOR. Post 8vo. 10s. 6d.

The Gladiators: a Tale of Rome and Judæa. By G. J. WHYTE MELVILLE. Crown 8vo. 5s.

Digby Grand, an Autobiography. By the same Author. 1 vol. 5s.

Kate Coventry, an Autobiography. By the same. 1 vol. 5s.

General Bounce, or the Lady and the Locusts. By the same. 1 vol. 5s.

Holmby House, a Tale of Old Northamptonshire. 1 vol. 5s.

Good for Nothing, or All Down Hill. By the same. 1 vol. 6s.

The Queen's Maries, a Romance of Holyrood. 1 vol. 6s.

The Interpreter, a Tale of the War. By the same. 1 vol. 5s.

Tales from Greek Mythology. By the Rev. G. W. COX, M.A. late Scholar of Trin. Coll. Oxon. Second Edition. Square 16mo. 3s. 6d.

Tales of the Gods and Heroes. By the same Author. Second Edition. Fcp. 8vo. 5s.

Tales of Thebes and Argos. By the same Author. Fcp. 8vo. 4s. 6d.

The Warden: a Novel. By ANTHONY TROLLOPE. Crown 8vo. 3s. 6d.

Barchester Towers: a Sequel to 'The Warden.' By the same Author. Crown 8vo. 5s.

The Six Sisters of the Valleys: an Historical Romance. By W. BRAMLEY-MOORE, M.A. Incumbent of Gerrard's Cross, Bucks. With 14 Illustrations on Wood. Crown 8vo. 5s.

Poetry and the Drama.

Moore's Poetical Works, Cheapest Editions complete in 1 vol. including the Autobiographical Prefaces and Author's last Notes, which are still copyright. Crown 8vo. ruby type, with Portrait, 7s. 6d. or People's Edition, in larger type, 12s. 6d.

Moore's Poetical Works, as above, Library Edition, medium 8vo. with Portrait and Vignette, 21s. or in 10 vols. fcp. 3s. 6d. each.

Tenniel's Edition of Moore's *Lalla Rookh,* with 68 Wood Engravings from Original Drawings and other Illustrations. Fcp. 4to. 21s.

Moore's Lalla Rookh. 32mo. Plate, 1s. 16mo. Vignette, 2s. 6d. Square crown 8vo. with 13 Plates, 15s.

Maclise's Edition of Moore's Irish *Melodies,* with 161 Steel Plates from Original Drawings. Super-royal 8vo. 31s. 6d.

Moore's Irish Melodies, 32mo. Portrait, 1s. 16mo. Vignette, 2s. 6d. Square crown 8vo. with 13 Plates, 21s.

Southey's Poetical Works, with the Author's last Corrections and copyright Additions. Library Edition, in 1 vol. medium 8vo. with Portrait and Vignette, 14s. or in 10 vols. fcp. 3s. 6d. each.

Lays of Ancient Rome; with *Ivry* and the *Armada.* By the Right Hon. LORD MACAULAY. 16mo. 4s. 6d.

Lord Macaulay's Lays of Ancient Rome. With 90 Illustrations on Wood, Original and from the Antique, from Drawings by G. SCHARF. Fcp. 4to. 21s.

Poems. By JEAN INGELOW. Sixth Edition. Fcp. 8vo. 5s.

Poetical Works of Letitia Elizabeth Landon (L.E.L.) 2 vols. 16mo. 10s.

Playtime with the Poets: a Selection of the best English Poetry for the use of Children. By a LADY. Crown 8vo. 5s.

The Revolutionary Epick. By the Rt. Hon. BENJAMIN DISRAELI. Fcp. 8vo. 5s.

Bowdler's Family Shakspeare, cheaper Genuine Edition, complete in 1 vol. large type, with 36 Woodcut Illustrations, price 14s. or, with the same ILLUSTRATIONS, in 6 pocket vols. 5s. each.

An English Tragedy; Mary Stuart, from SCHILLER; and Mdlle. De Belle Isle, from A. DUMAS,—each a Play in 5 Acts, by FRANCES ANNE KEMBLE. Post 8vo. 12s.

Rural Sports, &c.

Encyclopædia of Rural Sports; a Complete Account, Historical, Practical, and Descriptive, of Hunting, Shooting, Fishing, Racing, &c. By D. P. BLAINE. With above 600 Woodcuts (20 from Designs by JOHN LEECH). 8vo. 42s.

Col. Hawker's Instructions to Young Sportsmen in all that relates to Guns and Shooting. Revised by the Author's Son. Square crown 8vo. with Illustrations, 18s.

Notes on Rifle Shooting. By Captain HEATON, Adjutant of the Third Manchester Rifle Volunteer Corps. Fcp. 8vo. 2s. 6d.

The Dead Shot, or Sportsman's Complete Guide; a Treatise on the Use of the Gun, Dog-breaking, Pigeon-shooting, &c. By MARKSMAN. Fcp. 8vo. with Plates, 5s.

The Chase of the Wild Red Deer in Devon and Somerset. By C. P. COLLYNS. With Map and Illustrations. Square crown 8vo. 16s.

The Fly-Fisher's Entomology. By ALFRED RONALDS. With coloured Representations of the Natural and Artificial Insect. 6th Edition; with 20 coloured Plates. 8vo. 14s.

Hand-book of Angling: Teaching Fly-fishing, Trolling, Bottom-fishing, Salmon-fishing; with the Natural History of River Fish, and the best modes of Catching them. By EPHEMERA. Fcp. Woodcuts, 5s.

The Cricket Field; or, the History and the Science of the Game of Cricket. By J. PYCROFT, B.A. Trin. Coll. Oxon. 4th Edition. Fcp. 8vo. 5s.

The Cricket Tutor; a Treatise exclusively Practical. By the same. 18mo. 1s.

The Horse's Foot, and how to keep it Sound. By W. MILES, Esq. 9th Edition, with Illustrations. Imp. 8vo. 12s. 6d.

A Plain Treatise on Horse-shoeing. By the same Author. Post 8vo. with Illustrations, 2s.

General Remarks on Stables, and Examples of Stable Fittings. By the same. Imp. 8vo. with 13 Plates, 15s.

The Horse: with a Treatise on Draught. By WILLIAM YOUATT. New Edition, revised and enlarged. 8vo. with numerous Woodcuts, 10s. 6d.

The Dog. By the same Author. 8vo. with numerous Woodcuts, 6s.

The Dog in Health and Disease. By STONEHENGE. With 70 Wood Engravings. Square crown 8vo. 15s.

The Greyhound. By the same. With many Illustrations. Square crown 8vo. 21s.

The Ox; his Diseases and their Treatment: with an Essay on Parturition in the Cow. By J. R. DOBSON, M.R.C.V.S. Post 8vo. with Illustrations. [*Just ready.*

NEW WORKS PUBLISHED BY LONGMAN AND CO. 19

Commerce, Navigation, and Mercantile Affairs.

The Law of Nations Considered as Independent Political Communities. By TRAVERS TWISS, D.C.L. Regius Professor of Civil Law in the University of Oxford. 2 vols. 8vo. 30s. or separately, PART I. *Peace,* 12s. PART II. *War,* 18s.

A Dictionary, Practical, Theo- retical, and Historical, of Commerce and Commercial Navigation. By J. R. M'CULLOCH, Esq. 8vo. with Maps and Plans, 50s.

The Study of Steam and the Marine Engine, for Young Sea Officers. By S. M. SAXBY, R.N. Post 8vo. with 87 Diagrams, 5s. 6d.

A Nautical Dictionary, defining the Technical Language relative to the Building and Equipment of Sailing Vessels and Steamers, &c. By ARTHUR YOUNG. Second Edition; with Plates and 150 Woodcuts. 8vo. 18s.

A Manual for Naval Cadets. By J. M'NEIL BOYD, late Captain R.N. Third Edition; with 240 Woodcuts, and 11 coloured Plates. Post 8vo. 12s. 6d.

** Every Cadet in the Royal Navy is required by the Regulations of the Admiralty to have a copy of this work on his entry into the Navy.

Works of Utility and General Information.

Modern Cookery for Private Families, reduced to a System of Easy Practice in a Series of carefully-tested Receipts. By ELIZA ACTON. Newly revised and enlarged; with 8 Plates, Figures, and 150 Woodcuts. Fcp. 8vo. 7s. 6d.

On Food and its Digestion; an Introduction to Dietetics. By W. BRINTON, M.D. Physician to St. Thomas's Hospital, &c. With 48 Woodcuts. Post 8vo. 12s.

Adulterations Detected; or, Plain Instructions for the Discovery of Frauds in Food and Medicine. By A. H. HASSALL, M.D. Crown 8vo. with Woodcuts, 17s. 6d.

The Vine and its Fruit, in relation to the Production of Wine. By JAMES L. DENMAN. Crown 8vo. 8s. 6d.

Wine, the Vine, and the Cellar. By THOMAS G. SHAW. With 28 Illustrations on Wood. 8vo. 16s.

A Practical Treatise on Brewing; with Formulæ for Public Brewers, and Instructions for Private Families. By W BLACK. 8vo. 10s. 6d.

Short Whist; its Rise, Progress, and Laws: with the Laws of Piquet, Cassino, Ecarté, Cribbage, and Backgammon. By Major A. Fcp. 8vo. 3s.

Hints on Etiquette and the Usages of Society; with a Glance at Bad Habits. Revised, with Additions, by a LADY of RANK. Fcp. 8vo. 2s. 6d.

The Cabinet Lawyer; a Popular Digest of the Laws of England, Civil and Criminal. 19*th Edition,* extended by the Author; including the Acts of the Sessions 1862 and 1863. Fcp. 8vo. 10s. 6d.

The Philosophy of Health; or, an Exposition of the Physiological and Sanitary Conditions conducive to Human Longevity and Happiness. By SOUTHWOOD SMITH, M.D. Eleventh Edition, revised and enlarged; with New Plates. 8vo. [*Just ready.*

Hints to Mothers on the Manage- ment of their Health during the Period of Pregnancy and in the Lying-in Room. By T. BULL, M.D. Fcp. 8vo. 5s.

The Maternal Management of Children in Health and Disease. By the same Author. Fcp. 8vo. 5s.

Notes on Hospitals. By FLORENCE NIGHTINGALE. Third Edition, enlarged; with 13 Plans. Post 4to. 18s.

C. M. Willich's Popular Tables for Ascertaining the Value of Lifehold, Leasehold, and Church Property, Renewal Fines, &c.; the Public Funds; Annual Average Price and Interest on Consols from 1731 to 1861; Chemical, Geographical, Astronomical, Trigonometrical Tables, &c. Post 8vo. 10s.

Thomson's Tables of Interest, at Three, Four, Four and a Half, and Five per Cent, from One Pound to Ten Thousand and from 1 to 365 Days. 12mo. 3s. 6d.

Maunder's Treasury of Knowledge and Library of Reference: comprising an English Dictionary and Grammar, a Universal Gazetteer, a Classical Dictionary, a Chronology, a Law Dictionary, a Synopsis of the Peerage, useful Tables, &c. Fcp. 8vo. 10s.

General and School Atlases.

An Elementary Atlas of History and Geography, from the commencement of the Christian Era to the Present Time, in 16 coloured Maps, chronologically arranged, with illustrative Memoirs. By the Rev. J. S. BREWER, M.A. Royal 8vo. 12s. 6d.

Bishop Butler's Atlas of Modern Geography, in a Series of 33 full-coloured Maps, accompanied by a complete Alphabetical Index. New Edition, corrected and enlarged. Royal 8vo. 10s. 6d.

Bishop Butler's Atlas of Ancient Geography, in a Series of 24 full-coloured Maps, accompanied by a complete Accentuated Index. New Edition, corrected and enlarged. Royal 8vo. 12s.

School Atlas of Physical, Political, and Commercial Geography, in 17 full-coloured Maps, accompanied by descriptive Letterpress. By E. HUGHES, F.R.A.S. Royal 8vo. 10s. 6d.

Middle-Class Atlas of General Geography, in a Series of 29 full-coloured Maps, containing the most recent Territorial Changes and Discoveries. By WALTER M'LEOD, F.R.G.S. 4to. 5s.

Physical Atlas of Great Britain and Ireland; comprising 30 full-coloured Maps, with illustrative Letterpress, forming a concise Synopsis of British Physical Geography. By WALTER M'LEOD, F.R.G.S. Fcp. 4to. 7s. 6d.

Periodical Publications.

The Edinburgh Review, or Critical Journal, published Quarterly in January, April, July, and October. 8vo. price 6s. each No.

The Geological Magazine, or Monthly Journal of Geology, edited by T. RUPERT JONES, F.G.S. assisted by HENRY WOODWARD, F.G.S. 8vo. price 1s. 6d. each No.

Fraser's Magazine for Town and Country, published on the 1st of each Month. 8vo. price 2s. 6d. each No.

The Alpine Journal: a Record of Mountain Adventure and Scientific Observation. By Members of the Alpine Club. Edited by H. B. GEORGE, M.A. Published Quarterly, May 31, Aug. 31, Nov. 30, Feb. 28. 8vo. price 1s. 6d. each No.

INDEX.

ACTON's Modern Cookery 19
Afternoon of Life...................... 14
ALCOCK's Residence in Japan............. 15
Alpine Guide (The) 16
———— Journal (The) 20
APJOHN's Manual of the Metalloids...... 8
ARAGO's Biographies of Scientific Men ... 4
———— Popular Astronomy 7
———— Meteorological Essays 7
ARNOLD's Manual of English Literature.... 5
ARNOTT's Elements of Physics 8
Atherstone Priory 16
ATKINSON's Papinian 4
AYRE's Treasury of Bible Knowledge 13

BACON's Essays, by WHATELY 4
——— Life and Letters, by SPEDDING.... 3
——— Works, by ELLIS, SPEDDING, and HEATH............................... 4
BAIN on the Emotions and Will........... 6
——— on the Senses and Intellect 6
——— on the Study of Character 6
BAINES's Explorations in S.W. Africa 15
BALL's Guide to the Central Alps......... 16
———Guide to the Western Alps 16
BAYLDON's Rents and Tillages 13
BERLEPSCH's Life and Nature in the Alps.. 8
BLACK's Treatise on Brewing............. 19
BLACKLEY and FRIEDLANDER's German and English Dictionary.................. 5
BLAINE's Rural Sports................... 18
BLIGHT's Week at the Land's End 16
BOURNE's Catechism of the Steam Engine.. 12
——— Treatise on the Steam Engine.... 12
BOWDLER's Family SHAKSPEARE........... 18
Boyd's Manual for Naval Cadets 19
BRAMLEY-MOORE's Six Sisters of the Valleys 17
BRANDE's Dictionary of Science, Literature, and Art 9
BRAY's (C.) Education of the Feelings..... 7
——— Philosophy of Necessity......... 7
——— (Mrs.) British Empire 7
BREWER's Atlas of History and Geography 20
BRINTON on Food and Digestion 19
BRISTOW's Glossary of Mineralogy 8
BRODIE's (Sir C. B.) Psychological Inquiries 7
——— Works.................. 11
BROWN's Demonstrations of Microscopic Anatomy............................. 10
BROWNE's Exposition of the 39 Articles ... 13
——— Pentateuch and Elohistic Psalms 13
BUCKLE's History of Civilization 2
BULL's Hints to Mothers................. 19
——— Maternal Management of Children.. 19
BUNSEN's Analecta Ante-Nicæna 14
——— Ancient Egypt............. 2
——— Hippolytus and his Age 14

BUNSEN's Philosophy of Universal History 14
BUNYAN's Pilgrim's Progress, illustrated by BENNETT 11
BURKE's Vicissitudes of Families 4
BUTLER's Atlas of Ancient Geography 20
——— Modern Geography............. 20

Cabinet Lawyer........................... 19
CALVERT's Wife's Manual 14
CATS and FARLIE's Moral Emblems 11
Chorale Book for England 15
COLENSO (Bishop) on Pentateuch and Book of Joshua.......................... 13
COLLYNS on Stag-Hunting in Devon and Somerset 18
Commonplace Philosopher in Town and Country 6
Companions of my Solitude 6
CONINGTON's Handbook of Chemical Analysis 9
CONTANSEAU's Pocket French and English Dictionary 5
——— Practical ditto
CONYBEARE and HOWSON's Life and Epistles of St. Paul 14
COPLAND's Dictionary of Practical Medicine 10
——— Abridgment of ditto 10
COTTON's Introduction to Confirmation ... 14
Cox's Tales of the Great Persian War 2
——— Tales from Greek Mythology..... 17
——— Tales of the Gods and Heroes.... 17
——— Tales of Thebes and Argos 17
CRESY's Encyclopædia of Civil Engineering 12
CROWE's History of France............... 2

D'AUBIGNE's History of the Reformation in the time of CALVIN 2
Dead Shot (The), by MARKSMAN 18
DE LA RIVE's Treatise on Electricity 8
DENMAN's Vine and its Fruit 19
DE TOCQUEVILLE's Democracy in America 2
Diaries of a Lady of Quality.............. 3
DISRAELI's Revolutionary Epick 17
DIXON's Fasti Rboracenses 3
DOBSON on the Ox 18
DÖLLINGER's Introduction to History of Christianity 14
DOVE's Law of Storms 7
DOYLE's Chronicle of England 1

Edinburgh Review (The) 20
Ellice, a Tale........................... 16
ELLICOTT's Broad and Narrow Way........ 13
——— Commentary on Ephesians 13
——— Destiny of the Creature........ 13
——— Lectures on Life of Christ 13

Ellicott's Commentary on Galatians	13
——————— Pastoral Epist.	13
——————— Philippians, &c.	13
——————— Thessalonians	13
Essays and Reviews	14
Essays on Religion and Literature, edited by Manning	14
Essays written in the Intervals of Business	6
Fairbairn's Application of Cast and Wrought Iron to Building	12
——————— Information for Engineers	12
——————— Treatise on Mills & Millwork	12
First Friendship	16
Fitz Roy's Weather Book	7
Forster's Life of Sir John Eliot	3
Fowler's Collieries and Colliers	12
Fraser's Magazine	20
Freshfield's Alpine Byways	16
——————— Tour in the Grisons	16
Friends in Council	6
From Matter to Spirit	6
Froude's History of England	1
Garratt's Marvels and Mysteries of Instinct	9
Geological Magazine	8, 20
Gilbert and Churchill's Dolomite Mountains	15
Goodeve's Elements of Mechanism	11
Gorle's Questions on Browne's Exposition of the 39 Articles	13
Gray's Anatomy	10
Greene's Manual of Coelenterata	8
——————— Manual of Protozoa	8
Grove on Correlation of Physical Forces	8
Gryll Grange	16
Gwilt's Encyclopædia of Architecture	11
Handbook of Angling, by Ephemera	18
Hartwig's Sea and its Living Wonders	9
——————— Tropical World	9
Hassall's Adulterations Detected	19
——————— British Freshwater Algæ	9
Hawker's Instructions to Young Sportsmen	18
Heaton's Notes on Rifle Shooting	18
Helps's Spanish Conquest in America	2
Herschel's Essays from the Edinburgh and Quarterly Reviews	9
——————— Outlines of Astronomy	7
Hewitt on the Diseases of Women	10
Hinchliff's South American Sketches	15
Hind's Canadian Exploring Expeditions	15
——————— Explorations in Labrador	15
Hints on Etiquette	19
Holland's Chapters on Mental Physiology	6
——————— Essays on Scientific Subjects	9
——————— Medical Notes and Reflections	11
Holmes's System of Surgery	10
Hooker and Walker-Arnott's British Flora	9
Hooper's Medical Dictionary	11
Horne's Introduction to the Scriptures	13
——————— Compendium of ditto	13
Hoskyns's Talpa	12
Howitt's History of the Supernatural	6
——————— Rural Life of England	16
——————— Visits to Remarkable Places	16
Howson's Hulsean Lectures on St. Paul	13
Hughes's (E.) Atlas of Physical, Political, and Commercial Geography	20
——————— (W.) Geography of British History	7
——————— Manual of Geography	7
Hullah's History of Modern Music	3
Hymns from *Lyra Germanica*	15
Ingelow's Poems	17
Jameson's Legends of the Saints and Martyrs	11
——————— Legends of the Madonna	11
——————— Legends of the Monastic Orders	11
Jameson and Eastlake's History of Our Lord	11
John's Home Walks and Holiday Rambles	9
Johnson's Patentee's Manual	12
——————— Practical Draughtsman	12
Johnston's Gazetteer, or Geographical Dictionary	7
Jones's Christianity and Common Sense	7
Kalisch's Commentary on the Old Testament	5
——————— Hebrew Grammar	5
Kemble's Plays	18
Kennedy's Hymnologia Christiana	13
Kirby and Spence's Entomology	9
Lady's Tour round Monte Rosa	16
Landon's (L. E. L.) Poetical Works	17
Late Laurels	16
Latham's Comparative Philology	5
——————— English Dictionary	5
——————— Handbook of the English Language	5
——————— Work on the English Language	5
Leisure Hours in Town	6
Lewes's Biographical History of Philosophy	2
Lewis on the Astronomy of the Ancients	4
——————— on the Credibility of Early Roman History	4
——————— Dialogue on Government	4
——————— on Egyptological Method	4
——————— Essays on Administrations	4
——————— Fables of Babrius	4
——————— on Foreign Jurisdiction	4
——————— on Irish Disturbances	4
——————— on Observation and Reasoning in Politics	4
——————— on Political Terms	4
——————— on the Romance Languages	4
Liddell and Scott's Greek-English Lexicon	5
——————— Abridged ditto	5
Lindley and Moore's Treasury of Botany	9
Lister's Physico-Prophetical Essays	14
Longman's Lectures on the History of England	1
Loudon's Encyclopædia of Agriculture	12
——————— Cottage, Farm, and Villa Architecture	12
——————— Gardening	12
——————— Plants	9
——————— Trees and Shrubs	9
Lowndes's Engineer's Handbook	11

Lyra Domestica	15	Moore's Poetical Works	17
—— Eucharistica	15	Morell's Elements of Psychology	6
—— Germanica	11, 15	—————— Mental Philosophy	6
—— Messianica	15	Morning Clouds	14
—— Mystica	15	Morton's Handbook of Dairy Husbandry	12
—— Sacra	15	—————————————— Farm Labour	12
		—————————————— Prince Consort's Farms	12
		Mosheim's Ecclesiastical History	14
Macaulay's (Lord) Essays	2	Muller's (Max) Lectures on the Science of Language	5
——————— History of England	1	———————— (K. O.) Literature of Ancient Greece	2
——————— Laws of Ancient Rome	17	Murchison on Continued Fevers	10
——————— Miscellaneous Writings	6	Mure's Language and Literature of Greece	2
——————— Speeches	5		
——————— Speeches on Parliamentary Reform	5		
Macbrair's Africans at Home	8	New Testament illustrated with Wood Engravings from the Old Masters	11
Macdougall's Theory of War	12	Newman's Apologia pro Vitâ Suâ	3
McLeod's Middle-Class Atlas of General Geography	20	Nightingale's Notes on Hospitals	20
——————— Physical Atlas of Great Britain and Ireland	20		
McCulloch's Dictionary of Commerce	19	Odling's Course of Practical Chemistry	10
——————— Geographical Dictionary	7	—————— Manual of Chemistry	10
Maguire's Life of Father Mathew	3	Ormsby's Rambles in Algeria and Tunis	15
——————— Rome and its Rulers	3	Owen's Comparative Anatomy and Physiology of Vertebrate Animals	8
Malino's Indoor Gardener	9		
Maps from Peaks, Passes, and Glaciers	16		
Marshall's History of Christian Missions	2		
Massey's History of England	1	Packe's Guide to the Pyrenees	16
Maunder's Biographical Treasury	4	Paget's Lectures on Surgical Pathology	10
——————— Geographical Treasury	8	Parker's (Theodore) Life, by Weiss	3
——————— Historical Treasury	2	Peaks, Passes, and Glaciers, 2 Series	16
——————— Scientific and Literary Treasury	9	Pereira's Elements of Materia Medica	11
——————— Treasury of Knowledge	20	—————— Manual of Materia Medica	11
——————— Treasury of Natural History	9	Perkins's Tuscan Sculpture	11
Maury's Physical Geography	7	Phillips's Guide to Geology	8
May's Constitutional History of England	1	————— Introduction to Mineralogy	8
Melville's Digby Grand	17	Piesse's Art of Perfumery	12
——————— General Bounce	17	————— Chemical, Natural, and Physical Magic	12
——————— Gladiators	17	————— Laboratory of Chemical Wonders	12
——————— Good for Nothing	17	Playtime with the Poets	17
——————— Holmby House	17	Practical Mechanic's Journal	12
——————— Interpreter	17	Prescott's Scripture Difficulties	13
——————— Kate Coventry	17	Problems in Human Nature	14
——————— Queen's Maries	17	Pycroft's Course of English Reading	5
Mendelssohn's Letters	3	————— Cricket Field	18
Menzies' Windsor Great Park	13	————— Cricket Tutor	18
Merivale's (H.) Colonisation and Colonies	7		
——————— (C.) Fall of the Roman Republic	2		
——————— Romans under the Empire	2	Recreations of a Country Parson, Second Series	6
Meryon's History of Medicine	3	Riddle's Diamond Latin-English Dictionary	5
Miles on Horse's Foot	18	Rivers's Rose Amateur's Guide	9
——— on Horse Shoeing	18	Rogers's Correspondence of Greyson	6
——— on Stables	18	————— Eclipse of Faith	6
Mill on Liberty	4	————— Defence of ditto	6
——— on Representative Government	4	————— Essays from the Edinburgh Review	6
——— on Utilitarianism	4	————— Fulleriana	6
Mill's Dissertations and Discussions	4	————— Reason and Faith	6
——— Political Economy	4	Roget's Thesaurus of English Words and Phrases	5
——— System of Logic	4	Ronalds's Fly-Fisher's Entomology	18
Miller's Elements of Chemistry	10	Rowton's Debater	5
Monsell's Spiritual Songs	14		
Montagu's Experiments in Church and State	13		
Montgomery on the Signs and Symptoms of Pregnancy	10	Saxby's Study of Steam	19
Moore's Irish Melodies	17	————— Weather System	7
——— Lalla Rookh	17	Scott's Handbook of Volumetrical Analysis	10
——— Memoirs, Journal, and Correspondence	3	Scrope on Volcanos	8
		Senior's Biographical Sketches	4

SENIOR's Essays on Fiction	16
SEWELL's Amy Herbert	16
——— Ancient History	2
——— Cleve Hall	16
——— Earl's Daughter	16
——— Experience of Life	16
——— Gertrude	16
——— Glimpse of the World	16
——— History of the Early Church	2
——— Ivors	16
——— Katharine Ashton	16
——— Laneton Parsonage	16
——— Margaret Percival	16
——— Night Lessons from Scripture	14
——— Passing Thoughts on Religion	14
——— Preparation for Communion	14
——— Readings for Confirmation	14
——— Readings for Lent	14
——— Self-Examination before Confirmation	14
——— Stories and Tales	16
——— Thoughts for the Holy Week	14
——— Ursula	16
SHAW's Work on Wine	19
SHEDDEN's Elements of Logic	5
Short Whist	19
SIEVEKING's (AMELIA) Life, by WINKWORTH	3
SMITH's (SOUTHWOOD) Philosophy of Health	19
——— (J.) Voyage and Shipwreck of St. Paul	14
——— (G.) Wesleyan Methodism	2
——— (SYDNEY) Memoir and Letters	3
——— Miscellaneous Works	6
——— Sketches of Moral Philosophy	6
——— Wit and Wisdom	6
SOUTHEY's (Doctor)	5
——— Poetical Works	17
STEBBING's Analysis of MILL's Logic	5
STEPHENSON's (R.) Life by JEAFFRESON and POLE	3
STEPHEN's Essays in Ecclesiastical Biography	4
——— Lectures on the History of France	2
STONEHENGE on the Dog	18
——— on the Greyhound	18
STRICKLAND's Queens of England	1
TAYLOR's (Jeremy) Works, edited by EDEN	14
TENNENT's Ceylon	9
——— Natural History of Ceylon	9
——— Story of the Guns	12
Thalatta	16
Theologia Germanica	14
THIRLWALL's History of Greece	2
THOMSON's (Archbishop) Laws of Thought	4

THOMSON's (J.) Tables of Interest	20
TILLEY's Eastern Europe and Western Asia	15
TODD's Cyclopædia of Anatomy and Physiology	10
——— and BOWMAN's Anatomy and Physiology of Man	10
TROLLOPE's Barchester Towers	17
——— Warden	17
TWISS's Law of Nations	19
TYNDALL's Lectures on Heat	8
——— Mountaineering in 1861	16
URE's Dictionary of Arts, Manufactures, and Mines	12
VAN DER HOEVEN's Handbook of Zoology	8
VAUGHAN's (R.) Revolutions in English History	1
——— (R. A.) Hours with the Mystics	7
WARBURTON's Life, by WATSON	3
WARTER's Last of the Old Squires	16
WATSON's Principles and Practice of Physic	10
WATTS's Dictionary of Chemistry	9
WEBB's Celestial Objects for Common Telescopes	7
WEBSTER & WILKINSON's Greek Testament	13
WELD's Last Winter in Rome	15
WELLINGTON's Life, by BRIALMONT and GLEIG	3
——— by GLEIG	3
WESLEY's Life, by SOUTHEY	3
WEST on the Diseases of Infancy and Childhood	10
WHATELY's English Synonymes	4
——— Logic	4
——— Remains	4
——— Rhetoric	4
WHEWELL's History of the Inductive Sciences	2
WHITE and RIDDLE's Latin-English Dictionary	5
WILBERFORCE (W.) Recollections of, by HARFORD	3
WILLICH's Popular Tables	20
WILSON's Bryologia Britannica	9
WOOD's Homes without Hands	8
WOODWARD's Historical and Chronological Encyclopædia	2
YONGE's English-Greek Lexicon	5
——— Abridged ditto	5
YOUNG's Nautical Dictionary	19
YOUATT on the Dog	18
——— on the Horse	18

www.ingramcontent.com/pod-product-compliance
Lightning Source LLC
Chambersburg PA
CBHW032101220426
43664CB00008B/1090